The Economic Transformation of South China

The Economic Transformation of South China

Reform and Development in the Post-Mao Era

Edited by
Thomas P. Lyons
Victor Nee

East Asia Program
Cornell University
Ithaca, New York 14853

The *Cornell East Asia Series* publishes manuscripts on a wide variety of scholarly topics pertaining to East Asia. Manuscripts are published on the basis of camera-ready copy provided by the volume author or editor.

Inquiries should be addressed to Editorial Board, Cornell East Asia Series, East Asia Program, Cornell University, 140 Uris Hall, Ithaca, New York 14853.

Most of the papers in this volume were presented at "The Great Transformation in South China and Taiwan: Markets, Entrepreneurship, and Social Structure," a symposium held at Cornell University in October 1992.

To LT

Table of Contents

Introduction

Part 1. Development Patterns

Part 2. Institutional Change

Part 3. Taiwan-Mainland Economic Relations

Institutional Change and Regional Growth: An Introduction

Victor Nee

Since 1978 the southeastern coastal provinces of China have benefited the most from the economic reform policies emanating from Beijing. Post-Mao reformers targeted these provinces as the experimental grounds of their new development strategy. The creation of special economic zones and "open" cities, profit-sharing arrangements, and decentralization of economic decisions comprise the key institutional changes that paved the way for a rapid shift to markets in this region. Here marketization involved not only expansion of domestic markets, but also rapid incorporation in the global economy. In this respect, the geographical location of the southeastern coastal provinces proved decisive. Reliance on Hong Kong, Macao, and Taiwan to gain access to global markets, investment capital, entrepreneurial talent, and new technologies became a crucial part of the new coastal development strategy. This, combined with an ample supply of cheap labor and the willingness of local officials to negotiate favorable terms of investment, trade, and rent of land and facilities, produced an explosive—and unprecedented—growth rate.

Unlike the market transitions in Eastern Europe and the former Soviet Union, economic reforms in China were not coupled with far-reaching political restructuring. Instead, political institutions remained largely unchanged. The party organization of the 1980s formally played the same role as it did in the Maoist era. The state continued to operate within pre-reform administrative units and governance structures. Moreover, economic reform was not accompanied by fundamental change in the structure of property rights. In China there was no formal program for privatization of public property. Farmers still tilled state-owned land assigned to them by local cadres, and managers and workers continued to manufacture products in collective or state-owned enterprises. Rather than thoroughgoing political and economic changes conforming to familiar guidelines for establishing a market economy, the Chinese reforms were largely piecemeal, growing out of ad hoc responses to problems emanating from market-

1

induced economic growth.[1] As a result, the institutional framework for a market economy was at best partially constructed, and market institutions were often controverted by the dominant political and economic institutions of state socialism, rendering uninterrupted high-speed growth difficult to explain.

The relationship between institutional change and regional growth is the underlying theme of this book. Why does such change assume a regional character? What is the relationship between the dominant political and economic institutions of state socialism and new institutions emerging in the course of market reform? To what extent is institutional change path dependent? Lastly, what are the sources of such change in the South China regional economy and how is it diffused? The following chapters engage these difficult issues and suggest some tentative answers.

The authors contribute to the effort to explain the South China economic miracle by focusing attention on the spatial dimension of socioeconomic development, the path-dependent nature of institutional change, and the role of Hong Kong and Taiwan in the economic transformation of the mainland. The book is divided into three parts. In Part 1, G. William Skinner, Graham E. Johnson, Weng Junyi , and William L. Parish analyze the socioeconomic transformation of Guangdong and Fujian provinces, employing the tools of regional analysis. Part 2 offers case studies examining the limits and trajectory of institutional change. Thomas P. Lyons, Echo Heng Liang, and Su Sijin provide fine-grained analyses illustrating the evolutionary manner in which institutional environments change. Lastly, in Part 3, Chung Chin, Kao Charng and Henry Wan Jr. examine the role of Taiwan as a source of capital and technology and its potential as a model of economic development.

1. Spatial Dimensions of Regional Growth

Guangdong and Fujian provinces are rapidly emerging as the site of major manufacturing centers integrated with the global economy. Although Shanghai and other coastal provinces are competing mightily to displace their lead, the number of joint ventures and wholly foreign-owned firms in Guangdong and Fujian is unsurpassed in China. Significantly, as in China of the treaty port era, the sources of innovation come largely from abroad. These interact with internal pressures and incentives for change to set in motion an irreversible process of transformation.[2] Market transition for Guangdong and Fujian has been closely tied to rapid incorporation in the global market economy. The economic life-lines of these provinces are increasingly linked to the broader East Asian regional economy, making them less vulnerable to the ebb and flow of national macroeconomic policies emanating from Beijing.

A theoretical framework for regional analysis is presented in G. William Skinner's chapter on the Lingnan macroregion (Guangdong). He extends his earlier study of hierarchical regional space in the 1890s to the contemporary period, using 1982-85 county-level data. Empirically, Skinner demonstrates that there is a great deal of internal variation in the Lingnan macroregion, with some areas approaching the levels of development of South Korea and Taiwan and other areas showing conditions closer to that of Bangladesh. His analysis confirms a remarkable correspondence between levels of socioeconomic development and location in the regional system. Using a wide array of socio-economic indicators (i.e., industrialization, agricultural productivity, education, infant mortality, income inequality, fertility), Skinner shows that socioeconomic development rises as one moves from the rural periphery up through what he calls the hiearchical regional space (HRS) to the urbanized core. He concludes that inequality rooted in spatial location in the regional system is stark and immutable.

Skinner's regional systems theory builds on Christaller's seminal spatial model of North American farm communities and on core-periphery arguments developed by the German economist von Thünen. His key theoretical breakthrough comes from linking these ideas with diffusion theory: "My theory holds that it is the repetitive diffusion of myriad innovations through HRS, above all, that reproduces the regional-systems hierarchy through time." It is this insight that explains why regional differentiation does not wane in face of modernization, since innovations enter a regional system through its central metropolis and subsequently diffuse downward through a hierarchy of cities and across spatial distance to the periphery of the macroregion. Each wave of innovations thus reinforces the hierarchy of the regional system. As with the ripple of water emanating outward from a splash in a pond, the further from the center, the weaker the wave.

A key mechanism of diffusion is suggested in Graham E. Johnson's account of the role of Hong Kong in the economic transformation of the Pearl River Delta. His case studies detail substantial variation in village-level development in the Delta, and highlight the importance of network ties to villagers who emigrated to Hong Kong and beyond. One village with easy access to Guangzhou developed commercialized agriculture servicing the urban market; other villages closer to Hong Kong, with dense network ties to emigrants, developed export-oriented agriculture and light industry.

A village located further from Hong Kong, with fewer connections, experienced little change and remained firmly collectivist as in the pre-reform era, while a village beyond the immediate marketing range of Guangzhou, with high out-migration to North America, experienced less commercialization, though it received contributions to build public facilities from kinsmen overseas. Rather than diffusion flowing down through a nested hierarchy of cities and towns, these case studies point to the importance of direct network ties between the metropolis and rural communities. This finding need not, however, contradict Skinner's diffusion model insofar as only villages with close proximity to Hong Kong benefit from dense personal connections, whereas those at the periphery of the system must wait for innovations to arrive at the slower rate of diffusion specified by Skinner's model.

The economic transformation of the southeastern coastal provinces was largely the result of explicit state policies that favored this region over the inland provinces. Weng Junyi's chapter documents the history of past regional development strategies in Fujian province, which he suggests can be viewed as a microcosm of similar changes in the country as a whole. Prior to 1957, the coastal cities of Fujian were the centers of a fledgling industrial economy. From 1957 to 1978 Beijing and provincial authorities charted an inland development strategy for Fujian, in which investment capital for major industrial projects was channeled to inland cities. This was part of the "Third Front" policy that sought to shift industrial capacity to interior regions for military reasons. The magnitude of change in capital investment is seen in the case of Sanming prefecture, which received 2 percent of the province's capital construction funds prior to 1957, and 25 percent in the subsequent period of inland development. In the post-Mao years, the provincial government shifted the flow of investment capital from inland cities back to the coastal cities, reversing the pattern of investment that characterized the Maoist era.

That the consequences of the alternating coastal-inland-coastal development strategies were dramatic, Weng's analysis confirms—high-lighting the importance of government policy in the pattern of regional economic development. Policy-induced growth patterns are also seen in the direction of internal migration, from coastal cities to inland and back, and in changing strategic emphasis on agricultural and heavy and light industrial development prior to the 1980s. Not until 1984 does Weng's analysis indicate an absence of strategic sectors, and by implication a relaxation of a pattern of distorted growth associated with the Maoist era.

Rural industry is a sector that has grown rapidly in the reform era, in part as a result of government policy limiting reforms of urban land and labor markets. This growth has been supported by reformers who view rural industry as a virtual panacea to the problem of surplus rural labor power. They fear that if rural industries are not developed, footloose peasants lacking alternative employment might otherwise threaten to flood into hard pressed cities in search of jobs. William L. Parish employs comparative historical analysis to examine the effect of rural industrialization on rural-urban migration. His analysis focuses on the physical infrastructure, distribution of urban centers, and rural-urban income inequality of South Korea and Taiwan at similar stages of industrial take-off. He examines the experience of these developed East Asian economies for insights about Fujian's likely trajectory. As of 1990, Fujian lagged behind the Taiwan of 1967 in the quality of its infrastructure, and its rural-urban income gap was considerably higher than those of both South Korea and Taiwan. The experience of Taiwan in particular indicates that rural industrialization, even if it proceeds rapidly, can at best only lessen the rate of rural-urban migration.

Johnson's and Parish's analyses confirm Skinner's regional systems theory insofar as the level of commercialization and rural industrialization in Guangdong and Fujian decline as distance from a regional metropolis increases. The central coastal corridor of Fujian—especially after completion of the railway connecting the cities and towns between Fuzhou and Xiamen—may well rival the Pearl River Delta as an area of intense though dispersed industrial growth. The emergence of industrial districts, similar to the Third Italy or Silicon Valley phenomena, where dense concentrations of interwoven manufacturing and subsidiary industries supported by regional institutional arrangements (e.g., a league of corporatist local governments) assume global significance, highlights the importance of regional analysis of growth centers. Already entire industries, including primary manufacturers and their subcontractors, have moved from Hong Kong and Taiwan to the Pearl River Delta and the central coastal area of Fujian—reinforcing the view that these areas are destined to compete in the global economy as export enclaves mainly manufacturing products subcontracted by foreign firms. Such export enclaves have the potential of expanding their markets rapidly within the domestic economy as their greater manufacturing efficiency provides them with competitive advantages. A feature of industrial districts worldwide is the extent of their reliance on regional institutions and their relative autonomy from national centers of power.[3]

2. Path Dependence and Institutional Change

Rather than conceiving of the transition from state socialism in China as a linear progression to capitalism (albeit with a distinct East Asian flavor), we achieve greater realism by acknowledging the path-dependent nature of institutional change.[4] In the absence of regime change, the existing constitutional framework imposes formidable constraints on the emergence of a market economy. To be sure, communist local governments have presided over municipal economies in advanced capitalist countries, but the governance structures of a polity ruled by a communist party weakens market forces by imposing redistributive control over scarce resources.[5] Rather than a full-blown capitalist economy, the more likely outcome of economic reforms in China is a hybrid market economy that reflects the persistence of institutional forms stemming from a state socialist redistributive economy. This is seen in the entrepreneurial role of corporatist local governments.[6]

The transition period is likely to be protracted, even if there is eventually a change in political regime. This is because building the institutional framework for a modern market economy is an evolutionary process involving changing not only the formal institutions that govern economic action, but also the informal institutions that buttress the formal rules of the game. In the absence of corresponding changes in informal social practice, monitoring and enforcement entail such high transaction costs as to render the new rules ineffectual. Institutional change is complicated by the coexistence of multiple ownership forms—state, collective, and private—each supported by alternative governance structures that compete to dominate the institutional environment. In most urban areas state ownership remains the dominant form, while in rural towns and villages corporatist governments are active in promoting local economic development. Although growing rapidly, the private economy remains subordinate to the state and collective economies.

Weak market structures, poorly specified property rights, and institutional uncertainty characterize the transition economy; they are defining features of partial reform. Although markets stimulate the development of a private economy, entrepreneurs face high costs of transacting because property rights are weakly specified and enforced, and factor resources are costly to obtain through market channels relative to the subsidized prices of products supplied through the state allocation system. Thomas P. Lyons' chapter provides ethnographically rich accounts, from Fujian provincial newspapers, that document "not only dramatic institutional changes during the first decade of reform, but also difficulties of doing business within the context of new institutions and hazards that other regions may yet encounter as their reforms move forward." Lyons' case studies, which provide vivid descriptions of the insecurity of property rights, the difficulty of obtaining inputs, and the administrative barriers to commerce imposed by local governments, clearly illustrate the dilemma of partial reform in Fujian.

Evident from the newspaper reports of local conflict over property rights is an extensive reliance on contractual agreements to transfer rights to communal property to private entrepreneurs engaged in profit-making business ventures. This is clearly a pivotal change in the structure of property rights, representing an effort to privatize communal property within a constitutional framework that prohibits private ownership of land. The contracts are signed as binding long-term agreements between private agents and the corporate village—usually the village committee. In one case study, the outcome of a court litigation affirmed that contractual rights can be passed on to heirs. In another case court litigation affirmed rights to exclusive use of communal property even when formal contracts expired, so long as the entrepreneur paid his management fee to the village committee and continued to operate his business.

Conflicts over property rights typically have involved long-term contracts in which the entrepreneur increases the value and productivity of the communal property through personal investments and sound management. In one case study, fellow villagers then mobilized sentiment to annul the contract, believing that the entrepreneur was paying too little for the use of valuable communal property. In several case studies, villagers raided and carted off moveable assets; this was followed by efforts by the entrepreneurs to receive compensation for their losses. The village officials usually side with fellow villagers, and the entrepreneur must therefore turn to higher-level authorities to file grievances for losses suffered. In cases involving litigation in the county or prefectural courts, both sides might retain lawyers to represent them.

The results of formal arbitration appear to be binding; the problem comes in monitoring and enforcement. This is because the institution of legal contracts is poorly understood by villagers, who, Lyons reports, "were amazed to learn that dissolving a contract requires legal procedures, and couldn't understand why this is so."[7] The long-term lease contracts threaten a moral economy based on social norms of shared rights over communal assets. According to village custom, economic surplus gained from communal property ought to be shared by all villagers. For this reason, they view the lease contract as subordinate to deeper communal rights. So strong is this norm that in one case a mere handful of villagers succeeded in impeding a contract signed by the village committee and supported by practically everybody else in the village. It was only after the township party secretary intervened and a separate contract providing the entrepreneur with police protection was signed that he felt sufficiently secure to resume work. Fundamentally, the insecure property rights described in the case studies are rooted in the absence of constitutional rights to own land and in the weak enforcement capacity of the judicial system.

Another dilemma of partial reform stems from the continuing redistributive control over key inputs. Lyons focuses on the problem of the supply of chemical fertilizers to farmers, which brings to light the corruption pervasive in political markets. At each level of the supply bureaucracy fertilizer is siphoned off by redistributors who use it to reward clients and who also engage in arbitrage activity—selling subsidized fertilizer to illegal fertilizer merchants for windfall profits. As a result, farmers in Fujian were unable to obtain needed chemical fertilizer through redistributive channels, and instead were compelled to purchase artificially high-priced chemical fertilizer from illegal merchants, some of who also sold bogus fertilizer packaged with phony trademarks. These case studies document the higher transaction costs generated by resource dependence on redistributive institutions in the context of partial reform, and point to the institutional logic for deepening market reform.

Case studies depicting barriers to trade erected by local governments point to the legacy of Maoist policies that spawned autarkic local econo-mies.[8] Here Lyons describes the experiences of traders who confront a maze of legal and illegal barriers to trade in the form of local levies, taxes, and inspection stations that confiscate cargo and impose fines on the hapless trader. These and the accounts of social banditry and lawlessness highlight problems that stem from a weak regulatory capacity of the state as it shifts emphasis from managing a redistributive system to overseeing a market economy. Fragmented local markets reflect the cellular structure of local economies as they evolved out of the Maoist era. Their persistence, as Lyons suggests, attests to the need for a stronger federalist system in which the central government can intervene to enforce market-opening rules.[9]

In sum, these case studies support the view of institutional change as path dependent, with the emergent hybrid market economy remaining embedded in village customs and redistributive practices. They confirm the high transaction costs imposed on the private economy, stemming from still dominant socialist redistribution. Significantly, they do not refer to problems of economic agents working within the local corporatist economy, who I have argued enjoy a transaction cost advantage in the transition economy.[10]

As already noted, in the vastness of China's rural economy the extent of the shift to markets is highly variable. Villages closer to large urban centers are more likely to be embedded in a dense network of market institutions, while villages in the intermediate and peripheral areas may retain greater continuity with the institutional forms of the collectivist era. The redistributive power of village-level cadres may also vary considerably and correspondingly. My own research—conducted in 1985 in villages located in the "Golden Triangle" within marketing range of Xiamen, Zhangzhou, and Quanzhou—has pointed to a pronounced decline in the redistributive power of village-level cadres.[11] By contrast, Jean Oi found in villages she studied a rapid reconstitution of socialist redistributive power following decollectivization, particularly in villages that had developed rural industry.[12] Corporate villages with strong redistributive institutions were also found in my Fujian survey—but in a random sample of 30 villages, these comprised only a handful.[13]

Though the location of Echo Heng Liang's study—rural Jiangsu—is outside the southeastern coastal area, our main focus in this book, her findings are nonetheless relevant, and provide an interesting point of comparison. Employing logistic regression analysis of household contracting in three predominantly agricultural villages in Jiangsu, Liang established that village cadres used resources they controlled redistributively to provide farmers with incentives to produce quota grain for the state. Contracting households enjoyed a higher log-odds of being allotted more farm land, chemical fertilizer, and off-farm jobs than non-contracting households. Liang concluded that power remains centralized in village institutions controlled by cadres. Yet, unlike the collectivist era, the quota-production of grain cannot be mandated by administrative fiat; rather, agreement is arrived at through a semi-voluntary exchange. These findings are consistent with both Oi's claim of persistent redistributive power and market transition theory. That they are consistent with market transition theory is seen in the very low level of market penetration reported in these Jiangsu villages. Market grain sales accounted for less than 2 percent of total output. In other words, unlike the highly commercialized agriculture found in periurban counties of Fujian and Guangdong, there was virtually no shift to market coordination. This suggests that differences of opinion among scholars in respect to the persistent strength or decline of cadre power may well stem from variation in the extent of market penetration in the sites of research.[14]

A continuing shift from redistribution to markets—domestic and global—induces change in the comparative costs of governance. As the institutional environment changes through a thickening of market institutions—i.e., joint ventures with foreign firms, sub-contracting arrangements, financial institutions, marketing networks, marketized collective firms, and private firms—the relative cost of socialist redistribution increases, while hybrid marketized and private governance structures come to have a comparative advantage. This is evident in the poor performance of state enterprises relative to hybrid marketized firms. Sijin Su addresses such institutional change in urban industry, focusing on the transformation of state enterprises into marketized firms. Inside these firms, Su finds a multiplicity of organizational forms among the various subunits. The incentive for change comes from income disparity between subunits. Manager and employees are sensitive to differences in earnings within the firm. The basic salaries are invariant, as they are set according to a national wage scale; however, bonuses tend to vary considerably within and between firms. In general, the more market-dependent the firm or subunit, the larger the size of the bonus relative to the basic salary. Moreover, the size of bonuses is based on market performance, so that a particular employee's bonus depends on his or her work performance and the subunit's profitability. The gains of one subunit stimulate competitive imitation among other units. Each subunit is bound to the state enterprise or local government through discrete contract governance structures. Thus, for example, joint ventures utilize contracts negotiated by the foreign partner. According to Su, "Diffusion originates in foreign-invested firms for two major reasons. First, foreign partners tend to introduce international practices and management methods. Second, in their effort to attract foreign firms, both the central and local governments tend to introduce regulations favoring foreign-invested firms and accommodating their methods. Domestic firms, impressed by the success of foreign-invested firms, then seek to adopt similar methods." In this manner organizational innovations diffuse through the Chinese state enterprise.

3. Taiwan in the Making of a Market Economy in South China

The story of institutional change in Su's chapter points to the important role of Hong Kong and Taiwan in the transformation of the South China industrial economy. In recent years, the pace and scale of investment from Taiwan have increased dramatically, especially in Fujian, which benefits from geographical proximity and linguistic and cultural affinity with

Taiwan entrepreneurs. Investment activities of Taiwan businessmen in the coastal cities are widely evident, ranging from flashy real estate projects to export-oriented joint ventures. Bilateral trade is also thriving. Accompanying the surge in investment and trade has been a rapid diffusion of Taiwanese popular culture and business practices.

Prognosis for continued growth in investment and bilateral trade between Taiwan and the mainland is very good, according to both Chung Chin and Kao Charng. Driving Taiwan investment activities to the mainland were the exhaustion of surplus labor in Taiwan by the end of the 1970s, the escalating cost of domestic labor, and rapid currency appreciation. In order to remain competitive and retain their market share in the global economy, Taiwan exporters were compelled to seek lower-priced labor elsewhere. A seemingly limitless supply of cheap labor and low relative rents on land and buildings, coupled with the continued relaxation of political tensions between Beijing and Taipei, rendered the move to the mainland irresistible for Taiwan entrepreneurs. According to Chung, the pattern of Taiwan investment has created export enclaves that rely on home sources for inputs, machinery, and raw materials. Few domestic producers in the mainland were capable of supplying semi-products, components and parts; state enterprises were viewed as too inefficient; and a poor transportation system within China made it cheaper to ship components and raw material from Taiwan. In Chung's view, the extent of technology transfer to China is limited because much of this industrial activity is labor-intensive and technologically unsophisticated, and because the structure of the export enclave does not encourage sectoral linkages with the Chinese domestic economy. Only recently has there been an increase in capital-intensive projects.[15]

Kao, in turn, documents growth in bilateral trade with China —mostly triangular trade passing through Hong Kong or a third country elsewhere in Asia. Due to Taiwan's greater reliance on trade, the growth of trade with China has rendered Taiwan's economy more dependent on the mainland. Indeed, inducing greater dependence has been an explicit aim of Beijing's policy towards Taiwan.

Of particular interest is the small scale of Taiwan (and also Hong Kong) investments in the mainland. They typically involve owner-operators of family-owned businesses who retain close supervisory control of the mainland plant through an in-person manager. Rather than a small number of large joint ventures, there are instead large numbers of smaller firms dispersed in cities and townships. Although technology transfer is limited (since, as just noted, Taiwan has mainly exported labor-intensive industries), still the dispersed pattern of small investments is conducive to diffusion of management and business practices—the more so, given the close cultural identity between Taiwan managers and mainland employees and staff.

However, differences in political institutions between Taiwan and the mainland are likely to impose limits on both technological and organizational diffusion from Taiwan. Henry Wan Jr.'s chapter outlines the reasons to be cautious with respect to Taiwan's prospects as a model for mainland development. In his view, markets provide an effective matrix for transferring technology, but the "degree to which markets can assist economic development depends upon politico-social institutions." Despite the seeming similarity between the Nationalist Party (KMT) and the Chinese Communist Party, on the mainland obstacles to technology transfer are enormous and may prove insurmountable in the absence of regime change. In Taiwan, although political freedom was restricted, a conventional legal framework safeguarded personal freedoms. Moreover, the KMT ideology was not opposed to private enterprise or parliamentary democracy. A market economy was well established in Taiwan prior to the arrival from the mainland of the KMT. By contrast, the institutional structures of the mainland are at odds with a market economy. These include a communist party that must still pay homage to an out-moded ideology, continuing restrictions on change in institutions and laws, incorrigibly inefficient state enterprises, a government that is wedded to controlling the economy but whose capacity for governance has declined precipitously, and a ruling group with little motivation to carry out needed political reforms. The critical questions then are, "Will the government collapse, following in the footsteps of fellow communist regimes? Can a regime collapse while the economy booms? Can a communist government survive while state ownership withers away?"

4. Conclusions

Although there are reasons for caution in viewing Taiwan or Hong Kong as a model for China's overall transition to a market society, the main lesson imparted by regional systems theory is the need to examine the diffusion process as a regional rather than a national phenomenon. Here there is more reason for optimism. Diffusion of organizational and technological innovations can occur quickly even under conditions of partial reform. When private returns (the gains or losses to an individual in economic exchanges) are more in line with social returns (the gains or costs to society as a whole), improvements in economic performance are likely.[16] And many factors are contributing to increase private returns and incentives: profit-sharing arrangements through the extensive use of subcontracting within the firm, and bonus payments; opportunities for private entrepreneurship provided by expanding free markets; and the rapid increase in foreign and overseas investment and trade centered in special economic zones and "open cities."

In the context of a rapid shift to markets, gains from trade give rise to repeat transactions outside the boundaries of the redistributive economy. They also involve transactions across the supply bureaucracy, particularly in the early stages. Such exchanges, however, involve high transaction costs; if higher costs persist, they give rise to incentives and efforts to bypass the supply bureaucracy and develop market-based solutions.[17] Indeed, many agents in the move to markets are themselves from cadre background. Their market-making activities undermine incrementally the organizational integrity of the party, and pave the way for regime change. Initially transactions follow ad hoc procedures, but over time stable solutions emerge. The emergence of new norms and rules reflects solutions to collective action when rapid changes in the institutional environment render obsolete the old rules of the game. Much of the process of institutional change takes place at the subinstitutional level, involving face-to-face groups and informal arrangements.[18] Reliance on informal institutions and personal connections tends to congeal over time into routine action backed by monitoring and enforcement procedures. New norms and practices that are conducive to improved economic performance are more likely to be reinforced and institutionalized. This view of institutional change suggests that the diffusion of innovations relies to a large extent on processes that operate at the subinstitutional level. Here a matrix of social networks defines the paths of diffusion within and across institutional and organizational boundaries.[19]

The rise of regional industrial districts in Guangdong and Fujian indicates that institutional change and regional growth are closely linked. Though path dependent, there is little doubt that dramatic changes in institutional and organizational forms have taken place. Although national policy changes in Beijing have played a significant role in targeting these provinces as sites of special economic zones and "open" cities entitled to preferential policies, subsequent changes in the rules of the game were by no means all dictated from afar by the central government. Rather, as noted above, institutional change were incremental, involving changes in informal rules and embedded in social networks, and diffused unevenly within the region, more or less speedily or gradually. The crucial changes involve the diffusion of market institutions, ranging from hybrid contract governance structures in urban joint venture-firms to private rural credit cooperatives. A continuing shift from redistribution to markets induces change in the comparative cost of governance. As market institutions diffuse in the transition economy, such parameter changes result in relative increases in the cost of redistribution and reduction in the cost of transacting for marketized and private firms.

Notes

1. Cyril Lin, "Open-Ended Economic Reform in China," in Victor Nee and David Stark (eds.), *Remaking the Economic Institutions of Socialism: China and Eastern Europe* (Stanford: Stanford University Press, 1989), pp. 95-136; and Susan L. Shirk, *The Political Logic of Economic Reform in China* (Los Angeles: University of California Press, 1993).

2. Victor Nee and Peng Lian, "Sleeping with the Enemy: A Dynamic Model of Declining Political Commitment in State Socialism," *Theory and Society*, forthcoming April 1994.

3. Michael J. Piore and Charles F. Sabel, *The Second Industrial Divide: Possibilities for Prosperity* (New York: Basic Books, 1984); and Michael E. Porter, *The Competitive Advantage of Nations* (New York: Free Press, 1990).

4. Douglass C. North, *Institutions, Institutional Change, and Economic Performance* (Cambridge: Cambridge University Press, 1990).

5. Carlo Trigilia, "Small-Firm Development and Political Subcultures in Italy," *European Sociological Review*, 2, 1989, pp. 161-75.

6. Victor Nee and Sijin Su, "The Role of Political and Social Institutions: Informal Rights and Local Corporatism in China" (Cornell Working Papers on the Transitions from State Socialism, #93.1); Jean Oi, "Fiscal Reform and the Economic Foundations of Local State Corporatism," *World Politics*, 45, 1992, pp. 99-126; and Nan Lin, "Local Market Socialism: Reform in Rural China" (Cornell Working Papers on the Transitions from State Socialism, #93.5).

7. The view of law as based on flexible understanding of the human context or *renqing* is an old Chinese custom. For this reason, personal ties are much more important in binding contractual agreements than in the West.

8. Thomas P. Lyons, *Economic Integration and Planning in Maoist China* (New York: Columbia University Press, 1987).

9. See also Victor Nee, "Peasant Entrepreneurship and the Politics of Regulation in China," in Victor Nee and David Stark (eds.), *Remaking the Economic Institutions of Socialism: China and Eastern Europe* (Stanford: Stanford University Press, 1989), pp. 169-207.

10. Victor Nee, "Organizational Dynamics of Market Transition: Hybrid Forms, Property Rights, and Mixed Economy in China," *Administrative Science Quarterly*, 37, 1992, pp. 1-27.

11. Victor Nee, "A Theory of Market Transition: From Redistribution to Markets in State Socialism," *American Sociological Review*, 54, 1989, pp. 663-81.

12. Jean Oi, "The Fate of the Collective after the Commune," in Debra Davis and Ezra Vogel (eds.), *Chinese Society on the Eve of Tiananmen: The Impact of Reform* (Cambridge, MA: Harvard Contemporary China Series, 1990), pp. 15-36.

13. Victor Nee and Su Sijin, "Institutional Change and Economic Growth in China: The View from the Villages," *The Journal of Asian Studies,* 49, 1990, pp. 3-25.

14. Market transition theory predicts a covariation between persistent redistributive power and low levels of commercialization. Victor Nee, "Social Inequalities in Reforming State Socialism: Between Redistribution and Markets in China," *American Sociological Review,* 56, 1991, pp. 267-82.

15. Moreover, because many of the products manufactured in the export enclaves end up in the US market, trade friction between China and the United States is likely to escalate.

16. Douglass C. North, *Structure and Change in Economic History* (New York: Norton, 1981).

17. See Oliver E. Williamson, *Markets and Hierarchies* (New York: Free Press, 1975).

18. George C. Homans, *Social Behavior: Its Elementary Forms* (New York: Harcourt Brace Jovanovich, 1974).

19. See, for example, James S. Coleman, Elihu Katz, and Herbert Menzel, *Medical Innovations* (New York: Bobbs-Merrill, 1966).

Differential Development in Lingnan

G. William Skinner

1. Introduction

In this paper I use a model of spatial differentiation to analyze levels of development in Lingnan, the largest macroregional economy in southern China.[1] Level of development is held to be a function of position within the internally differentiated structure of regional systems at various levels of the economic hierarchy.

China's macroregional economies have deep historical roots. In an earlier analysis, I showed that high-order regional economies took shape within the major physiographic regions associated with drainage basins.[2] The core-periphery structure that characterized these macroregional systems at the beginning of the modern era was manifest in myriad ways.[3] Such key resources as arable land, population, and capital investment were concentrated in the lowland riverine cores of drainage basins, thinning out toward their mountainous peripheries. Agriculture was more intensive and productivity higher in core areas, due to fertility migration through deforestation, erosion and deposition, and to the greater potential for irrigation and reclamation in lowlands as against uplands. In addition, regional cores enjoyed major transport advantages vis-à-vis peripheral areas. The density of the transport network and the efficiency of transport both varied from high in the inner core to low in the far periphery. Regional systems of cities also reflected and reinforced core-periphery differentiation, with high-order cities concentrated in core areas and urbanization levels low in the peripheries. It follows from these contingencies that the local economies of core areas were consistently more commercialized than those of peripheral areas. In virtually all respects, then, the macroregional economy climaxed in the urbanized inner core, where the density of economic transactions was highest, where markets of all kinds were most developed, where financial and wholesaling services were concentrated, and where industrial production was highest.

The metropolises that served as apex cities of macroregional economies were but the highest level of a more or less integrated hierarchy of central places that extended down to rural market towns.[4] The marketing systems centered on those towns, each typically encompassing 15-20 villages, constituted the basic building blocks of the economic hierarchy.[5] Central places at each ascending level served as the nodes of ever more extensive and complex socioeconomic systems. Such systems at any one level were articulated with those at the next higher level through an intricate overlapping network.[6] Macroregional economies such as that of Lingnan may be seen as the culmination of this hierarchical structure of local and regional systems.

It is central to the regional-systems argument that internal differentiation analogous to the core-periphery structure of macroregional economies characterizes nodal systems throughout the lower reaches of the hierarchy. Each local and regional system, then, is a territorially based system of human interaction. In the last analysis, a given system is manifested as patterned movements—flows of goods and services, of money and credit, of messages and symbols, and of persons in their multifarious roles and statuses. The town or city at the system's center serves to articulate and integrate activity in space and time.

This paper is the first report of an analysis that applies this regional-systems model to contemporary China.[7] Does the conceptualization of China's regional structure as a cumulative hierarchy of ever more inclusive town- and city-centered systems, developed initially to model a mature premodern agrarian society, still hold for the partially modernized, much more developed, and significantly less agrarian China of the 1980s? Have the macroregional economies of late imperial times persisted into the post-Mao era, and, if so, how have their boundaries changed? Has the internal core-periphery differentiation within regional systems at a given level been weakened or sharpened by modernizing processes? How stark is spatial inequality in contemporary Lingnan, as indicated by the range of variation between the most advanced and most backward areas? To what extent is the patterning of development and underdevelopment shaped by topography? And how does that patterning relate to the administrative map of provinces, prefectures, and municipalities?

It is possible to pursue these and related questions in some detail only because of the outpouring of disaggregated data that began in the early 1980s. In my earlier regionalization of China as of the 1890s, I had little to go on in the way of urban or county-level data. I analyzed the central-place system on the basis of painstakingly gathered and inferred town populations plotted on maps showing the contemporaneous transport grid.[8]

I based my delineation of regional systems and their core-periphery structure primarily on population density, arguing that in an agrarian society population density mirrored agricultural productivity and provided a rough index of the availability of resources that could be used in the struggle for wealth, status, and power. There was plenty of good county-level data on the Qing system of field administration, which I used to good effect in analyzing its regional basis, but that should not obscure the fact that the regional analysis *per se* was a seat-of-the-pants effort relying extensively on hunches and inferences from topography.[9]

This time around, data for counties and central places are relatively abundant, providing a far more reliable basis for analyzing the urban hierarchy and delineating regional systems. These rich data make it possible for the first time to distinguish the territorial extent of macroregional economies from their respective physiographic macroregions and to analyze their internal structures in some detail. Whereas the earlier study modeled the core-periphery structure of a macroregional economy as a simple dichotomy, the present analysis delineates seven zones to capture the full range of differentiation from the innermost core to the farthermost periphery.

2. Regional-Systems Theory

The theory on which this analysis rests was developed through modifying the unrealistic assumptions of location theory in accordance with the general features of large-scale drainage basins. These include (1) systematic progression in terrain types from a mountainous far periphery to a lowland, riverine inner core; (2) the formal characteristics of river systems, including tributary structure and erosion/deposition processes; and (3) systematic variation in the relevant resource base—that is, in the naturally occurring phenomena that can be used in the production processes of an agrarian society.

Modeling the central-place hierarchy of a regional system is approached by elaborating Christaller's model.[10] This involves the introduction of (what from a regional-systems perspective would be) theoretically expected spatial variations in (1) population density, (2) market dependency or commercialization, (3) transport efficiency, and (4) ruggedness of terrain.[11] Modeling the core-periphery structure of a regional system is approached by elaborating von Thünen's model.[12] This involves the introduction of (what from a regional-systems perspective would be) theoretically expected spatial variations in (1) population density,

(2) technical knowledge, (3) knowledge of the state of the market, (4) transport efficiency, (5) land fertility, (6) production functions, (7) the aspirations and living standards of rural producers, (8) nonfarm labor and nonfarm land use, and (9) economies of scale. The two elaborated models in conjunction bring us close to a theoretical picture of the hierarchy of economic central places and associated nodal territorial systems.

This spatial framework is termed *hierarchical regional space* (hereafter HRS), and a third major ingredient of regional-systems theory is a respecification of diffusion theory in terms of HRS.[13] Innovations of all kinds, I argue, are typically introduced in or near high-order cities and diffuse through HRS as modeled. That this should be so was anticipated by Hägerstrand.[14] Cautioning against overreliance on a "surface wave" model, he wrote: "A closer analysis shows that the spread along the initial 'frontier' is led through the urban hierarchy. The point of introduction in a new country is its primate city; sometimes some other metropolis. Then centers next in rank follow. Soon, however, this order is broken up and replaced by one where the neighborhood effect dominates over the pure size succession." By neighborhood effect, Hägerstrand refers to diffusion from a city directly to its rural hinterland. My model, of course, predicts that diffusion will proceed simultaneously along both paths—down the central-place hierarchy *and* out from central places into their rural environs. As a particular innovation spreads, spatial differentiation through HRS becomes ever more pronounced for a time, but eventually peaks out and declines and, as saturation is approached, becomes negligible. Meanwhile, other innovations introduced in the metropolis have begun to spread. In the course of development, modern innovations in many contingently related sequences are continually being introduced in the metropolis, generating successive diffusion waves through HRS. My theory holds that the repetitive diffusion of myriad innovations through HRS is a major mechanism for reproducing the regional-systems hierarchy through time.

3. Methods and Procedures

An initial step of the present analysis was to assign cities to functional levels in a hierarchy of economic central places. Known as central-place analysis, this endeavor is technical and painstaking.[15] The more and better the data about cities and towns and about the trade and transport links between them, the more reliable the analysis. In the case of China as of end-year 1984, we have digitized mapped data on the transport network, know the nonagricultural populations of over 6000 cities and towns, and have additional economic, social, and institutional data for the largest 300 cities.[16] For levels in the hierarchy I use the same terminology as in my previous analysis: central metropolis, regional metropolis, regional city, greater city, local city, and central (market) town. Once all cities and towns with a nonagricultural population greater than 1500 were assigned to levels, counties were classified according to the level and configuration of towns they contained and according to the proportion of the population that was urban.[17] This is the basis for classifying counties into six levels according to place in city- and town-centered systems, one dimension of the data matrixes introduced below.[18] This classification effectively places counties along an urban-rural continuum.

The method used to delineate regional systems and their core-periphery structure disaggregates artificial high-order administrative units (in this case, provinces and prefectures) into lower-order county-level units, and reaggregates the latter in accordance with human interaction patterns in HRS. The research strategy followed is largely inductive, *a priori* decisions being avoided insofar as possible. Rather, the disaggregated data themselves (always viewed in relation to landscape features) are allowed to establish the levels, to define the limits of the systems at each level, and to differentiate their internal nodal structure. To determine macroregional boundaries, I created an omnibus index from a wide range of variables, transformed it to remove urban effects, and displayed the index values on a county outline map.[19] System boundaries were then drawn through pathways of counties with the lowest values. A similar index was then created for each macroregional system separately, from variables most strongly intercorrelated within that system.[20] It too was transformed to remove urban effects and displayed on county outline maps.[21] With adjustments to achieve full geographic coherence, zonal boundaries in the core-periphery structure were drawn to minimize variation within zones while maximizing the difference in means between zones. This process yielded a seven-fold zoning of Lingnan's core-periphery structure.

4. Spatial Differentiation in the Course of Modernization

How early modernization affects spatial differentiation is a controversial issue. One set of arguments holds that most modernizing processes serve to reduce regional differentiation. (1) Modern industry relies heavily on minerals, fossil fuels, and hydroelectric power—resources whose location (as a matter of physical geography) is unlikely to coincide with fertile farmland. Furthermore, in siting new industries, Chinese policymakers have at times placed strategic considerations above the economic calculus of comparative advantage.[22] On both counts, then, industrialization would disrupt the locational logic of a premodern agrarian society. (2) The rationale for modeling China's regional structure as a hierarchy of semi-autonomous regional systems, including core-periphery differentiation, rests heavily on the high (yet variable) cost of unmechanized transport, travel, and communication. Thus, the rapid expansion of mechanized transport— think of rail lines and highways being laid across macroregional boundaries—and of aspatial modes of communication—telegraph, telephone, fax—ought on first principles to mute spatial differentiation, both within and between systems. (3) The vast growth of interregional trade, facilitated by the expansion of mechanized transport, would inevitably strengthen the national economy at the expense of regional economies, and reduce the relative autonomy of subsystems at all levels of the hierarchy. (4) Finally, the continuing extension of modern facilities to the remote peripheries of regional systems ought to reduce and eventually eliminate traditional elements of backwardness. As schools are introduced into every village and as the expanding road network brings peripheral areas into wider markets, illiteracy would be reduced and living standards improved in regional peripheries, thereby decreasing core-periphery differentiation. This homogenization process, moreover, may even extend to modern features: by now, we are told, virtually every village in China can boast a radio.

Against these views, a set of countervailing arguments yield quite different expectations. (1) Transport efficiency and cost-distance remain powerful determinants of industrial location and trade flows even after mechanized transport has been extended throughout a regional economy. Water transport along navigable rivers and canals still has significant cost advantages over rail and truck transport. And it is much cheaper to build overland routes in the plains than across mountain ranges. (2) The arguments cited above about the effects of interregional transport and trade overlook the fact that transport modernization and trade growth have proceeded within as well as between regions. At any given level of the hierarchy, one might find that while the internal transport net has been greatly extended and upgraded, interregional routes, despite mechanization and upgrading, have not been appreciably intensified. At any given level, it is an empirical question whether interregional trade has outpaced intraregional trade, or vice versa. It may be argued, in short, that what counts is the relative balance between levels, not the simple fact of interregional growth. (2) Modern communications retain a good deal of regional centrality. Radio and TV transmitters, normally sited on the outskirts of cities, create catchment areas similar to the circulation areas of urban newspapers. In any case, the distribution of telephones, radios, TV sets, and fax machines would almost certainly reflect the differentiated spatial structure of developmental level. (3) Rather more generic is the argument that modernization processes involve the continual introduction of innovations in metropolises and their diffusion down to lower-order cities and out through their hinterlands. The diffusion of any one innovation at first sharpens spatial differentiation, only to mute it later on as the innovation spreads throughout the region. Long before saturation is reached, however, new innovations introduced at the center have begun their differentiating work. Before radios have saturated a region, TVs are spreading. And, of course, the argument is no less cogent when applied to economic, social, and cultural innovations, be they new forms of accounting, contraceptive use, or female literacy. William Lavely has ably documented the successive diffusion through regional space of female literacy, primary education, and secondary education.[23]

In a word, my analysis supports the second set of arguments. Each of the late imperial macroregional systems persists to the present. Needless to remark, major structural changes have occurred—in the urban system, the transport grid, the sectoral composition of the economy, among others—and at least some changes are apparent in the territorial extent of each macroregional system. Nonetheless, the continuities are striking. The central metropolises (apex cities) of all nine macroregional economies remain unchanged. With one exception, each of those spatial economies reveals a clear pattern of core-periphery differentiation which echoes that of late imperial times. And virtually all indicators suggest that spatial differentiation is sharper in the 1980s than it was a century earlier.

While a comprehensive overview of China's contemporary regional structure cannot be presented here, it will be helpful to place Lingnan comparatively within the range of agrarian China's nine macroregional systems. On almost all indicators of level of development, my analysis places either the Lower Yangzi (LY) or Manchuria (MC) at the head of the list. If these are the most advanced economies overall, then Yungui (YG) is indubitably the most backward. On most indicators as of the mid-1980s, Lingnan (LN) fell near the middle of the range. For instance, Lingnan ranked fifth overall in grain yields (tons per 10,000 mu, 1985: LY 3080, LN 2297, YG 1913) and in mean total farm income (yuan per capita, 1982: MC 250, LN 140, YG 95). As of 1982, Lingnan ranked fifth in level of urbanization (MC 33.1 percent, LN 12.7 percent, YG 10.3 percent, with urban specified as towns with a nonagricultural population of 3000+), sixth in proportion of the population outside agriculture (MC 37.4 percent, LN 16.8 percent, YG 12.3 percent), and sixth in per-capitized GVIAO (gross

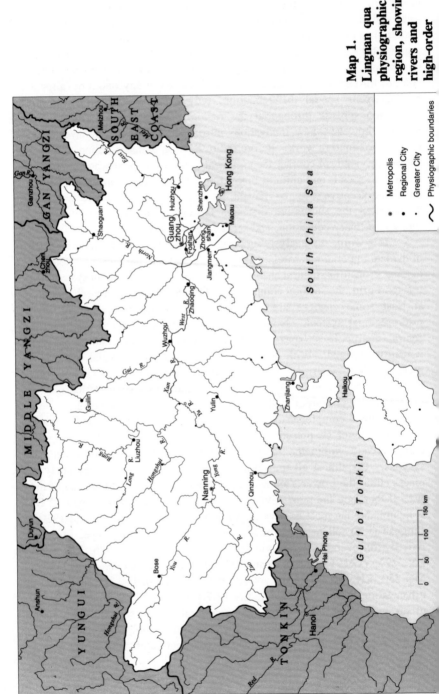

**Map 1.
Lingnan qua
physiographic
region, showing
rivers and
high-order**

* Metropolis
• Regional City
· Greater City
〜 Physiographic boundaries

YUNGUI

MIDDLE YANGZI

GAN YANGZI

SOUTH EAST COAST

TONKIN

South China Sea

Gulf of Tonkin

Anshun
Duyun
Bose
Guilin
Liuzhou
Nanning
Qinzhou
Hanoi
Hai Phong
Haikou
Zhanjiang
Yulin
Wuzhou
Zhaoqing
Jiangmen
Guangzhou
Foshan
Zhongshan
Macau
Shenzhen
Hong Kong
Huizhou
Shaoguan
Chenzhou
Meizhou
Ganzhou

East R.
Mei R.
North R.
West R.
Gui R.
Xun R.
Rong R.
Long R.
Hongshui R.
You R.
Zuo R.
Yong R.
Gan R.
Hongshui R.

0   50   100 150 km

value of industrial and agricultural output: LY 959 yuan, LN 469 yuan, YG 370 yuan). In absolute terms, Lingnan's total population in 1982, some 87 million, made it the sixth most populous macroregional system, while its GVIAO, 55 billion yuan, showed it to be the fifth largest macroregional economy in terms of output.

5. Lingnan: How It Shapes Up in the 1980s

Lingnan *qua* physiographic region is depicted in Map 1. The regional boundary is drawn along the crests of the mountains that surround the basin drained by the rivers debouching through the Pearl River Delta. At only one point does the physiographic boundary cross a river—namely, the Hongshui, whose upper drainage is usually considered part of the Yungui Plateau. Physiographic Lingnan is bordered to the east by the Han basin of the Southeast Coast, to the northeast by the Gan basin (the Gan Yangzi region), to the north by the Xiang and Yuan basins of the Middle Yangzi, to the northwest by the Yungui plateau, and to the southwest by the Red River basin of Vietnam.

The limits of the Lingnan macroregional economy as revealed by this analysis are shown in relation to the physiographic region on Map 2; the physiographic boundary is shown only where it does not coincide with the boundary of the socioeconomic system. On the facing page, Map 3 shows the macroregional limits juxtaposed with provincial boundaries. A quick tour counterclockwise around the rim of the system will serve to define its limit in relation both to physiography and to administrative geography.

It is notable (in Map 3) that the Chaozhou/Jiayingzhou area of eastern Guangdong—that is, the Han-basin system whose regional city is Shantou (Swatow)—remains outside the Lingnan economy. However, a coastal corner of that physiographic region (consisting of Haifeng *xian* and part of Lufeng *xian*) has been "captured" by Lingnan. To the northeast, the Lingnan economy has expanded to include a considerable portion of the southern Gan basin in Jiangxi; the incorporated areas, it may be noted, are largely Hakka-speaking.

Along the Hunan frontier, the socioeconomic boundary generally follows the drainage divide, with the exception of the portion near Guilin. While Guilin's city system, whose extent is brought out very clearly by the 1980s data, falls wholly within Guangxi province, it straddles the physiographic boundary, with about half falling in the Gui river basin and half in the upper basin of the Xiang. Interestingly enough, my analysis shows the entire city system to be more closely integrated into the Middle Yangzi

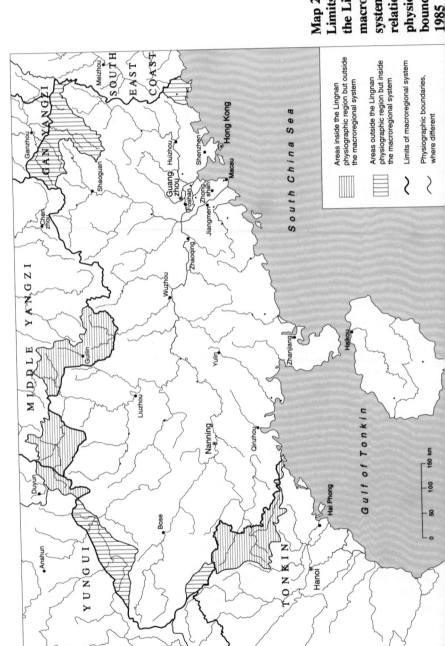

Map 2.
Limits of
the Lingnan
macroregional
system in
relation to
physiographic
boundaries,
1985

Areas inside the Lingnan physiographic region but outside the macroregional system

Areas outside the Lingnan physiographic region but inside the macroregional system

Limits of macroregional system

Physiographic boundaries, where different

MIDDLE YANGZI

GAN YANGZI

SOUTH EAST COAST

YUNGUI

TONKIN

South China Sea

Gulf of Tonkin

Anshun
Duyun
Ganzhou
Chenzhou
Meizhou
Shaoguan
Guilin
Liuzhou
Bose
Nanning
Wuzhou
Zhaoqing
Guangzhou
Foshan
Huizhou
Shenzhen
Zhongshan
Macau
Hong Kong
Jiangmen
Yulin
Qinzhou
Zhanjiang
Haikou
Hai Phong
Hanoi

0   50   100   150 km

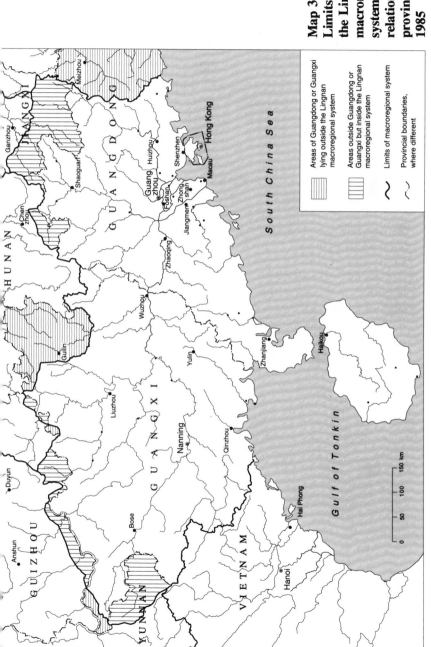

**Map 3.
Limits of
the Lingnan
macroregional
system in
relation to
provinces,
1985**

Areas of Guangdong or Guangxi lying outside the Lingnan macroregional system

Areas outside Guangdong or Guangxi but inside the Lingnan macroregional system

Limits of macroregional system

Provincial boundaries, where different

South China Sea

Gulf of Tonkin

HUNAN

GUANGXI

GUANGDONG

GUIZHOU

YUNNAN

VIETNAM

Ganzhou

Meizhou

Shaoguan

Chen

Guilin

Liuzhou

Nanning

Bose

Duyun

Anshun

Wuzhou

Yulin

Qinzhou

Zhanjiang

Haikou

Hai Phong

Hanoi

Guang Zhou

Huizhou

Foshan

Zhong shan

Shenzhen

Hong Kong

Macau

Jiangmen

Zhaoqing

0 50 100 150 km

economy than into the Lingnan economy, whence its exclusion from the present analysis.

Two discrepancies may be seen along the Guizhou frontier. The Duliu river basin above Congjiang (which falls in physiographic Lingnan) has been "lost" to the Lingnan economy, with the eastern portion incorporated into the Middle Yangzi economy, and the western (upriver) portion incorporated into the Yungui economy. Farther southwest, a strip of territory along the upper Hongshui (which falls physiographically in Yungui) has been incorporated into Lingnan. In accordance with physiography, Lingnan's macroregional economy extends into southeastern Yunnan. Along the Vietnam border, a small corner of the Red River drainage basin is incorporated into Lingnan's regional economy, while a much more extensive portion of physiographic Lingnan (namely, the upper Zou river basin) lies across the international border and has been incorporated into the Tonkin macroregional economy of Vietnam.

Although details must be eschewed here, most of these differences between regional economy and physiographic region may be explained in terms of the transport network: the construction of specific routes which afford particular frontier areas more efficient access to cities and markets on the other side of the nearby physiographic boundary. Shifting focus from trees to the forest, we may note that less than a tenth of the territory of physiographic Lingnan lies outside the macroregional economy. Broadly speaking, then, Lingnan *qua* socioeconomic system is largely coterminous with the physiographic region.

Map 4 (the fold-out at the end of this volume) displays the seven zones of Lingnan's core-periphery structure, as revealed through the procedures described above. It should be clear that we are dealing with a continuum from Guangzhou and its immediate environs in the Pearl River Delta to a far periphery along Guangxi's western borders with Yunnan and Guizhou. How many cuts one makes in this continuum is an arbitrary decision; in the present project, I have consistently been making the core-periphery analyses as fine-grained as county-level data permit. (This has meant seven zones in the Upper Yangzi and Lingnan but, for instance, only six in Yungui and five in the Southeast Coast.) Given the conceptual and empirical continuum, the precise location of zonal "boundaries" is unimportant, and I have accordingly drawn them in generalized fashion. However, the overall picture of core-periphery differentiation has a strong empirical basis, as the data to follow will show. In level of development, Lingnan's Zone 1, the inner core, is comparable to the Four Dragons, whereas Zone 7, the far periphery, resembles Nepal.[24]

6. Data Matrixes

We have seen that any locality fits into a hierarchy of multiple levels. Given this kind of structure, it will not do to present findings concerning internal differentiation within a macroregional system, say, without controlling on variation through lower-order nodal systems. Furthermore, the overall model predicts that variation at the macroregional level will be echoed or replicated at lower levels. The nature of the methodological problem that is posed by a system hierarchy of this kind may be illustrated by focusing on a regional-city system that is wholly included in Lingnan's far periphery (Zones 6 and 7). The regional city of Bose is sited at the head of navigation on the Yu River in far western Guangxi. Its maximal hinterland extends to the limits of the macroregion on three sides, but to the east and southeast it abuts two other regional-city systems within Lingnan. The developmental level of the fourteen counties that lie wholly or partly in Bose's hinterland varies systematically, declining from the city itself in all directions toward the rim of the city system. In terms of the omnibus index developed for Lingnan as a whole, county values moving upriver to the northwest are 101.3 (Bose *xian*), 89.2, 83.8. Moving downriver to the southeast, the progression is 101.3, 97.6, 96.4, 93.8. The counties in Bose's hinterland that are situated upriver from the city fall in Zone 7, the farthermost periphery, whereas Bose itself and the downriver portion of its hinterland fall in Zone 6 of the macroregional core-periphery structure. Thus, while city-system differentiation in the upriver portion of Bose's hinterland echoes and reinforces macroregional differentiation, the downriver portion shows node-to-rim differentiation that countervails the periphery-to-core differentiation of the more inclusive macroregional system. The gradient of index values is steep where decline is predicted for both hierarchical levels, but only gradual where the decline predicted for the city system is countervailed by the rise predicted for the macroregional system.

A simple way around this methodological problem is to cross-tabulate the data to show variation through the macroregion *and* through lower-level city systems at the same time. The figures of this paper are based on such cross-tabulations. We may take as an example the first chart of Figure 1. In the manner described, all counties have been classified into seven zones according to their positions in the core-periphery structure, and each is positioned in *columns* of the chart according to its geographic position in regional space. The six *rows* of this chart represent comparable zoning within lower-order city-centered systems. Each county has been assigned

Mechanization

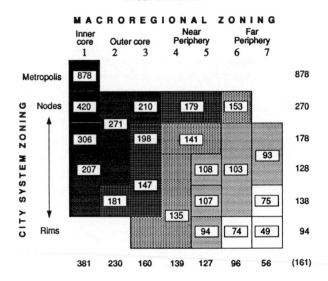

Irrigation

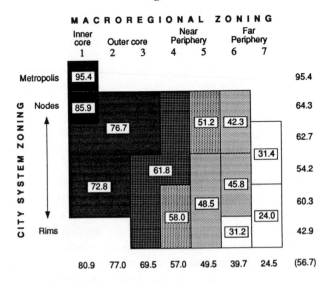

Figure 1. Agricultural Inputs

Upper chart: Mechanization, in watts per mu of cultivated land, 1985. Lower chart: Irrigated land as a share of cultivated land, in percent, 1985.

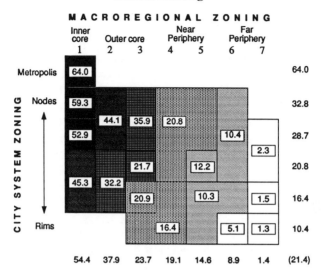

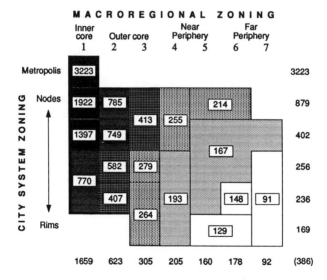

Figure 1 (continued). Agricultural Inputs

Upper chart: Tractor-plowed land as a share of cultivated land, in percent, 1985. Lower chart: Electricity use, in 100 watt-hours per mu, 1985.

to one of six classes according to its urbanization index and the hierarchical level and configuration of its towns.

The irregular outline of the chart reflects the fact that cells at the upper right and lower left are empty—no cases fall in them. In my previous analysis, I argued that in late imperial times higher-order cities were concentrated in cores and might be entirely absent from the periphery; this is obviously still true of Lingnan.[25] In this chart, the top row consists of only one cell, which in turn contains only one case, the municipality that includes Guangzhou. (If data were available, Hong Kong, which already in 1982 functioned as a second metropolis of the Lingnan regional economy, would also fall in this cell.) As is true of all other central metropolises in China, Guangzhou is situated in the inner core, so that its cell is positioned in the first column (Zone 1); since the remaining zones of the core-periphery structure lack any comparable urban unit, the other cells in this row are empty and excluded from the chart. The second row has an empty (and hence missing) cell at the far right; this tells us that none of the counties in the far periphery contains a high-order city. The two missing cells at the lower left attest the lack of any inner-core counties that fall into the most rural class of counties. The rural rims of city systems in the inner core typically fall in the outer core of the macroregional system.

To summarize, then, both dimensions of the chart refer to spatial position, and together they "model" hierarchical regional space, bringing together in the same cell counties similarly situated within the internally differentiated macroregional system. The upper-left cell containing Guangzhou municipality represents one extreme of internal differentiation: the most urbanized unit of the inner core. The other extreme is found at the diagonally opposite cell, which contains counties that are doubly peripheral: situated in the far periphery of the macroregional system and also at the rural rim of component city-centered systems. Attributes that vary monotonically through the upper reaches of hierarchical regional space will, in charts so constructed, show a steady progression of mean values from the upper-left cell to the lower-right cell, yielding a more or less diagonal patterning.

Before turning to my findings, we would do well to inspect more closely the structure of the charts I have just introduced. We may continue to focus on the first chart of Figure 1, where data on agricultural mechanization are presented. The highest level of mechanization (a mean of 878 watts per mu) is found in the periurban areas of Guangzhou municipality at the upper left, while the lowest level (49 watts per mu) is found in the diagonally opposite corner. If we take any pathway across the chart, moving downward and/or to the right, the values get smaller. So, going around the rim of the chart clockwise, we see the following progression: 878, 271, 210, 179, 153, 93, 75, 49. Going around the chart in the opposite direction, counterclockwise, we see 878, 420, 306, 207, 181, 147, 135, 94, 74, 49. Similarly, pathways that go directly across the chart also yield a steady downward progression. This monotonic pattern is imposed on the data by a non-parametric fitting procedure that consists essentially of combining cells representing contrary movements. As a result, a chart with more and smaller groupings of cells indicates sharper differentiation in HRS than does a comparable chart with fewer and larger groupings of cells.

More importantly, this non-parametric fitting procedure brings out with particular clarity differences in the salience of variation in the two dimensions. So, to compare the first two charts of Figure 1, we may first conclude that the mechanization of agriculture is more finely graded in HRS than is the proportion of land irrigated. More importantly, we can say that, while mechanization is fairly well differentiated within city systems as well as the macroregion, in the case of irrigation city-system variation is muted by comparison with macroregional variation. For the most part, the diagonals are close to the vertical in the irrigation chart, enabling us to conclude that, while irrigation varies in HRS, it does so much more sharply through the core-periphery structure of macroregions than within city systems. Let us contrast the chart for irrigation with that for the population of each county's largest town (Figure 5). Here, the diagonals are very nearly horizontal bars, indicating greater salience through the space of city-systems. It could hardly be otherwise with an urban variable, of course, and the reason for reproducing this chart here is to show that urbanization *does also* vary through macroregional space when place in city systems is controlled.

7. Spatial Differentiation in Level of Development

To this point, we have developed a geographically specific empirical model of Lingnan's regional structure and introduced a cross-tabular matrix designed to facilitate the display of data ordered in accordance with the systems hierarchy. We are now positioned to address the main argument of the paper—namely, that the HRS model effectively differentiates the relative level of development in its various aspects. In the case of each attribute, the expectation is that its "advanced" or "developed" or "modern" manifestation will characterize the urbanized inner core, with a monotonic progression through HRS to the most rural counties of the far periphery,

34

Grain Yields

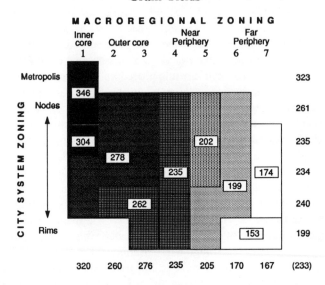

Meat Production

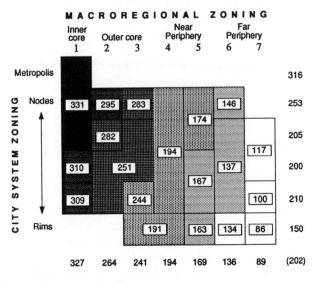

Figure 2. Agricultural Outputs

Upper chart: Mean yield of all grains, in tons per 1000 mu of sown area, 1985. Lower chart: Meat output, in tons per 100,000 rural population, 1985.

whose extreme values reflect backwardness and underdevelopment. We may begin with economic development.

Figure 1 displays data on four agricultural inputs, all indexed in relation to cultivated land. The weakest relationship shown is that for irrigation, where the proportion of cultivated land under irrigation in the urbanized core is "only" 3.4 times that in the rural far periphery. The overall level of irrigation in Lingnan, 56.7 percent, is relatively high, reflecting high levels of rainfall, relatively gentle gradients in the river system, and long growing seasons that facilitate multiple cropping of rice.[26] While the overall extent of irrigation has undoubtedly increased under the PRC, the spatial differentiation shown in the second chart of Figure 1 probably differs only slightly from that obtaining a century earlier. As already noted, variation through macroregional space is much sharper than that through city-system space, reflecting no doubt the importance for hydrology of large-scale topography within the Lingnan drainage basin. Note in particular that differentiation is modest throughout the regional core, which lies largely in riverine lowlands. The very moderate differences within each core-periphery zone by place in city systems point to the relative inelasticity of irrigation *qua* factor of production in relation to urban demand.

Mechanization, tractor plowing, and farm electricity use are all modern inputs. Their sharp differentiation through HRS conforms closely with the proposed model of innovation diffusion. The difference between the two extremes across HRS is over 17-fold for farm mechanization, 35 times for electricity use, and 49 times for the proportion of tractor-plowed land. (Use of chemical fertilizer, another modern input, shows a 5-fold difference across HRS.) There are, of course, important topographic limitations to the extension of tractor plowing, which partly accounts for the low proportions in the periphery. But the clear evidence of response to urban demand indicates room for further growth in each of these modern inputs.

It follows from spatial variation in soil fertility and agricultural intensity (as indexed by factor inputs) that agricultural productivity would also vary systematically through HRS. The first chart of Figure 2 displays the findings for grain yields, which more than double across HRS. It may be noted that the precise pattern of differentiation in HRS closely resembles that for irrigation (and also that for fertilizer use, not shown here), and in fact, in a differently designed analysis to be published elsewhere, I am able to show that irrigation and fertilizer are the two most important determinants of grain yields. The data on meat output, displayed in the second chart of Figure 2, reveal sharper and more monotonic differentiation

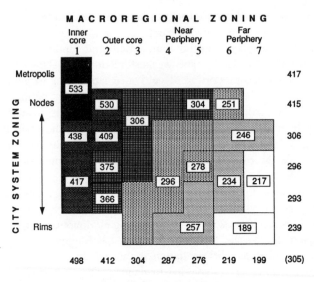

Figure 3. Gross Value of Agricultural Output

Note: Adjusted GVAO, in yuan per rural capita, 1985.

through HRS (a nearly 4-fold increase across the chart) and, as one might expect, considerable responsiveness to urban demand. A generalized indicator of agricultural productivity, the net value of agricultural output per rural capita, is displayed in Figure 3. For agricultural productivity as a whole, it appears, position within city systems is very nearly as salient as position within the macroregional core-periphery structure.

The spatial distribution of industry as against agriculture is clearly reflected in the two charts of Figure 4. With 78.9 percent of the labor force in agriculture, we see (setting aside the not-too-meaningful figure for Guangzhou municipality) variation from 58.9 percent in the most highly urbanized portion of the inner core to 93.8 percent in the most rural areas of the far periphery. While the proportion of farmers declines steadily with city-system location throughout the region, differentiation through the core-periphery structure is monotonic only in the three core zones. The only differentiation seen through the four zones of the regional periphery is at the two extremes (counties containing the nodal cities, on the one hand, and counties at the rural rims of city systems, on the other). By comparison, the distribution of the industrial population in HRS (the second chart of Figure 4) is much sharper and more nearly monotonic. The proportion of the employed population in industry varies across the HRS chart from a minuscule 1.2 percent in the most rural and remote counties to over 46

Agricultural Labor Force

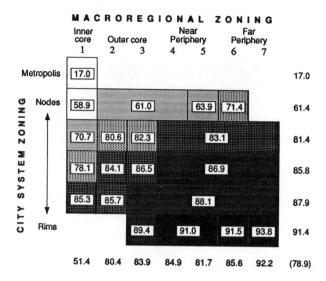

Industrial Labor Force

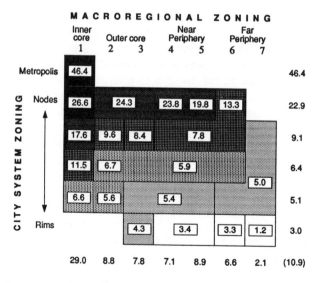

Figure 4. Occupational Structure

Upper chart: Agricultural population as share of employed population, in percent, 1982. Lower chart: Industrial population as share of employed population, 1982.

38

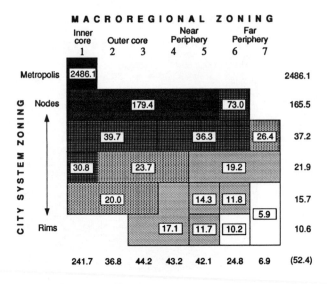

Figure 5. Size of Largest Town

Note: Mean non-agricultural population of the largest town in each county-level unit, in thousands, 1984.

percent for Guangzhou municipality. (I should note that when the proportion of the employed population in neither industry nor agriculture is displayed, the spatial patterning is similar to that for the industrial population. The major component of this residual category is commerce, and the sharp variation across HRS from 5 percent in the rural far periphery to over 36 percent in Guangzhou indicates that commerce, too, is a significant component of the pervasive spatial differentiation of the Lingnan economy.)

It goes without saying that the distribution of industry and commerce would closely mirror position within city systems. However, as Figure 4 shows, the numerical strength of the industrial labor force varies not only through the node-to-rim structure of city systems but also through the core-periphery structure of the macroregional economy. This reflects not only the greater urbanization of regional core as against periphery, but also a gradient in rural industry through HRS, from underdeveloped in the far periphery to highly developed in the inner core. Figure 5 documents this important point for one urban variable, the mean population of the largest city/town in each county-level unit.

I have not yet inputted data on industrial production *per se*, but Figure 6 sets out the finding for industrial and agricultural productivity

39

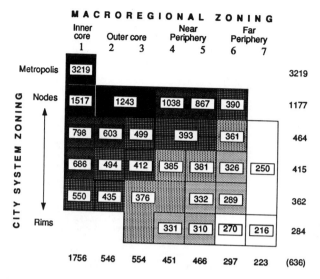

Figure 6. Gross Value of Industrial and Agricultural Output
Note: GVIAO, in yuan per capita, 1982.

combined. These data for per-capitized GVIAO show an astonishingly close approximation of perfect monotonicity through HRS as modeled here. They provide the best summary indicator now available of the spatial structure of Lingnan's regional economy.

There are, of course, many other economic propositions that deserve a rigorous test. For some of these, relevant county-level data have not yet been released, and for others I have not yet been able to track down or input the necessary data. Transport is a particularly egregious omission. The relevant propositions, which would almost certainly be smartly upheld, are that the density of the transport network, the volume of freight and passengers carried by it, the mean technological level of the transport mix, and transport efficiency would all covary through HRS. The overall model of a regional economy predicts that the density of economic transactions would be highest in the urbanized inner core, where markets of all kinds would be most fully developed. A general argument, not yet respecified for a market-socialist economy, is that revenue collection, both of the land tax and of commercial levies, would be most efficient (in the sense of greater tax take per unit of administrative effort) in urbanized inner cores, declining steadily through HRS to the rural periphery. Among the reasons are the high levels of productivity and income per capita and the high density of taxable units (households, farms, firms, marketplaces, etc.) per unit of area.

Illiteracy

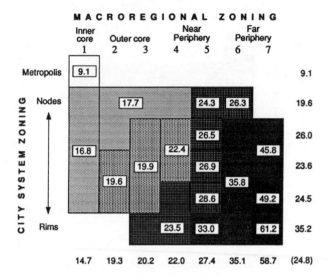

Junior Middle Schooling

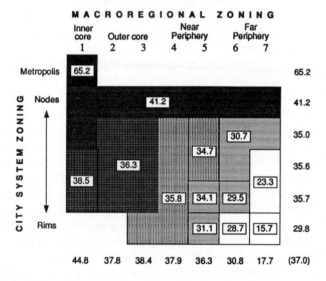

Figure 7. Education

Upper chart: Illiterate as share of population aged 12+, in percent, 1982. Lower chart: Those educated to junior middle school or higher as share of population aged 15+, in percent, 1982.

Turning to socioeconomic attributes, we might first call attention to the social significance of the findings already presented concerning occupational structure: opportunities for nonfarm employment increase steadily as one moves from the rural far periphery to the urbanized inner core, reflecting an ever more complex division of labor.

Figure 7 sets out findings on educational opportunity and attainment. In Guangzhou municipality, illiteracy has been reduced to less that 10 percent, and nearly two-thirds of the adult population has attended junior middle school. However, both literacy and level of educational attainment drop off sharply as one moves down the central-place hierarchy and out into the hinterlands of lower-order cities and towns. Note that in the most rural counties of the far periphery over 60 percent of adults remained illiterate as of 1982 and only 16 percent had attended junior middle school. (Given the well documented gender gap in educational attainment, we may assume that in these spatially disadvantaged counties at least three-quarters of all women over age 12 were illiterate.) Particulars of the spatial patterning indicate that urban residence counts for a lot, and that differentiation at these low levels of educational attainment is sharper in the regional periphery than in the core. This reflects the fact that primary schools are now found in all but the least favored villages, whereas junior middle schools are concentrated in central places. Data on higher levels of educational attainment, not presented here, document the consequence of pronounced urban bias in the distribution of secondary schools and universities. In the case of university graduates, variation through space is accounted for almost entirely by position within city systems, place in the macroregional core-periphery structure being largely irrelevant.

If illiteracy is one prime negative indicator of quality of life, infant mortality is clearly another.[27] My findings on this critical variable are set out in Figure 8. Here we see in Guangzhou municipality a very creditable rate of 10 per thousand, with a fairly gradual downward gradient through the upper reaches of HRS. The gradient steepens outside the cities in the periphery, reaching 80 per thousand (almost certainly a severe undercount) in the most rural and remote counties.[28]

Poverty is often taken as the third of the trinity of negative indicators of quality of life. The best index of overall poverty in my present data set is the income per capita of the agricultural population. (It goes without saying that excluding the urban population understates the degree of economic inequality.) The findings, displayed in Figure 9, document sharp differentiation in income levels through HRS. The mean income of farmers in most counties of the far periphery was *one-tenth* that of periurban farmers in Guangzhou municipality.

42

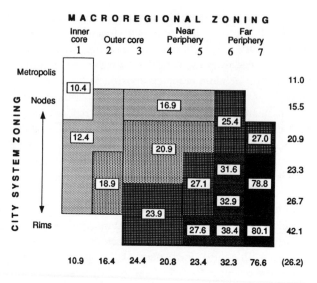

Figure 8. Infant Mortality

Note: Deaths during the first year of life, per 1000 births, 1981.

Turning now to demographic development, we must first clarify the nature of demographic and family "modernity." The demographic transition involves change from an "inefficient" regime of high fertility and high mortality to a more efficient demographic regime of low fertility and low mortality. The implications of this transition for change in the structural complexity and size of Chinese families are ambiguous. In the short run, declines in fertility may be offset by declines in infant and child mortality, though in the longer run the net effect of sustained fertility decline is to reduce the mean size of conjugal units. Declines in adult mortality tend to delay family division and hence increase the mean complexity and size of households at any point in time. This effect, however, may be offset by another modern, quasi-demographic trend—namely, the rise in age at marriage, which delays the domestic-cycle transition from conjugal to more complex forms and hence decreases the mean complexity and size of households at any point in time. Two other "modern" trends in Chinese family life have a less ambiguous effect on mean household complexity and size. One is the increase in neolocal marriage, and the other is an emerging change in the domestic cycle. In this increasingly accepted new form of the domestic cycle, when a daughter-in-law is brought in for a second son, one or the other of the junior conjugal units hives off to form an independent family, thereby inhibiting the formation of joint families and increasing the

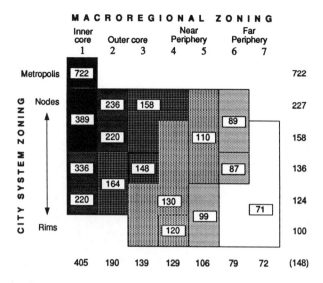

Figure 9. Farm Income

Note: Total annual income of the agricultural population, in yuan per capita, 1982.

overall proportion of stem and conjugal families.[29] Both structural changes serve to depress the mean complexity and size of households. On balance, then, we may take small household size as an indicator of family modernity.

We are now ready to test the proposition that demographic and family modernity vary systematically through HRS. For purposes of this paper, infant mortality (already presented in Figure 8) will have to stand in for overall mortality. (The crude death rate, which I have also calculated for 1981, shows a similar pattern in HRS, its level doubling from the one extreme in the urbanized inner core to the other in the rural far periphery.)

Data on fertility also vary sharply through HRS, as shown in Figure 10. The child-woman ratios displayed in the upper chart reveal that fertility during the preceding five years (that is, 1977-81) varied systematically from 53 children per 100 women of child-bearing age in the urban inner core to 166 children in the rural far periphery, a 3-fold increase across HRS. The general fertility rate, exhibited in the lower chart, presents a similar pattern for 1981 births alone; in this case, the rate increases 3.5 times from one extreme of HRS to the other.

These sharp findings on fertility speak to a controversy in the literature on the Chinese fertility decline. On the one hand, Martin King Whyte and William L. Parish have argued that the government's birth planning policies "have simply accelerated changes that could have been

Child-Woman Ratios

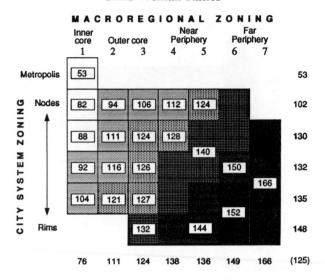

General Fertility Rates

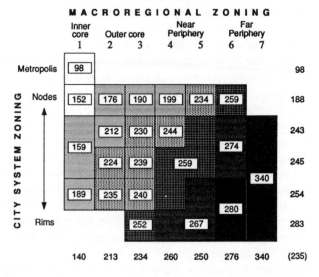

Figure 10. Fertility

Upper chart: Children aged 0-5 years, per 1000 women aged 15-45, 1982. Lower chart: Births per 1000 women aged 15-45, 1981.

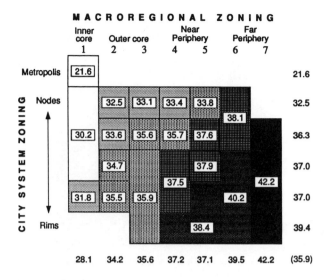

Figure 11. Age Structure

Note: Population aged 0-14 years as share of total population, in percent, 1982.

expected to occur as a result of industrialization, urbanization, and other forms of modern social change."[30] On the other hand, Arthur P. Wolf strongly argues the more usual position that the rapid fertility decline in the PRC is "largely the result of direct and forceful government intervention."[31] It is, in fact, quite remarkable that the patterning of fertility in HRS so closely replicates that of socioeconomic variables indexing "modern social change": the more modern the locality, the greater the shortfall between government targets and popular behavior. At the same time, we must also recognize that the HRS model in all likelihood captures consistent spatial differences in local policy and enforcement. Still, one could argue quite plausibly that departures from policy in implementation were in effect concessions forced by popular resistance, whose strength in different localities might reflect rather closely the level of development-cum-modernity.

Persistent spatial differentiation in fertility is likely to produce spatial differentiation in age structure. That this is true of Lingnan is apparent from Figure 11. Here we see that the proportion of young people, in this case those under 15 years of age, steadily increases through HRS, progressing from under 22 percent in Guangzhou municipality to nearly twice that in the far periphery. On the assumption that most children under 15 are living with their parents, these differences translate directly into

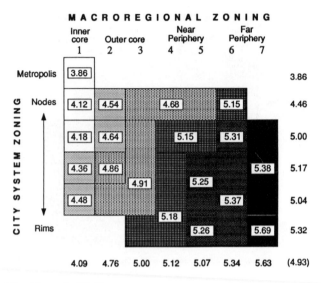

Figure 12. Household Size

Note: Mean number of persons per family household, 1982.

systematic spatial differentiation in the number of children per conjugal unit. Data on household size *per se* are displayed in Figure 12. The progression of mean family size across HRS revealed in this chart reflects systematic differences not only in the number of children (i.e., the size of conjugal units) but also in family complexity (i.e., the number of conjugal units per household). Though the two effects cannot be disentangled here, it appears likely that families in the higher reaches of HRS are both smaller and less complex—that is, more modern on both counts.

It remains to say a word about migration, a demographic phenomenon that is both inherently spatial and central to regional development. The obvious regional-systems formulation posits net migration flows from hinterland to node within systems at various levels, from lower-order to higher-order central places, and in general from the periphery toward the core. If this hypothesis were borne out, we would find the highest rates of net in-migration in the urbanized inner core, graded diagonally across HRS to low rates or net out-migration in the most rural counties of the far periphery—that is, the pattern we have found for all other developmental variables. When we look at Lingnan data on net migration (Figure 13), we see a sharp pattern but one distinct from that of any other variable displayed in this paper. Net out-migration characterizes the counties at lower left rather than at lower right, and the monotonic upward progression of values

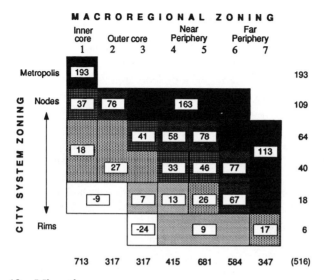

Figure 13. Migration

Note: Index of net in-migration, 1982.

is from lower left to upper right, rather than from lower right to upper left. We see sharp differentials within city systems throughout the region, attesting rural-to-urban and rural-toward-urban migration, but (holding position in city systems constant) net in-migration is heavier the more *peripheral* the city's position within the macroregion. It is as if a portion of migrants from the countryside were deflected from the most desirable destinations (the regional cities of the core) toward more peripherally situated towns. This feature of the distribution is, we may infer, the consequence of governmental restrictions on migration to municipalities; for the most part, migrants appear to have headed for the nearest central place that was a permissible destination. However, some other factor must be adduced to account for the attractiveness of all but the most rural counties of the far periphery to in-migrants. New employment opportunities there may be associated with the expansion of mining, lumbering, and possibly sheep grazing.

8. Conclusions

Definitive conclusions must await the completion of the China-wide project. Nevertheless, this analysis of Lingnan alone suffices to point up certain advantages of the regional-systems approach.

I have shown that the various aspects or manifestations of development (economic, social, educational, welfare, demographic, etc.) vary together through Lingnan's regional structure. The overall level of development rises through ascending levels of the systems hierarchy and from periphery to node within systems at each level. This implies that the developmental process proceeds within the arenas of local and regional systems, so defined. This finding is also consistent with the conceptualization of regional structure as a cumulative hierarchy of ever more inclusive town/city-centered systems.

With respect to method, the following observations are in order. (1) Recourse to disaggregated data is necessary to reveal the shape of China's regional economies. Data aggregated to the level of prefectures or provinces are too crude to do the job. (2) Simply plotting socioeconomic index values on a county-outline map will not reveal regional systems with any clarity because of their hierarchical structure. What appears as patchwork to the eye may in fact be the result of (often countervailing) variation at two or more levels of the systems hierarchy. Thus, as we have shown, analytical controls of city-system variation are necessary to reveal the full extent of core-periphery differentiation within a macroregional economy. (3) When virtually all aspects of development covary systematically through HRS, as shown here for Lingnan, we have an empirical situation that may confound widely used analytical procedures. For instance, ecological analyses employing regression models may be misleading as to cause and effect if spatial differentiation is not brought explicitly into the design. In the absence of spatial controls, the results can be largely an artifact of which few of the scores of indicators of development the investigator selected for inclusion in his/her regression models. While I have not sought to establish causal flows in this paper, its findings alert us to the desirability of building explanatory models on a prior regional systems analysis.

The systems hierarchy may be thought of as a "deep structure" unrecognized by the "natives"—that is, by the participants whose differentiated transactions constitute its very substance. Nonetheless, it is quite real—not imposed by the analyst, but rather revealed through an inductive methodology. As I have suggested for Lingnan, both the territorial extent and the internal structure of macroregional economies are subject to continual flux, responding to fortuitous events and deliberate policies, to the patterning of transport improvements and of trade expansion—in short, to changes of all kinds, exogenous as well as endogenous. If we think of Lingnan as a kind of self-organizing system, then it appears to have a certain built-in inertia.

The systems hierarchy is, so to speak, masked by the administrative hierarchy of provinces and prefectures, which has long had cognitive salience not only in China but also among outside analysts. Regional development is usually investigated by comparing provinces or groupings of provinces. But what can be said about level of development in Guangdong as a whole that is not misleading? It is not the province that is highly developed, but rather Lingnan's inner core. Guangdong's counties are found in each of the seven zones of Lingnan's core-periphery structure, and Guangxi's counties miss out on only Zone 1, the innermost core.

Nor does the usual contrast drawn between the developed coastal provinces and the underdeveloped interior provinces stand up in the face of regional analysis. Well over half of the coastal areas of Lingnan fall in the underdeveloped periphery, a finding that also holds for the China coast as a whole. To be sure, a global comparison of China's macroregional economies shows some of those abutting on the coast (Manchuria, the Lower Yangzi, and Lingnan) to be more advanced than some of those in the interior (the Upper Yangzi and especially Yungui). But the major fault line in the geography of China's development is not that of coast as against interior. It is core versus periphery within China's macroregional economies. Lingnan's far periphery is not much better off than the worst in all of China proper (Yungui's far periphery), and Lingnan's inner core is not far behind the very best (the Lower Yangzi's inner core). There is, moreover, nothing ad hoc about this stark patterning in level of development, ranging from that of poor Third World countries at the one extreme to that of newly industrializing countries at the other. Rather, the differentiation is both systematic and systemic.

Notes

1. I am grateful to Dudley L. Poston, Jr., and William R. Lavely for sharing data and data sources. Special thanks are due to Bill Chu for computation and to Sherry Smith-Williams for research assistance. The maps were prepared by Chessy Si, the charts by Sherry Smith-Williams. Precursors of this paper were delivered at the Contemporary China Studies Seminar, University of Hong Kong, and the Symposium on the Great Transformation in South China and

Taiwan, Cornell University; on both occasions I benefited from the criticism of participants. Griffith Feeney and Susan Mann were kind enough to provide a critical reading.

2. G. William Skinner, "Urban Development in Imperial China," in G. William Skinner (ed.), *The City in Late Imperial China* (Stanford: Stanford University Press, 1977), pp. 9-17. See also G. William Skinner, "The Structure of Chinese History," *Journal of Asian Studies*, 44(2), 1985.

3. G. William Skinner, "Regional Urbanization in Nineteenth-Century China," in Skinner, *The City*, pp. 216-18; G. William Skinner, "Cities and the Hierarchy of Local Systems," in Skinner, *The City*, pp. 286-88.

4. Skinner, "Cities and the Hierarchy of Local Systems," pp. 275-86.

5. G. William Skinner, "Marketing and Social Structure in Rural China, Part I," *Journal of Asian Studies*, 24(1), 1964.

6. For an analysis through seven levels of the hierarchy in one regional economy, see Skinner, "Cities and the Hierarchy of Local Systems," pp. 288-98.

7. The overall project is supported by the National Science Foundation (Grant no. 91-122939).

8. That analysis also used data on goods and services available in particular towns. For the procedures followed in assigning central places to levels in the economic hierarchy, see Skinner, "Cities and the Hierarchy of Local Systems," Appendix.

9. Skinner, "Cities and the Hierarchy of Local Systems," pp. 307-46.

10. Walter Christaller, *Zie zentralen Orte in Süddeutschland* (Jena: Gustav Fisher, 1933); translated by Carlisle W. Baskin as *Central Places in Southern Germany* (Englewood Cliffs, NJ: Prentice-Hall, 1966).

11. Skinner, "Cities and the Hierarchy of Local Systems," pp. 276-85; John U. Marshall, *The Structure of Urban Systems* (Toronto: University of Toronto Press, 1989), Chapter 6.

12. Johann Heinrich von Thünen, *Der isolierte Staat in Beziehung auf Landwirtschaft und Nationalökonomie* (Berlin, 1826); translated by Carla M. Wartenberg as *Isolated State* (Oxford: Pergamon, 1966). See also Michael Chisholm, *Rural Settlement and Land Use* (New York: Wiley, 1962); D. W. Harvey, "Theoretical Concepts and the Analysis of Agricultural Land Use in Geography," *Annals of the Association of American Geographers*, 56, 1966; and John R. Tarrant, *Agricultural Geography* (New York: Wiley, 1974).

13. See John C. Hudson, *Geographical Diffusion Theory* (Evanston: Northwestern University, 1972); and Andrew D. Cliff et al., *Spatial Aspects of Influenza Epidemics* (London: Pion, 1986).

14. Torsten Hägerstrand, "Aspects of the Spatial Structure of Social Communication and the Diffusion of Information," *Papers of the Regional Science Association*, 15, 1966, p. 27.

15. For a lucid exposition of the rationale and methodology of central-place analysis, see Marshall, *Structure of Urban Systems*, Chapters 5-7.

16. The transport network was vectorized from 1:1,000,000 sheet maps of China published by Xi'an Ditu Chubanshe. The vectorized database is used courtesy of Lawrence W. Crissman, Director of the Australian Centre of the Asian Spatial Information and Analysis Network, Griffith University. Data on municipalities and *zhen* are taken from *China Urban Statistics 1985* (London: Longman, 1985) and *Zhongguo chengzhen renkou ziliao shouce* (Beijing: Ditu Chubanshe, 1985), respectively.

17. If the areal units of analysis were sufficiently small (townships, say), one could simply classify them by the level of the highest-order central place. However, county-level units, a bit large for the purpose at hand, often contain more than one important town—so that, for example, one must distinguish counties with a greater city and two local cities from those with a greater city and only one local city or none.

18. The relatively small number of cases in any one macroregional economy permits no more than six classes. Class intervals were chosen, *inter alia*, to maximize the homogeneity of each class on the level and configuration variable. Thus, for example, county-level units containing a regional city are all in Class 2, and counties lacking even one central market town are all in Class 6.

19. It should be emphasized that the objective of the analysis presented here is to achieve the best possible delineation of China's regional structure, and for that purpose one should use all available information. A Spearman correlation matrix of all socioeconomic variables in the dataset (excluding structural urban variables) was analyzed to identify the dozen or so most highly intercorrelated variables, which (reduced by dropping a few variables to avoid overrepresentation of any one class—say, agricultural inputs) were taken as components of the omnibus index. It goes without saying that when one pursues substantive analyses and/or tests hypotheses, more restrictive regionalizations are required to avoid tautology. So, for instance, in the larger research project of which this is a part, we plan an analysis of agriculture that uses a regionalization based on occupance density and an analysis of demographic processes that uses a strictly economic regionalization.

20. The omnibus macroregional index developed for Lingnan is based on nine highly intercorrelated substantive variables. These are measures, respectively, of farm mechanization, irrigated area, electricity use, meat output, farm income, agricultural productivity, illiteracy, child-woman ratios, and age structure. In this regard, it might be noted that, for any given macroregional system, all socioeconomic variables (at least all those in my dataset) that intercorrelate with high coefficients turn out to covary through HRS.

21. In practice, procedures involve more iterations than described here. For instance, the nth adjustment of the MRI (macroregional index) may slightly alter the positioning of the macroregional boundary. But if a couple of counties are thereby dropped or added, at least part of the analysis must be redone. At the same time, the separate macroregional analyses must be reconciled. So, regional analysis of the Middle Yangzi is unlikely to yield a southern boundary (at least not on the first try) that is identical to the northern boundary indicated by the Lingnan analysis. This consideration introduces further criteria (and complications) into the end-stage fine tuning.

22. The most notable example is the massive program of investment in the interior macroregions carried out for military reasons between 1964 and 1971. Whenever halfway feasible, industrial sites in the mountainous periphery were preferred to those in regional cores. See Barry Naughton, "The Third Front: Defence Industrialization in the Chinese Interior," *China Quarterly*, no. 115, September 1988. For Maoist programs to disrupt the economic rationality of local marketing systems, see G. William Skinner, "Rural Marketing in China: Repression and Revival," *China Quarterly*, no. 103, September 1985.

23. William R.Lavely, Zhenwu Xiao, Bohua Li, and Ronald Freedman, "The Rise in Female Education in China: National and Regional Patterns," *China Quarterly*, no. 121, March 1990, pp. 61-93. Lingnan is one of three macroregions given comparative treatment. Lavely's research design was (unavoidably) anachronistic in that he classified counties in accordance with my earlier regionalization. If the study were redone using the regional framework provided by this paper, one would expect sharper findings.

24. That these rough comparisons are not too wide of the mark is suggested by the following illustrative data. Lingnan's far periphery (FP) and Nepal as a whole exhibit comparably low urbanization rates (Lingnan's FP 6.8 percent in 1984, Nepal 8.1 percent in 1981), high proportions of agriculturalists in the employed population (Lingnan's FP 92.2 percent in 1982, Nepal 91.1 percent in 1981), low proportions of cultivated land under irrigation (Lingnan's FP 24.5 percent in 1985, Nepal 23.7 percent in 1981), high rates of adult illiteracy (Lingnan's FP 61.2 percent in 1982, Nepal 72.2 percent in 1981), and very young age structures (Lingnan's FP 42.19 percent aged 0-14 in 1982, Nepal 41.35 in 1981). Lingnan's inner core (IC) and South Korea as a whole exhibit comparably high proportions of the employed population in industry (Lingnan's IC 29.0 percent in 1982, South Korea 29.0 percent in 1980), high levels of fertilizer use in agriculture (Lingnan's IC 254.7 kilograms per hectare in 1985, South Korea 281.7 in 1982), low rates of adult illiteracy (Lingnan's IC 14.7 percent in 1982, South Korea 7.3 percent in 1980), balanced age structures (Lingnan's IC 28.1 percent aged 0-14 in 1982, South Korea 29.7 percent in 1984), and low rates of infant mortality (Lingnan's IC 10.9 per thousand in 1981, South Korea 16.0 in 1991). The data on Nepal and South Korea are drawn from George T. Kurian (ed.), *Encyclopedia of the Third World*, 3d ed. (New York: Facts on File, 1987); World Bank, *World Development Report 1983* (New York: Oxford University Press, 1983); World Bank, *World Development Report 1985* (New York: Oxford University Press, 1985); World Bank, *World Development Report 1987* (New York: Oxford University Press, 1987); *Population Monograph of Nepal* (Kathmandu: Central Bureau of Statistics, 1987); and *Statistical Yearbook of Nepal* (Kathmandu: Central Bureau of Statistics, 1987).

25. Skinner, "Cities and the Hierarchy of Local Systems," pp. 286-87.

26. Lingnan ranks fourth in this regard. The proportion of farmland under irrigation is 78.4 percent in the Lower Yangzi, 67.5 percent in the Southeast Coast, and 61.0 percent in the Middle Yangzi. At the other extreme, only 16.7 of the farmland in Manchuria is irrigated.

27. For a pioneering effort to develop a quality-of-life index using county-level data, see Walter H. Aschmoneit, "Life-Quality Index of China," in Jörgen Delman et al. (eds.), *Remaking Peasant China* (Aarhus: Aarhus University Press, 1990), pp. 204-14.

28. Because of leakage in data collection, the rates implicit in the 1981 data understate the actual level of infant mortality. In her book *China's Changing Population* (Stanford: Stanford University Press, 1987), Judith Banister indicates that the undercount must be at least 30 percent overall. To the extent that the recording of infant deaths varies systematically through HRS, we may expect records to be more complete in the urbanized core than in the rural periphery. Thus, if the rate shown for the urban inner core is understated by 20 percent (so that the reported rate of 10 implies an actual rate of 12), that of the far periphery might be understated by 40 percent (so that 80 implies 112). In all probability, then, Figure 8 understates the degree of spatial differentiation in infant mortality.

29. With respect to the Lingnan core, see Sulamith H. Potter and Jack M. Potter, *China's Peasants: The Anthropology of a Revolution* (Cambridge: Cambridge University Press, 1990), Chapter 10; and Anita Chan, Richard Madsen, and Jonathan Unger, *Chen Village: The Recent History of a Peasant Community in Mao's China* (Berkeley: University of California Press, 1984), Chapter 7.

30. Martin King Whyte and William L. Parish, *Urban Life in Contemporary China* (Chicago: University of Chicago Press, 1984), p. 191.

31. Arthur P. Wolf, "The Preeminent Role of Government Intervention in China's Family Revolution," *Population and Development Review*, 12, 1986, p. 101.

Open for Business, Open to the World: Consequences of Global Incorporation in Guangdong and the Pearl River Delta

Graham E. Johnson

1. Introduction

China's economic and political problems in the thirty-year period after 1949 were major.[1] The Soviet-inspired developmental strategy of the 1950s created institutional rigidities that persisted, despite the effort to create Chinese-style socialism after 1958.[2] Ill-considered policies such as the Great Leap Forward in 1958, political chaos during and after the Cultural Revolution, and the leftist tendencies of the Gang of Four period in the 1970s created a succession of economic and political crises.

In late 1978, with Deng Xiaoping firmly in control of the Chinese state, massive tampering with the machinery of economic control that had been in place since the 1950s was attempted. A new "open door" policy was created. A cautious opening to the forces of the market and the global economy occurred. In the search for a recipe for economic success, the coastal regions of south and southeast China were given a degree of autonomy to develop innovative responses to China's perceived crisis, which was seen in large part as a failure to improve the material well-being of the population. Part of the effort resulted in negotiations to resume sovereignty over Hong Kong and Macao.

Hong Kong's political status will change with the resumption of Chinese sovereignty over the territory in 1997, and British colonial control will come to a formal end. In the late twentieth century, Hong Kong has a distinctive and major role in the global economy—which, in the decade since reform in China began in 1979, has become central to China's incorporation into the world economic system. One hundred and fifty years of British administration in Hong Kong has had a profound impact on the territory. It has created a distinctive social system that cannot readily and expeditiously be incorporated into the existing economic, political and social structures in China itself. Negotiations between the governments of China and Britain therefore attempted to create a legal and political structure for the Hong Kong region ("the Basic Law") to take into account Hong Kong's historical development and its role in China's own economic future.[3]

This paper will outline some of the features that have made Hong Kong distinctive, especially over the past forty years, and the role that it has come to play in the economic transformation of Guangdong province. It will describe how Hong Kong's fractured links with its hinterland in the period before 1979 had a pronounced effect on its own economic performance. These links have changed significantly since economic reform began in China in 1979 and since the Anglo-Chinese agreement on the future of the territory was signed. Hong Kong has been a major element in the transformation of its hinterland. I will discuss the impact of connections between Hong Kong and its hinterland through an examination of five localities in the Pearl River delta region. I will indicate that where Hong Kong connections are intense there has been major structural change as production systems are incorporated into the global economy. The entrepreneurial activities with Hong Kong partners are a key to economic transformation. Where partnership is lacking, structural change is muted. In parts of Hong Kong's hinterland where the extensive links are with Overseas Chinese (*huaqiao* or *huayi*) in contrast to Hong Kong "compatriots" (*tongbao*), while the impact of those connections is substantial, especially for the social infrastructure, they have not resulted in fundamental economic restructuring.

2. Chinese Development Strategies, Guangdong, and the Pearl River Delta Region

The economic transformations as a consequence of policy initiatives since 1979 have been substantial in all the coastal provinces of China.[4] They have been especially marked in Guangdong, which has become firmly incorporated into the global economy and has assumed a particular role in the new international division of labor.[5] Major rural economic change has occurred as a consequence of incorporation into the world system. There has been a shift from a relatively insulated, state-dominated economic system to one that is open to outside influences, and in which rural households and communities have assumed, or re-assumed, control over production activities.

Economic opportunity in nonagricultural production has been expanded throughout rural China and has had major consequences for peasant households, which can deploy their members into an array of new economic activities. The major changes in China's rural development policies and their impact in a variety of regional contexts since 1979 have been extensively documented.[6]

Guangdong, located strategically along China's south coast, is a large province of substantial geographic, economic, and cultural diversity. Its economic core is the Pearl River delta, with Guangzhou as its regional center. The delta also contains Hong Kong and Macao and two of the three Special Economic Zones that were located in Guangdong after the promulgation of the new "open door" policies in 1979. Outside the delta, the province is mountainous and therefore relatively poor, with inadequate communications and a pronounced linguistic diversity.

Guangdong is one of China's great economic regions, ranking third in terms of the total value of production at the onset of the 1990s. Overall economic growth rates have been rapid since the middle of the 1980s in contrast with earlier periods, especially the decade and a half after the beginning of the Cultural Revolution (1965-79). (See Tables 1 and 2.) As China's "southern gate," Guangdong has consistently attracted the bulk of China's foreign investment since the reform period began, which has had consequences for the province as a whole but especially in the Pearl River delta region.[7] The province's trade performance has been significant in the reform decade, accounting for slightly less than a fifth of China's domestic exports at the end of the 1980s (Table 1).

Aggregate statistics for Guangdong province, although impressive, mask the performance of the delta region, which since early 1985 has been designated an "Open Economic Region" (*jingji kaifang qu*).[8] The delta region occupies a commanding position in the Guangdong provincial economy. It has built on its advantageous location, closely proximate to Hong Kong and, through it, to the world economy. Before 1978, it was unable to take full advantage of its long tradition of commercialized production but nonetheless was the major provincial producer of cash crops such as sugar cane, fruits, and vegetables, and of fish and silk cocoons. In the wake of rural reform, its agricultural sector has flourished under the newly liberalized policies. While sericulture in the central delta region has declined, the production of fish, fruits, and vegetables—destined both for the domestic market and for Hong Kong/Macao and beyond—has expanded dramatically.

The major transformation in the rural sector, however, has not been in agriculture. Rapid economic growth has occurred as the rural sector has shifted to an emphasis on nonagricultural production. Entrepreneurial energies have been released in a flurry of industrial growth. This was concentrated, initially, in certain regions of the delta. The central delta

Table 1. Guangdong Province: Selected Indicators, 1952-90

	1952	1965	1978	1985	1990
Population (millions)	29.1	38.7	50.6	56.7	62.5
non-agricultural	5.1	6.8	8.2		14.7
Labor Force (millions)	12.7	16.4	22.8	27.3	31.2
non-agricultural	2.3	3.2	5.2	6.9	8.5
GVIAO (billion yuan)	3.6	10.0	27.4	65.8	165.2
agriculture	2.1	3.6	7.4	15.3	22.2
industry	1.5	6.4	20.0	50.5	143.0
Foreign Trade (billion USD)	n.a.	0.3	1.6	5.4	16.3
exports	0.1	0.3	1.4	3.0	10.6
GNP per Capita (yuan)	102	196	319	825	1812
Average Wage (yuan)			789[a]	1393	2929
Rural Income per Capita (yuan)			274[a]	495	1043
Commodity Output					
grain (million tons)	7.97	12.27	13.29	15.09	18.96
sugar cane (million tons)	2.65	5.23	8.35	18.35	20.93
fruit (million tons)	0.17	0.20	0.29	1.16	3.29
aquatic products (million tons)	n.a.	0.35	0.66	1.09	2.08
pork (million tons)			0.63[a]	0.98	1.45
cloth (million meters)	77	148	227	246	459
bicycles (thousands)		120.1	622.5	2051	2963
sewing machines (thousands)	5.6	142.5	450.6	1600	970.5
televisions (thousands)			17.2	1084	3216

59

Table 1, continued

	1952	1965	1978	1985	1990
washing machines (thousands)			4.9[b]	779	1430
refrigerators (thousands)			2.6[a]	235.4	1057

a. 1980.
b. 1979.

Sources: Guangdong sheng tongji ju, *Qianjinzhong de guangdong: 1949-1988 nian guangdong shehui jingji fazhan qingkuang [Guangdong Forging Ahead: The Character of Guangdong's Social and Economic Development, 1949-88]* (Hong Kong: Dadao wenhua, 1989); Guangdong sheng tongji ju, *Guangdong tongji nianjian 1992 [Guangdong statistical yearbook 1992]* (Beijing: Zhongguo tongji, 1992); Guangdong nianjian bianzuan weiyuanhui, *Guangdong nianjian 1991 [1991 Guangdong yearbook]* (Guangzhou: Guangdong renmin, 1991).

region from Guangzhou south to Macao and the Zhuhai Special Economic Zone and the eastern corridor to Hong Kong and the rapidly expanding Shenzhen area were the major areas of economic activity at the outset of the reform period. These developments were possible partly because national policy allowed the province considerable autonomy to pursue innovative measures to seek capital and to retain foreign exchange earnings. The central and eastern Pearl River delta regions were also able to mobilize extensive links with kinsmen and fellow-countrymen who live in Hong Kong and Macao. The western delta region renewed links with kinsmen and fellow-countrymen both in Hong Kong and overseas, especially in North America.

The entire delta region has long been an area of out-migration. From the mid-nineteenth century large numbers of emigrés from south and southeast China worked as unskilled laborers in the Americas, southern Africa, and Southeast Asia. The western reaches of the delta region are the ancestral homeland of the great majority of Americans and Canadians of Chinese origin. Under different circumstances, a large number of delta residents left for Hong Kong in the late 1940s and early 1950s, and many contributed to Hong Kong's economic transformation after 1950.

In the 1980s, the entrepreneurial skills and capital of these emigrés were actively sought by their Guangdong kinsmen and fellow-countrymen. Kinship connections and local loyalties have become a central part of local development initiatives. In the process, the delta region has become firmly linked to the global economy through its Hong Kong connections. It has

60

Table 2. Guangdong Province: Selected Growth Rates, 1952-90

	Average Annual Growth Rate (%)		
	1952-65	1965-78	1978-90
Population	2.2	2.1	1.8
non-agricultural	2.2	1.5	5.0
Labor Force	2.0	2.6	2.6
non-agricultural	2.6	3.8	4.2
GVIAO	8.2	8.1	16.2
agriculture	4.2	5.7	9.6
industry	11.8	9.2	17.8
Foreign Trade		13.7	21.3
exports	8.8	9.4	18.4
GNP per Capita	5.2	3.8	15.6
Commodity Output			
grain	3.4	0.6	2.6
sugar cane	5.4	3.7	8.0
fruit	1.3	2.9	22.4
aquatic products		5.0	10.0
pork			8.7[a]
cloth	5.2	3.3	6.0
bicycles		13.5	13.9
sewing machines	28.3	9.3	6.6
televisions			54.6
washing machines			67.5[b]
refrigerators			82.4[a]

Note: All growth rates estimated from initial and terminal observations only.

a. 1980-90.
b. 1979-90.

Sources: See Table 1.

Table 3. The Pearl Delta Regional Economy, 1990

	Open Economic Region[a]	Guangzhou Urban Area	Shenzhen SEZ	Zhuhai SEZ	Total	Share in Province (percent)
Population (millions)[b]	16.56	3.94	0.88	0.33	21.71	34.8
GVIAO (billion yuan)	69.19	26.02	14.21	3.72	113.14	68.5
agriculture	7.55	0.41	0.04	0.08	8.08	36.4
industry	61.63	25.62	14.17	3.64	105.06	73.5
Exports (billion USD)	3.39	1.23	2.95	0.46	8.13	77.0
GVIAO per Capita (yuan)	4178	6604	16,148	11,272	5211	

a. The Pearl River Delta Open Economic Region is composed of 28 *xian* and municipalities and excludes the "urban" area of Guangzhou and the Shenzhen and Zhuhai Special Economic Zones. Guangzhou's dependent *xian* (Panyu, Zengcheng, Huaxian, and Conghua) and the dependent *xian* of Shenzhen and Zhuhai (Baoan and Daomen, respectively) are included in the open economic region.

b. Includes temporary residents without official residence permits.

Sources: Guangdong sheng tongji ju, *Guangdong tongji nianjian 1991*; Guangdong sheng tongji ju, *Qianjinzhong de guangdong*.

thus begun to share with other parts of East and Southeast Asia some of the developmental characteristics that McGee has described as the "desakota process," in which an intense mixture of agricultural and non-agricultural activities stretches along linear corridors between large city cores. The process, McGee indicates, typically occurs in regions, characterized by high population densities, that were formerly dominated by wet rice agriculture.[9] The Pearl River delta constitutes one of these desakota regions (Table 3).

3. Hong Kong: From Entrepot to Entrepreneur

Hong Kong was created as a consequence of the expansion of European capitalism into East Asia in the mid-nineteenth century, when China was forcibly opened to the full force of economic processes that it was incapable of incorporating without massive economic, political, and social disruption. China reluctantly became a part of the "world system," and Hong Kong played a key role in Chinese economic history in the century that followed, along with a set of "Treaty Ports" created in the wake of the Anglo-Chinese conflict that ceded Hong Kong, "in perpetuity," to the British.[10]

British procedures were dominant in the Treaty Ports along the China coast and especially in Shanghai, Hong Kong's illustrious twin on the Yangzi, until the Second World War fundamentally affected global economic and political forces. The British dominated China's two great commercial deltas from the mid-nineteenth century, and British merchants (and perhaps other merchants of European origin) found commercial dealings there, enforceable in British courts, a more reliable alternative to the older arrangements of the trading season in Guangzhou, subject to the whim of Chinese government officials, and an enforced sojourn in Portuguese Macao, whose government was at best indifferent to the needs of the China traders.

The first phase of Hong Kong's history effectively ended in 1941, the centennial of its creation as a British possession, when it came under Japanese occupation. The occupation of Hong Kong was severe in its impact.[11] In 1945, when it ended, Hong Kong's role in the world economy began to undergo a major transformation. Structural changes in the global economy created opportunities for the territory that could scarcely have been imagined at the moment of its liberation from occupation by Japan.

The immediate consequence of civil war in China and the formation of the People's Republic of China was the flight of capital and entrepreneurial skill to Hong Kong. There was also a massive out-migration of people from throughout China but especially from its Pearl River delta hinterland. Chinese capital and entrepreneurial skill, ample supplies of (cheap and hard working) labor, and an interventionist governmental structure were key factors in creating the economic system that emerged in the 1950s and 1960s.

From the early 1950s, China moved in a distinctive "socialist" direction and, for a complex of reasons, was significantly insulated from the global economy for the succeeding thirty years. As a consequence, Hong Kong's relationship to its hinterland changed. Vogel has suggested that Hong Kong "lost" its hinterland in 1950 in the wake of the formation of the People's Republic of China.[12] The entrepot trade with China, which had been Hong Kong's *raison d'être* from its beginnings as a British colony, ended with the Japanese occupation in 1941. It recovered during the chaotic period of the Chinese civil war in the late 1940s, but was compromised by China's domestic policies and pressures on the Hong Kong government by American foreign policy dictates after 1950.

Table 4. Hong Kong in Developmental Context: Basic Indicators, 1990

Country or Region	Population (millions)	GNP per Capita (USD)	Growth Rate (percent)[a]	Life Expectancy (years)
Hong Kong	5.8	11,590	6.2	78
Singapore	3.0	11,160	6.5	74
South Korea	42.8	5400	7.1	71
Taiwan	20.1	7512	7.8	74
China	1133.7	370	5.8	70
India	849.5	350	1.9	59
OECD	776.8	20,170	2.4	77
Japan	123.5	25,430	4.1	79
Poland	38.2	1690	n.a.	71
Hungary	10.6	2780	n.a.	71
Low-Income Countries[b]	1075.1	320	1.7	55
Middle-Income Countries[b]	1087.5	2220	2.2	66

a. Average annual growth rate of GNP per capita, 1965-90.
b. World Bank categories; low-income group excludes China and India.

Sources: World Bank, *World Development Report 1992* (New York: Oxford University Press, 1992); *Chung-hua min-kuo t'ung-chi nien-chien 1990 [Republic of China Statistical Yearbook 1990]* (Taipei: Executive Yuan, 1990).

Hong Kong survived as a capitalist enclave on China's southernmost border despite the restrictions on the China trade. In the thirty years after the formation of the People's Republic and the economic difficulties that it created for Hong Kong, an efficient and prosperous manufacturing economy assumed an increasingly important role in a global economy, itself undergoing a major restructuring. Its developmental path was paralleled by those of Taiwan, South Korea, and Singapore (the Asian "NICs") and exhibited rapid economic growth.[13] By 1980, Hong Kong had a GNP per capita on par with some southern European economies and bettered in Asia by only Japan and oil-rich Brunei (and closely matched by Singapore). Its economic advance and its material well-being stood in great contrast to those of China, a contrast that remained even after the advances in China during the 1980s (Table 4).

4. Consequences for Hong Kong

From its beginnings, Hong Kong has been critically dependent on developments in China. The establishment of the People's Republic of China compromised the entrepot trade. The in-migration of entrepreneurial talent and an enormous pool of labor, from Hong Kong's hinterland and beyond, contributed to a major economic transformation beginning in the 1950s. China's long periods of relative isolation from global economic forces only intensified Hong Kong's efforts to create a new accommodation with a changing international economy. The reform period in China after 1979, and especially the commitment to seek new economic paths in Guangdong, had a profound effect on Hong Kong, which had become a major Asian industrial center by the time the reform effort in China got underway.

The motor of Hong Kong's development from the 1950s was manufacturing. It began with textiles—in large measure a consequence of the relocation of Shanghai interests in the late 1940s.[14] Hong Kong entrepreneurs, with extensive assistance from the Hong Kong government, responded readily to changing world market conditions. The role of the Hong Kong government seems critical. It certainly assisted in a conventional fashion through trade promotion and also bargained decisively in terms of international agreements to ensure that Hong Kong's manufactured goods entered the global marketplace. Less obvious were the domestic policies of the Hong Kong government, the most strategic being the system of subsidized public housing, which had major consequences for wage rates and allowed Hong Kong to remain competitive in the global economy. The highly interventionist role of the Hong Kong government in creating the social infrastructure that assisted the efforts of Hong Kong entrepreneurs to respond creatively to a rapidly changing global economy has often been overlooked in accounting for the economic success of "Adam Smith's other island."[15]

Up to the mid-1960s, textiles were dominant in terms of both (industrial) employment and Hong Kong's domestic export performance. There was a gradual shift from textiles to garments and clothing accessories beginning in the mid-1960s, and by the mid-1980s Hong Kong was one of the major global producers of fashionable clothing. Other technological possibilities were rapidly incorporated. In the late 1960s plastics made their appearance, and in the late 1970s electronics products (including digital clocks and watches) were added to a very substantial electrical goods industry.

Manufacturing is still one of the largest components of GDP and employment. Its share, however, has been declining. Manufacturing comprised fully 40 per cent of GDP in 1965, declined to 31 per cent in 1971, was a little over 20 per cent throughout the 1980s, and is now less than 17 per cent. Its share of the labor force had declined to 26 percent by 1991.[16]

Hong Kong's economy has changed both as a consequence of global forces and, since 1979, because of its changing economic relations with an outward-looking China and its rapidly changing hinterland, with which it has become increasingly integrated and which is now an important location for much of the industrial capacity that was so central to Hong Kong's own economic history from the 1950s until the 1970s.

Hong Kong became a major financial center in the 1970s. This was in part due to changes in the nature of the global economy, which saw the production of key manufactured goods shift away from Europe and North America to East and Southeast Asia. The tertiary sector in Hong Kong had assumed major proportions as early as 1970. Transport, storage and communications, finance, insurance, real estate, business services, and the growing tourist industry became increasingly important in the 1970s, and total employment in these areas grew from about 40 per cent in 1970 to almost 50 per cent in 1980. With reform in China, the tertiary sector continued to expand; its employment share was 63 per cent in 1991. Almost 53 per cent of Hong Kong's GDP derived from finance and banking, trade, and transport services in 1990.

Trade has always been the life-blood of Hong Kong. The China trade never ceased to be of importance; China remained an important source of Hong Kong's imports, even as Hong Kong's domestic exports sought other markets. Entrepot trade, although not insignificant, was of only modest proportions until the late 1970s. After 1980, entrepot trade with China was reborn. The volume of Hong Kong's trade increased dramatically in the 1980s, and the composition of Hong Kong's trading partners changed (Tables 5 and 6). In particular, China and Hong Kong became each other's largest trading partners.[17] China's domestic export trade grew dramatically, to US$52.54 billion at the end of the 1980s, of which 41.7 per cent was conducted with Hong Kong.

The dramatic growth rates that the Hong Kong economy began to enjoy in the 1980s were due to a renewed relationship with China and, especially, with Hong Kong's Guangdong hinterland. Hong Kong's GNP

Table 5. Hong Kong's External Trade, 1955-91

Year	Imports	Domestic Exports	Reexports	Total Trade
1955	3.72	2.53		6.25
1965	8.97	5.03	1.50	15.50
1970	17.61	12.35	2.89	32.85
1978	63.01	40.71	13.12	116.84
1980	111.65	68.17	30.07	209.89
1986	275.96	153.98	122.64	552.48
1988	498.80	217.66	275.41	991.87
1991	778.98	231.06	534.84	1544.88

Note: All data in billion Hong Kong dollars. Until 1959, reexports were included in domestic exports and were not reported separately.

Source: Hong Kong Government, *Hong Kong: Annual Report* (Hong Kong: Government Printer, various years).

had experienced steady growth through the 1960s and into the 1970s—from US$750 million in 1960 to $2.5 billion in 1965 and $11.74 billion in 1977. GNP reached some $38.56 billion in 1986, and $81.56 billion in 1991; GDP per capita increased from US$6,971 in 1986 to $14,102 in 1991. As a consequence of this rapid growth, substantial investable funds were generated, and Hong Kong entrepreneurs became truly global in their activities and, like other entrepreneurs in East Asia, began to have an impact on economies where they hitherto had had only little involvement.[18]

During the 1980s, the conditions of production changed for Hong Kong, and high wage rates compromised Hong Kong's ability to efficiently produce commodities that demanded large amounts of labor. Plastics and textiles, for example, diminished in importance for the Hong Kong economy and the Hong Kong labor force. While the character of Hong Kong's economy changed, Hong Kong entrepreneurs did not relinquish control over profitable production lines, the output from which was in great demand in the affluent societies of the First World. They increasingly shifted such lines out of Hong Kong. Some went to Malaysia, Thailand, and other parts of Southeast Asia, and a few to Africa—but most went to China. Hong Kong entrepreneurs were culturally most comfortable in China, and most familiar with their largely Cantonese-speaking hinterland in the Pearl River

67

Table 6. Hong Kong: External Trade by Major Trading Partners, 1955-91

	Imports		Domestic Exports		Reexports	
1955	China	24	Malaya	15		
	Japan	14	U.K.	10		
	U.K.	12	China	7		
1965	China	26	U.S.A.	34	Japan	17
	Japan	17	U.K.	17	Singapore	14
	U.S.A.	11	China		Indonesia	10
	U.K.	11			U.S.A.	6
					China	4
1970	Japan	24	U.S.A.	42	Japan	20
	China	16	U.K.	12	Singapore	14
	U.K.	12	Germany	8	U.S.A.	8
			China		China	
1978	Japan	23	U.S.A.	34	Japan	17
	China	17	Germany	11	Singapore	11
	U.S.A.	12	U.K.	11	Indonesia	9
	Taiwan	7	China		U.S.A.	8
					China	2
1980	Japan	23	U.S.A.	33	China	15
	China	20	Germany	11	U.S.A.	10
	U.S.A.	12	U.K.	10	Indonesia	9
	Taiwan	7	China	2	Singapore	8
1986	China	30	U.S.A.	42	China	33
	Japan	20	China	12	U.S.A.	18
	Taiwan	9	Germany	7	Japan	5
	U.S.A.	8	U.K.	6	Taiwan	5
1988	China	31	U.S.A.	34	China	35
	Japan	17	China	18	U.S.A.	18
	Taiwan	9	Germany	7	Japan	6
	U.S.A.	8	U.K.	7	Taiwan	5
1991	China	38	U.S.A.	27	China	29
	Japan	16	China	24	U.S.A.	21
	Taiwan	10	Germany	8	Japan	6
	U.S.A.	8	U.K.	7	Germany	6

Note: Figures show share of each partner, in percent.

Sources: See Table 5.

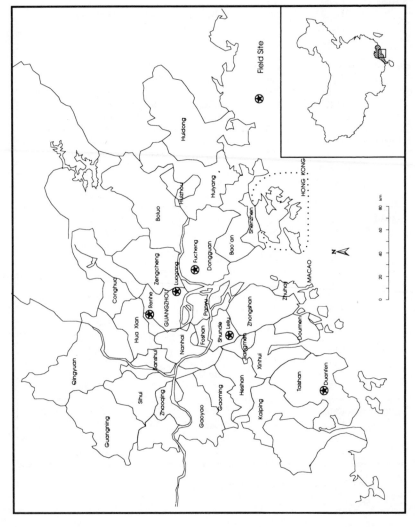

**Map 1.
The Pearl River
Delta Region**

delta region. Some factories were relocated from Hong Kong to the new Shenzhen Special Economic Zone (built in Hong Kong's image and resembling the new towns of Hong Kong's own New Territories), but most went beyond the zone to the Pearl River delta itself. Hence, Hong Kong entrepreneurs became central to the economic well-being of localities within the hinterland, to which they were often connected by ties of kinship and sentiment.

5. The Pearl River Delta Region: Five Examples

Hong Kong entrepreneurs, in concert with Guangdong officials at various administrative levels, have taken full advantage of the flexibility implicit in the reform measures to begin a process that has fundamentally changed the economy of the Pearl River delta region and, by the early 1990s, the surrounding areas. I will now describe some of the effects of development since the reforms began in five locations across Hong Kong's Pearl River delta hinterland. (See Map 1.)

I chose these locations in the 1970s in different policy circumstances when the links between Hong Kong and its hinterland were still strained and tenuous.[19] Each was administratively a commune and all had some distinguishing characteristics. Duanfen, located in southern Taishan *xian* (since early 1993, a *shi*) in the western delta, is a center of out-migration to North America.[20] Leliu in Shunde *xian* (now a *shi*), in the central delta, had a distinctive cash-cropping economy and possessed some unique cultural characteristics.[21] Luogang and Renhe are close to Guangzhou, located in Baiyun *qu* (formerly the "Suburban District" of Guangzhou). Luogang is mountainous but long famous for its fruit production. Renhe, a grain specialist area to the north, was known for its radical political character during the Cultural Revolution when it was the Dongfeng (East Wind) commune; coincidentally, it is a major source of migration to Canada. Fucheng, in Dongguan *shi* (formerly *xian*) is a major source of migrants to Hong Kong.[22]

The economies of the five units and the villages that compose them have changed substantially since reform got underway in 1979.[23] Key factors affecting the exact nature and extent of economic transformation in each unit have been the indigenous economy, leadership, and location. Since the reform initiatives got underway, linkages with emigrés in Hong Kong or Macao or in Overseas Chinese communities have become of increasing importance. The extent of change in the Hong Kong hinterland varies from locality to locality, depending on the extent and nature of the emigré involvement in the local economy. For some localities there are no connections at all and fundamental structural change is therefore largely absent.

Duanfen, located in southern Taishan, is distant from Guangzhou and Hong Kong and its prospects for growth and development were, until recently, hampered by inadequate communications. As an Overseas Chinese area, it suffered from almost the moment of its incorporation into the People's Republic of China; overseas connections were political liabilities for much of the three decades 1949-79, especially during the Cultural Revolution. After 1979, overseas links were viewed in a positive light, and many of the harsh political judgments that had colored local policy options were reversed. Duanfen has remained an agricultural economy firmly based on grain production, with a substantial dependence on remittances from abroad—although its economic base has diversified. Cash crops such as fruit and sugar cane, and the raising of poultry, have become widespread. Duanfen has prospered since reform but its incorporation into the world system has not occurred on the same scale as with other units in central and eastern portions of the Pearl River delta. This is partly due to its location but also to the particular nature of its overseas links.

Leliu, in the central region of the delta, has had a distinctive economy based on fish farming, the production of sugar cane, and sericulture. There are no rice paddies in Leliu. Its commercialized (and export-oriented) agricultural production allowed its peasant cultivators to enjoy relative prosperity even before the reform period. It was an area of extensive out-migration to Hong Kong before 1949, and links with its out-migrants were revitalized in the wake of reform. A young and dynamic leadership sought to involve the entrepreneurial energies of Hong Kong in its economic transformation. Its agricultural economy, especially fish farming, has remained buoyant, although sericulture has been eliminated as a consequence of pollution and low prices for cocoons. Leliu's agriculture, though buoyant, has been overwhelmed by dramatic growth in non-agricultural production. The market towns of Shunde have become centers of light industrial production, allowing its households to enjoy some of the highest incomes in rural China.[24]

Luogang is located off the main highway that links Guangzhou to eastern Guangdong, at the eastern edge of Baiyun *qu* of Guangzhou Municipality.[25] Formerly part of Panyu *xian*, Luogang has a long history of specialization in fruit production. Changes in pricing policies and release from the highly bureaucratic purchase and supply of fruit allowed its peasant cultivators to substantially increase household income throughout much of the 1980s. The region did not have a history of extensive out-migration, and the local economy saw little growth in its small enterprise sector at the outset of the reform period. Its villages remained firmly agricultural and their proximity to major markets (especially Guangzhou) allowed them to take full advantage of new commercial opportunities and profit from higher prices paid to fruit growers. In the early stages of reform, Luogang's fruit specialists were recruited to assist other localities throughout the delta diversify their grain-based economies by moving into highly profitable citrus production. Grain production also remained important in Luogang, and its proximity to centers of labor demand (especially in construction) allowed villagers to seek employment opportunities outside agriculture.

At the end of the 1980s, newly established citrus groves came into production and fruit prices tumbled. Construction experienced a downturn, and the Pearl River delta's labor suffered competition from the enormous influx of outsider migrants. Luogang natives returned to their villages, and the local cadres looked to economic diversification as the mechanism to continue their economic success. The enterprise sector began to grow, and an export orientation exploiting the Hong Kong connection became central to local success.

Renhe is located at the northern edge of Baiyun *qu*. It has a large and dense population, which was largely engaged in grain production, and enjoyed a good deal of success, under the "grain-first" policies of the 1970s. Renhe lies beyond the zone of intense vegetable cultivation developed to meet the needs of the Guangzhou market and has relatively little involvement in cash cropping, although it has had some success in raising poultry. Its out-migration was substantial in the past and there are significant numbers of its natives overseas and in Hong Kong. Its industrial capacity at the *zhen*, village, and individual levels has grown since the reform period, often in cooperation with Hong Kong entrepreneurial interests. Yet the degree of Renhe's incorporation into the broader economy of the delta region is less extensive than that of other units in the central delta region or closer to Guangzhou or Hong Kong. The capacity of the local economy to absorb surplus labor is limited. Large numbers of men, especially those under forty years of age, have left the area to seek work in Guangzhou and elsewhere in the delta, leaving the management of the agricultural economy in the hands of women and older men, with, at the outset of the 1990s, substantial sub-contracting of the land to non-provincial outsiders.

Fucheng extends in a wedge to the south and east from Dongguan City (*shi*). The economic growth of Dongguan since the reform period got underway has been quite remarkable. Fucheng has fully shared in the transformation of the entire *shi*—which has benefitted from its close proximity to the Shenzhen Special Economic Zone and Hong Kong.[26] Dongguan has utilized the investment resources and skills of its emigrés in Hong Kong, who have provided much of the capital for the extensive array of enter-prises, both industrial and agricultural, that has transformed the rural economy.

Fucheng has over 400 enterprises, whose foreign exchange earnings in 1990 totalled over HK$100 million. They include subsidiaries of Hong Kong manufacturers of plastics, garments, electronics, and toys, whose products are virtually all destined for the world market. Fucheng also makes large shipments of vegetables to the Hong Kong market and of fruit to both Hong Kong and domestic markets throughout China.

These five units are broadly representative of the Pearl River delta region. They extend across the delta, representing differing production regimes—historically influenced, but also consequences of different leadership strategies and different developmental possibilities in the wake of reform. I will first outline the consequences of reform for the central and eastern delta regions (what Vogel calls "the inner delta") and will then comment on developments in the western reaches of the delta, where Overseas Chinese, rather than Hong Kong, connections are dominant.[27]

The reform process has turned on "openness," and the external connections that localities possess are often based on kinship. The presence or absence of kinsmen outside the village and the broad communities that villages form have been decisive for the development process. Kinsmen have become sources of investment and entrepreneurial skill. Yet it is important to distinguish between the effects of kinsmen who are resident in Hong Kong or Macao and those who are Overseas Chinese. Unquestionably, areas in the western delta region have benefitted in particular ways from extensive Overseas Chinese linkages. The substantial, and growing, funds that have flowed into the region from North America and elsewhere (including Hong Kong) have been channelled into projects such as roads, bridges, and public buildings (of which schools and hospitals are most common). In other parts of the delta, investment funds and entrepreneurial energies that have derived from Hong Kong (and a lesser degree Macao), by contrast, have been directed towards the creation of productive enterprises and have had a major and direct effect on local systems of production.

The consequences for economic change in the eastern and central delta regions, where the presence of Hong Kong and Macao-based kinsmen is predominant, can be readily contrasted with those in the western delta region, where the proportion of Overseas Chinese kinsmen and Overseas

Chinese households is larger. Fundamental economic change, as a consequence of the entrepreneurial activities of Hong Kong-based kinsmen, has been greater in the central and eastern delta regions. The greater the degree of incorporation into the global economy, the greater the effect on the local economy.

6. The Central and Eastern Delta Region: Hong Kong Connections

The central and eastern delta regions have been most advantageously located to take full advantage of new policy options. These regions were historically highly commercialized and open to a variety of external links. The assumptions of development policy for much of the thirty years after 1949 compromised these connections, and local economies turned inwards under intense pressure from the Chinese state.[28] Peasant resistance was substantial but the degrees of maneuverability were highly constrained.[29] Possibilities for economic innovation changed after 1979.

Wantong, a large multi-surname village (formerly brigade) in Fucheng, Dongguan, responded quickly to the changed circumstances after 1979. The village had thrived under collectivization, and a dynamic and highly respected leadership had organized major land reclamation during the Great Leap Forward, resulting in high grain yields and relatively high per capita incomes even before 1979. Its Party Secretary was transferred to the commune level shortly before the reforms got underway. Working closely with a *xian* leadership committed to exploring new economic relationships, he argued—with considerable success—for mobilization of capital and entrepreneurial resources among the substantial number of local emigrés in Hong Kong. The area was helped by its proximity to the growing Shenzhen SEZ and the dramatic improvement in road communications with Hong Kong.

The consequences of local economic transformation have been major. There has been little mobility of local labor away from Fucheng as village economies have intensified.[30] Only 34 per cent of the indigenous labor force in Wantong is engaged strictly in household-managed agricultural production. The rest works in enterprises, the bulk of which are run by the village as collective entities. Although there is no single lineage base to the village (as in neighboring Zengbu), there is an intense local loyalty.[31] It is a loyalty that was furthered during the period of agricultural collectivism in the 1960s and the 1970s, and heightened with the extensive involvement of Hong Kong-based emigrés in the village economy throughout the 1980s and into the 1990s.

Wantong's links to the global economy are direct. Much of the output of village-run enterprises, in such industries as garments and plastics, is destined for Hong Kong and for re-export to Europe and North America. All the former brigades in Fucheng have established industrial estates with new plants, and with dormitory facilities for the largely immigrant work force, at a cost far below that prevailing in Hong Kong. The physical dispersion of much of the Hong Kong manufacturing sector to the Pearl River delta hinterland has been to units of which Fucheng, and the villages like Wantong comprising it, are typical examples.[32]

Not all the village-run enterprises in Wantong have been industrial. Vegetables were cultivated year-round for the Hong Kong market by an enterprise working jointly with a Hong Kong-based entrepreneur, who had left the village shortly after 1949. It employed wage workers, the bulk of whom were villagers. Its operations were much reduced after 1990 as vegetable production in Baoan, attached to Shenzhen and much closer to Hong Kong, became more cost efficient and as the industrial base of Wantong further expanded.

The village has also moved into tourism in a major way. In concert with another Hong Kong-based native and with the leisure needs of Hong Kong residents clearly in mind, it has created a "holiday village" complete with villas, a handsome restaurant, and a variety of leisure activities. The local economy is thus closely integrated with the world system through Hong Kong and has become acutely aware of new consumption patterns in increasingly affluent Hong Kong, another index of the desakota character of the broad region of which it is part.

The village of Tsimkong, in Luogang, has also prospered in the reform period—but not as a consequence of global incorporation through Hong Kong links, as in Wantong. Tsimkong's major comparative advantage derives from a long history of growing fruit (oranges, litchi, and pineapple). Reform of the price system and the resurgence of private fruit marketing has caused rapid increases in household incomes. Economic strategy in Tsimkong is less elaborate than in Wantong; it involves maximum allocation of household labor into highly commercialized agricultural production. There is little out-migration and a virtual absence of kin abroad or in Hong Kong or Macao. The Tsimkong economy has therefore responded largely to changes in the domestic market, and to growing opportunities as a consequence of increases in disposable income throughout the region (themselves largely an effect of Hong Kong-inspired economic activities). Some of Tsimgong's fruit output, of litchi in particular, is destined for Hong Kong.

At the end of the 1980s, the domestic market changed and was no longer as buoyant for the villages of Luogang as it had been for much of the decade. Villagers returned from their temporary sojourns as fruit-growing specialists or as construction workers. Cadres at various levels sought to augment the enterprise base. At the *zhen* level, Hong Kong connections were sought and garment factories established. A large and modern pharmaceutical plant has begun operation, using local sugar cane to produce the base for Chinese herbal "tonics," largely for export. At the village level, two enterprises are notable. One raises a highly desirable black-skinned chicken for export to the markets of Hong Kong and Southeast Asia. It is a joint enterprise with Hong Kong interests and a provincial-level marketing organization located in Guangzhou. The second, employing skilled craftsmen from Zhejiang, manufactures Chinese-style ebony and rosewood furniture, primarily for export to Hong Kong, Taiwan, and Overseas Chinese areas (where such furniture is in high demand). This, once again, represents geographical dispersion of an economic activity once well-represented in Hong Kong—an activity that has become increasingly difficult to maintain there, due to cost increases.

The experience of Tsimkong, and of Luogang more generally, demonstrates that collectively-organized village enterprises cooperating with Hong Kong entrepreneurs are beginning to have an impact even in localities that for much of the 1980s profited only indirectly from the increasing influence of Hong Kong over its hinterland. Progress in local economies in the delta region increasingly requires access to the Hong Kong market and an involvement with Hong Kong entrepreneurial interests.

7. The Central and Eastern Delta Region: Lack of Connections

Two other sample villages, although located in the eastern and central delta regions, lack extensive penetration by Hong Kong interests. The consequences of the absence of those links is instructive.

Leliu, like other former communes in Shunde in the heart of the delta region, has benefitted very substantially from its Hong Kong links. Naamshui has been less involved in the economic transformation of Leliu than other villages in the *zhen*. There has been a persistent inability to develop industrial enterprises and thereby diversify the village economy. As a consequence, a large portion of the labor force remains in agricultural production; some 40 percent, including most of the men under 40, have left the village and often Leliu itself. They work as carpenters, decorators, and temporary workers in construction and in commerce and transportation.

They regularly return to the village, but they have no continuing role in village-based production activities. The village agricultural economy is dominated by women, despite the demise of sericulture, and older men who have contracted fish ponds, either individually or (more commonly) in cooperation with men from other households.

Households in Naamshui make a steady living. Income per capita was about 1400 yuan in 1990, slightly below the level of Leliu as a whole. One reason for the failure to diversify the village economy is that it is in a remote corner of the *zhen*, although it has been linked by road to the administrative center of Leliu and to Daliang, the county town, for more than a decade. Its Hong Kong emigrés are relatively few in number, and the village lacks, or fails to make full use of, the "connections" (*guanxi*) that have been so critical for the success of other villages in Shunde. There is an intense village solidarity, and the organization of production does not differ dramatically from its form in the 1960s and 1970s. Fish production is organized around cooperative principles, and income from the contracted fish ponds is distributed on an annual basis. The collective health care system works well; there are pensions, and there are only two "five-guarantee" households in the village. Naamshui was extremely successful during the dominance of the Dazhai model; its agricultural economy is efficient, and its commitment to collective welfare very strong. Some households in the village (intriguingly, with former "landlord" political status) have been extraordinarily entrepreneurial and have prospered. They are, however, exceptional, as the village as a collectivity has chosen to remain aloof from the larger changes sweeping the area around it. In the reform era, there is no single model of success that dominates; whether a village does or does not emulate others is for that village to decide.

Ngawu, in Renhe, has also changed less dramatically than some other villages in the delta region. It, too, is firmly agricultural and has only a small enterprise sector. In the past it was also deeply committed to certain ideological positions and may not have grasped with wholesale enthusiasm some of the ideas of the reform period. A significant proportion of its (male) labor force is working outside the village. Ngawu has large numbers of households with relatives abroad. They are, however, Overseas Chinese, many resident in Canada. The impact of Overseas Chinese kinsmen on local economies, as I will indicate below, does not typically translate into economic transformation of the kind experienced in those parts of the delta where Hong Kong emigrés are most numerous.

Ngawu has not been able to fully capitalize on the opportunities implicit in reform policies and to transform its system of production. A large proportion of the households remain in subsistence production. Only a few village households have members working in *zhen*-managed enterprises, and there are only a few enterprises at the village level to absorb local surplus labor. The out-migration of household labor is therefore substantial—and predominantly male. Villagers have sought employment in construction projects, either in Guangzhou or Shenzhen. Many of these have been Hong Kong joint ventures. The village economy may therefore benefit significantly, but indirectly, from the broader penetration of the delta economy by Hong Kong.

The long-term prospects for continued prosperity in Renhe are somewhat compromised by its failure to significantly expand its export-oriented enterprise sector. In the mid-1980s it created an amusement park, in cooperation with an entrepreneur who had left the region for Hong Kong in the early 1950s. The park has not been a success. Communications with Guangzhou are poor, and the patrons never materialized in sufficient numbers to make it viable. The leadership in Renhe is well aware that outside investment is central to a strong economic performance in the future. Its difficulties were only furthered when its most industrialized area separated and formed a smaller *zhen* in 1987.

Renhe's specialty has been grain farming, and this is unlikely to bring gains in the 1990s. The indigenous population is increasingly reluctant to engage in field agriculture, and already some 400 outsider households have subcontracted land in Renhe. The indigenous labor force will sojourn, unless major internal economic change persuades them to remain in the area. This will be possible only when larger numbers of entrepreneurs, preferably with a Hong Kong or Taiwan base, can be persuaded to invest.[33]

8. The Western Delta Region: The Overseas Chinese Connection

The distinctive western delta region is the homeland of many North Americans of Chinese origin.[34] Overseas Chinese have remained fiercely loyal to their ancestral points of origin, and thus have been willing to donate to homeland projects even after decades abroad. Local leaders in production units throughout the region have encouraged the involvement of emigrés in local economic development and other projects since the reform initiatives began. Overtures to natives of the region resident abroad have met with substantial success, though the consequences have been markedly different from those in the central and eastern delta regions. Overseas Chinese connections have not resulted in economic transformation, but have markedly improved the social infrastructure.

The great majority of households in Duanfen have relatives overseas, and are described as "Overseas Chinese dependents" (*qiaojuan*). The closeness of kinship determines the amount of support that relatives abroad will provide. A close kinship relationship will increase the possibility of obtaining an immigration visa and of joining kinsmen abroad through family reunification programs. *Qiaojuan* households whose kinsmen are more distantly related may receive remittances from their relatives abroad but have little opportunity to migrate. They have significant advantages when compared to non-*qiaojuan* households, who have the fewest resources and are therefore reliant upon their own abilities. Remittances to *qiaojuan* households can become working capital, and their connections with relatives abroad can be a source of capital inputs.

Since 1979, *qiaojuan* families have been leaving in large numbers as part of family reunification policies in such countries as Canada and the United States. As a consequence, there is a considerable amount of property standing empty, often managed by the remaining (distant) *qiaojuan* kinsmen. Such properties can be used as an economic resource; access to capital by distant *qiaojuan* households has allowed them to contract formerly collectively-managed facilities (such as orchards, general stores, and repair shops) at the village level and thereby augment their participation in agriculture with private production activities. The private sector is much more extensive in the western delta and highly collectivized rural industrialization, particularly at the village level, is much smaller when compared to the central and eastern delta regions.

The willingness of many Overseas Chinese to commit substantial funds to public projects in the homeland has depended on resolution of outstanding grievances. One was the return of property that had been seized during the land reform. There was also the closely related issue of political status emerging from the land reform process. Chinese abroad had suffered a good deal of discrimination, living and working in societies that only rarely granted them full participation. They remitted funds earned in occupations that were often either of low status or within the ethnic subeconomy. Because such remittances were put into land and housing in China, during land reform the Overseas Chinese were judged to be "landlords" and their properties were confiscated.[35] Many working-class Chinese abroad bitterly resented this, which was perceived as a social injustice. Their relatives in China, prevented by discriminatory immigration legislation from leaving China, suffered from their political labels for much of the thirty years after land reform. These two issues were substantially resolved by the mid 1980s.

The fate of lineage organizations was another nagging question. Before 1949, the western delta region was characterized by a highly elaborate lineage organization.[36] It was compromised by land reform, in which lineage property was confiscated; by the time of the Cultural Revolution, if not before, the ancestor cult was emasculated. In the 1980s, throughout the Pearl River delta region but especially in the western part, lineages have been revived. Graves have been repaired, rituals are performed at the graves of apical ancestors, ancestral halls have been restored or rebuilt, ritual feasts occur in the halls once more, lineage libraries have been refurbished, and lineage officers have begun to act as agents for lineage members, similar to the way the administrators of lineage trusts intervened on behalf of members in the period before 1949.

Restoration work is made possible by donations from local and external contributors. The major donations come from abroad. Funds are remitted through a network that is worldwide—but energized from Hong Kong. This network is maintained by a sophisticated and widespread communications system. The western delta region generates a large stream of local publications, focusing on the reliance of local areas upon contributions from kinsmen and fellow countrymen overseas in maintaining local integrity. Local history and local tradition are emphasized; while economic advances receive careful attention, they are seen to be in harmony with a local cultural base.

The funds that flow into the western delta region, substantial though they are, are not put primarily into economic enterprises, as they are in the central and eastern delta regions. Their impact is, nonetheless, substantial. The public facilities in the traditional areas of Overseas Chinese are superior to those in any other rural region in Guangdong (and possibly in China as a whole). The details of social structure in this region differ significantly from other regions because of the long history of migration to an array of overseas locations and a long history of concern with the fate of the homeland by Chinese abroad. That concern was strained by intemperate policies toward Overseas Chinese and their dependents over a thirty year period, but it was not dissipated. Homeland loyalties have been encouraged in the reform period, and Overseas Chinese have responded enthusiastically.

The Hong Kong connection is crucial in developments in the western delta region. Hong Kong has become a global center for an array of economic forces. It has also become the center for concentrating and organizing the homeland sentiments of Overseas Chinese—and for encouraging their involvement, once again, in their points of ancestral origin.

9. Conclusion

Hong Kong has an extensive set of economic and cultural links to its hinterland, particularly the Pearl River delta region, which has been transformed since economic reform was initiated in China in 1979. Rapid economic growth in the region has been fueled by industrial and tertiary sector growth in which Hong Kong investment, entrepreneurial skill, and management expertise have been extensively utilized. The key figures are Hong Kong-based emigrés who, having left China in anticipation of, or shortly after, the formation of the People's Republic of China, responded to calls to return to their native places. Their identity with ancestral areas is strong even after a three-decade sojourn in Hong Kong. Equally, however, the appeals from their home areas present an economic opportunity, as the global economy continues its restructuring and as Hong Kong's economy undergoes change. No region of China has developed as rapidly as the delta has, especially after the mid-1980s. The major stimulus has been Hong Kong. The territory and the prime movers in its economic success, primarily drawn from the Pearl River delta region, have assumed a key role in the innovative policies formulated in Guangdong; Hong Kong became the catalyst drawing the Guangdong provincial economy into the global economy after 1979.

I have examined the connectedness of Hong Kong to the transformation of its hinterland through the experiences of five rural localities in the Pearl River delta region. They extend from Taishan in the western reaches of the delta, the historic homeland of North Americans of Chinese descent, through Shunde in the highly commercialized central delta, with its historic focus on cash crops and its export orientation, to Dongguan in the eastern delta, long a point of out-migration to Hong Kong and, in the contemporary period, deeply influenced by creation of the Shenzhen Special Economic Zone. The experiences of the five localities show different aspects of regional transformation in the 1980s and distinct responses to the possibilities of reform.

The eastern and central delta regions, which include the Special Economic Zones of Shenzhen and Zhuhai, have benefitted most dramatically from the activities of Hong Kong (and to a lesser degree, Macao) emigrés. There has been massive economic transformation of the central and eastern delta region as a consequence of emigré investment in productive enterprises.

The Hong Kong connection is no less important for the Overseas Chinese areas of the western delta region, though the economic effects for these Overseas Chinese areas are less immediately obvious. Here as elsewhere in the delta, Hong Kong-based natives of the region, along with kinsmen and fellow countrymen in Overseas Chinese areas around the world (and especially in North America), have resumed with great intensity the contacts with the homeland that were compromised by government policy toward Overseas Chinese dependents (*qiaojuan*) after the Land Reform of the early 1950s. In the Overseas Chinese areas there has been major investment in social infrastructure—roads, schools, hospitals, and public buildings.

The regional economy that is now emerging, energized by Hong Kong's enormous entrepreneurial capacities, is split across distinct administrative and political systems. After 1997 the political and administrative barriers will be diminished, although it is unlikely that Hong Kong's economic dominance will lessen. There is clearly an important cultural distinctiveness between Hong Kong and its hinterland that only widened in the thirty years after 1950. It has narrowed substantially since 1980, as Hong Kong and its hinterland have become increasingly integrated. Hong Kong's domination of its hinterland will likely remain well beyond 1997—and those who lack Hong Kong connections will likely be disadvantaged.

Notes

1. A preliminary version of this paper appeared in *1989: Rivista di Diritto Pubblico e Scienze Politiche 3* (February 1993), pp. 233-74. My thanks to Victor Nee for insightful comments.

2. See Nicholas Lardy, "Dilemmas in the Pattern of Resource Allocation in China, 1978-1985," in Victor Nee and David Stark (eds.), *Remaking the Economic Institutions of Socialism: China and Eastern Europe* (Stanford: Stanford University Press, 1989), pp. 278-305.

3. *A Draft Agreement between the Government of the United Kingdom of Britain and Northern Island and the Government of the People's Republic of China on the Future of Hong Kong* (Hong Kong: Government Printer, 1984) specifies the broad mechanisms. A set of annexes dealing with China's policy towards Hong Kong, the nature of the Sino-British liaison group, and land leases, plus the exchange of memoranda between the British and Chinese governments, can all be found in F. Ching, *Hong Kong and China: For Better or Worse* (New York: China Council of the Asia Society and the Foreign Policy Association, 1985). The basic law was approved by the National People's Congress in April 1990, in an atmosphere changed significantly by the events

in China and reaction to them in Hong Kong during the spring of 1989. A draft of the basic law with commentary appears in William McGurn (ed.), *Basic Law, Basic Questions* (Hong Kong: Review Publishing Company, 1988). See also G. Hicks, *Hong Kong Countdown* (Hong Kong: Writers and Publishers Cooperative, 1989) for views written before June 1989. The perception from Taipei is expressed in Jurgen Domes and Yu-ming Shaw, *Hong Kong: A Chinese and International Concern* (Boulder: Westview Press, 1989). A recent Canadian view is Jules Nadeau, *Hong Kong 1997: Dans la Gueule du Dragon Rouge* (Montreal: Editions Quebec/Amerique, 1990).

4. Dali Yang, "China Adjusts to the World Economy: The Political Economy of China's Coastal Development Strategy," *Pacific Affairs*, 65(1), Spring 1991, pp. 42-64.

5. David Thorns, "The New International Division of Labor and Urban Change: A New Zealand Case Study," in M. P. Smith (ed.), *Pacific Rim Cities in the World Economy* (New Brunswick and Oxford: Transaction Books, 1989), pp. 68-101.

6. See the essays in William L. Parish (ed.), *Chinese Rural Development: The Great Transformation* (Armonk, NY: Sharpe, 1985); Keith Griffin, *Institutional Reform and Economic Development in the Chinese Countryside* (London: Macmillan, 1984); Elizabeth Perry and Christine Wong (eds.), *The Political Economy of Reform in Post-Mao China* (Cambridge: Harvard, 1985), pp. 1-194; Robert F. Ash, "The Evolution of Agricultural Policy," *China Quarterly*, no. 116, December 1988, pp. 529-55; Jörgen Delman, Clemens S. Ostergaard, and Flemming Christiansen, *Remaking Peasant China: Problems of Rural Development and Institutions at the Start of the 1990s* (Aarhus: Aarhus University Press, 1990); David Zweig, "Internationalizing China's Countryside: The Political Economy of Exports from Rural Industry," *China Quarterly*, no. 128, December, 1991, pp. 716-41.

7. Yang Dali, "Patterns of China's Regional Development Strategy," *China Quarterly*, no. 122, June 1990, p. 248.

8. The core of the delta is composed of the two municipalities (*shi*) of Foshan and Jiangmen, which were created out of the former Foshan prefecture, in the early period of reform. The western part of the delta is composed of Enping, Taishan, Kaiping, Xinhui (from which the bulk of the North American Chinese population traces its ancestry), Doumen, and Heshan. The central delta region extends from Guangzhou south and includes Nanhai, Panyu, Shunde and Zhongshan, and also mountainous Gaoming and Sanshui. The eastern delta

region consists of Dongguan and Baoan, adjacent to the Shenzhen Special Economic Zone and Hong Kong. In 1987 the administrative definition of the "Open Economic Area" was expanded up the West River to Zhaoqing *shi*, north of Guangzhou, to include Hua *xian* and Conghua *xian*, and eastward to include much of what had formerly been Huiyang prefecture. Most of these new additions are not strictly delta; they are mountainous and Hakka-speaking. They had begun to share in the prosperity of what is known as "the small delta," the original, essentially Cantonese-speaking, core. For a discussion of the "small" and "large" delta, see *Guangdong sheng nianjian 1989 [1989 Guangdong Yearbook]*, pp. 252-53, 492, and 496. Official statistics on the delta, large or small, exclude Guangzhou's urban area (which includes still largely rural Baiyun *qu*) and the two special zones. I have included them.

9. T. G. McGee, "Urbanasasi or Kotadesasi? Evolving Patterns of Urbanization in Asia," in L. Ma, A. Noble, and A. Dutt (eds.), *Urbanization in Asia* (Honolulu: University of Hawaii Press, 1989), pp. 93-108; T. G. McGee, "The Emergence of Desakota Regions in Asia: Expanding a Hypothesis," in N. Ginsburg, B. Koppel, and T. G. McGee (eds.), *The Extended Metropolis: Settlement Transition in Asia* (Honolulu: University of Hawaii Press, 1991), pp. 3-26.

10. For a popular account of the early period, see M. Collis, *Foreign Mud* (London: Faber and Faber, 1946). The most thorough scholarly analysis is still John K. Fairbank, *Trade and Diplomacy on the South China Coast* (Cambridge: Harvard University Press, 1953). See also F. Wakeman, *Strangers at the Gates* (Berkeley: University of California Press, 1967).

11. On the Japanese occupation, see H. J. Lethbridge, "Hong Kong under Japanese Occupation: Changes in Social Structure," in I. C. Jarvie (ed.) in consultation with J. Agassi, *Hong Kong: A Society in Transition* (London: Routledge and Kegan Paul, 1969), pp. 77-126; G. B. Endacott (edited by, and with additional material by, A. Birch), *Hong Kong Eclipse* (Hong Kong: Oxford University Press, 1978); J. Luff, *Hong Kong: The Hidden Years* (Hong Kong: South China Morning Post, 1967); Lai-Hung Kwan, "The Charitable Activities of Local Chinese Organizations During the Japanese Occupation of Hong Kong, December 1941-August 1945," in D. Faure, J. Hayes, and A. Birch (eds.), *From Village to City* (Hong Kong: Centre of Asian Studies, University of Hong Kong, 1984), pp. 178-90.

12. Ezra Vogel, *One Step Ahead in China: Guangdong Under Reform* (Cambridge: Harvard University Press, 1989), pp. 44-47.

13. For a broad account of some of the issues in a global context, see J. Kolko, *Restructuring the World Economy* (New York: Pantheon, 1988). On the issues for the NICs in particular, see M. A. Bienefeld, "The International Context for National Development Strategies and Opportunities in a Changing World," in M. E. Bienefeld and M. Godfrey (eds.), *The Struggle for Development: National Strategies in an International Context* (New York: John Wiley, 1982), esp. pp. 49-53. Also see P. L. Berger and Hsiao Hsin-huang, *In Search of an East Asian Developmental Model* (New Brunswick: Transaction Books, 1988).

14. Wong Siu-lun, *Emigrant Entrepreneurs: Shanghai Industrialists in Hong Kong* (Hong Kong: Oxford University Press, 1988).

15. Some have argued that Hong Kong represents the vindication of a classical "laissez-faire" approach to economic growth; see H. Smith, *John Stuart Mill's Other Island: A Study of the Economic Development of Hong Kong* (London: Institute of Economic Affairs, 1966). An extension of the argument can be found in A. Rabushka, *Hong Kong: A Study in Economic Freedom* (Chicago: Chicago University Press, 1979). Such arguments are critically analyzed in M. Castells, L. Goh, and R. Y-W. Kwok, *The Shek Kip Mei Syndrome: Economic Development and Public Housing in Hong Kong and Singapore* (London: Pion Press, 1990), esp. pp. 58-117.

16. See Ho Lok-sang, "Labour and Employment," in Joseph Y. S. Cheng and Paul C. K. Kwong, *The Other Hong Kong Report: 1992* (Hong Kong: Chinese University Press, 1992), pp. 191-212.

17. See Yun-wing Sung, *The China-Hong Connection: The Key to China's Open-Door Policy* (Cambridge: Cambridge University Press, 1991), pp. 104-63. On the nature of the new trading policies and their problems, see the fascinating chapter by John Kamm, "Reforming Foreign Trade," in Vogel, *One Step Ahead*, pp. 338-92.

18. See G. E. Johnson, "The Impact of Hong Kong Migration on the Chinese Community of Vancouver," in R. Skeldon (ed.), *Reluctant Exiles: Hong Kong Chinese Communities Abroad* (Armonk, NY: Sharpe, forthcoming).

19. The study of the region began in the mid-1970s when some limited field work in China became possible. For a very preliminary study, see Elizabeth Johnson and Graham Johnson, *Walking on Two Legs: Rural Development in South China* (Ottawa: International Development Research Centre, 1976).

20. Administrative redefinition has been constant during the reform period. Starting in the late 1970s the creation of the Special Economic Zones saw the formation of the new municipalities (*shi*) of Shenzhen, Zhuhai, and Shantou. Foshan prefecture was divided into two *shi*, Foshan and Jiangmen, and by the middle of the 1980s all former prefectures had become *shi*. Zhongshan *xian*, adjacent to the Zhuhai SEZ, became a *xian*-level *shi* in 1984, and Dongguan assumed *shi* status in 1987. In 1992 and 1993, a number of economically advanced *xian*, including Shunde, Nanhai, and Panyu in the central delta region and Taishan and Kaiping in the western delta were elevated to *shi* status. While each remained part of its higher level "municipality," changed administrative status allowed some substantial degree of autonomy with respect to seeking hard currency investment.

21. The distinctive ecological features of Shunde (and of Leliu in particular) are described in Kenneth Ruddle and Zhong Gongfu, *Integrated Agriculture-Aquaculture in South China: The Dyke-Pond System of the Zhujiang Delta* (Cambridge: Cambridge University Press, 1988).

22. For much of the 1980s I interviewed cadres at a variety of administrative levels associated with the units. In the summer of 1986 I selected five villages from among the units, based on my general knowledge of them. Using the household records, I drew random samples of village households and administered a standard questionnaire. The work was funded by a research grant from the Social Sciences and Humanities Research Council of Canada. The Chinese Academy of Social Sciences gave me every assistance. In Guangdong I was greatly helped by the Guangdong Academy of Social Sciences and by the Department of Sociology at Zhongshan (Sun Yat-sen) University. I express my thanks to Li Ruichang and Chen Daojin and to Professor He Zhaofa. Mr. Tan Xiaobing assisted me in collecting the data. His efforts are greatly appreciated.

23. Some general findings are indicated in the following: G. E. Johnson, "The Production Responsibility System in Chinese Agriculture: Some Examples from Guangdong," *Pacific Affairs*, 55(3), Fall 1982, pp. 430-52; G. E. Johnson, "1997 and After: Will Hong Kong Survive? A Personal View," *Pacific Affairs*, 59(2), Summer 1986, pp. 237-54; G. E. Johnson, "Rural Transformation in South China? Views from the Locality," *Revue Europeene des Sciences Sociales*, Tome 27 (no. 84), 1989, pp. 191-226.

24. I have explored some of these issues in "The Political Economy of Chinese Urbanization: Guangdong and the Pearl River Delta," in Gregory Guldin (ed.), *Urbanizing China* (Westport, CT: Greenwood Press, 1992), pp. 185-220.

25. For a broad account of Baiyun *qu* (formerly the "Suburban District"), see Guangzhou nianjian bianzuan weiyuanhui, *Guangzhou nianjian 1991 [Guangzhou Yearbook 1991]* (Guangzhou: Guangdong renmin, 1991), pp. 552-54.

26. The performance of Dongguan is detailed in Zhonggong zhongyang bangongting, *Dongguan shinian: 1979-1988 [Dongguan Ten Years: 1979-1988]* (Shanghai: Shanghai renmin, 1989). Fucheng's performance is detailed at pp. 219-20.

27. Ezra Vogel, "Guangdong's Dynamic Inner Delta," *The China Business Review,* September-October 1989, pp. 56-62.

28. Helen Siu, *Agents and Victims in South China: Accomplices in Rural Revolution* (New Haven: Yale University Press, 1989), describes the consequence of state policies from the 1950s for citrus and fan palm production in Xinhui. Xinhui is on the highly commercialized eastern edge of the western delta region. Siu's field sites are in and around the *xian* city. The arguments that she makes for Huancheng can be appropriately made for much of the central and eastern delta regions. Even where cash-cropping was extensive, its development was compromised by the emasculation of peasant marketing after 1956, and especially after the Great Leap Forward.

29. See David Zweig, "Struggling over Land in China: Peasant Resistance after Collectivization, 1966-1986," in Forrest D. Colburn (ed.), *Everyday Forms of Peasant Resistance* (Armonk, NY: Sharpe, 1989), esp. pp. 153-62, for an account of peasant resistance to collectivist policies in the Lower Yangzi region.

30. On the contrary, growth in the number of enterprises in the *zhen* as a whole (there were 346 enterprises in 1987, of which 118 were wholly engaged in processing of materials for the international market [*wailai jiagong*]) has resulted in the recruitment of several thousand workers from outside the area, many of whom are neither Cantonese speakers nor natives of Guangdong.

31. See S. H. Potter and J. M. Potter, *China's Peasants: The Anthropology of a Revolution* (New York: Cambridge University Press. 1990), esp. pp. 251-69. Zengbu is across the river from Wantong, the village in Fucheng that I surveyed, and draws the bulk of its brides from the village.

32. Wantong is the village in Fucheng most familiar to me. It is not necessarily the most dramatic example of change in Fucheng. Tsimtau [Qiantou] is even more astonishing in terms of the number and diversity of its enterprises. See my remarks on this example in "Rural Transformation in

South China?" (note 23, above), pp. 206-07. Tsimtau now distributes 100 yuan per month from enterprise profits to all indigenous members of the village.

33. In the summer of 1991, a delegation from Renhe visited North America and organized meetings with emigrés from the region. They brought well-produced brochures explaining regulations for investment in Renhe and the possibilities for both assisting the native place and also turning a profit. See the comment on some of the efforts by the Renhe government to deal with its poorer villages by helping them establish export processing facilities in *Guangzhou Nianjian 1991*, p. 554. In the summer of 1992 I visited a large shoe factory established with investment from Taiwan. Significantly, the bulk of its workforce was recruited locally.

34. I have benefitted from numerous conversations, about the western delta region, with Dr. Woon Yuen-fong of the University of Victoria. She has generously shared her findings from Chikan in Kaiping *xian*. See her "Social Change and Continuity in South China: Overseas Chinese and the Guan Lineage of Kaiping County, 1949-1987," *China Quarterly*, no. 118, June 1989, pp. 324-44; "International Links and Socio-economic Development of Modern China: An Emigrant Community in Guangdong," *Modern China*, 16(2), 1990, pp. 139-72; and "From Mao to Deng: Life Satisfaction among Rural Women in an Emigrant Community in South China," *Australian Journal of Chinese Affairs*, no. 25, January 1991, pp. 139-69.

35. See Glen D. Peterson, "Socialist China and the *Huaqiao*: The Transition to Socialism in the Overseas Chinese Areas of Rural Guangdong, 1949-1956," *Modern China*, 14(3), July 1988, pp. 309-35.

36. Woon Yuen-fong, *Social Organization in South China, 1911-1949: The Case of the Kuan Lineage in K'ai-p'ing County* (Ann Arbor: Center for Chinese Studies, University of Michigan, 1984).

Economic Growth in Fujian Province: A Growth Center Analysis, 1950-91

Weng Junyi

1. Introduction

Over the past decade, South China has become one of the most rapidly growing regions in the world. Of course, this growth has not been evenly spread: a few cities and counties have made truly remarkable achievements and have played disproportionate roles in driving the economic growth of the entire region. Shenzhen, Guangzhou, and the Pearl River Delta (all in Guangdong province) and Xiamen (in Fujian) are now among the most conspicuous growth centers in South China.

This paper will examine the emergence and development of such growth centers, the changing constellation of growth centers over time, the development strategy behind the observed pattern, and the implications of the pattern in terms of sectoral and spatial disparities. The paper focuses upon Fujian province, which captures in microcosm some important dimensions of the larger regional development path of China since 1949; in particular, Fujian has undergone internally a transition from inland development to coastal development, mirroring a similar transition in China as a whole.

We proceed as follows. Before beginning the empirical analysis, Section 2 briefly examines the evolution of regional policies impinging directly upon the spatial pattern of growth in Fujian. Section 3 then identifies the growth centers in Fujian during various subperiods of 1950-91 and, in particular, documents the shifts first to inland centers and then from inland back to coastal centers. Section 4 examines the sectoral roots of growth center development, via a shift-share analysis, and Section 5 examines the impact of growth centers on intercounty disparities in productive capacity and living standards, via a decomposition of Gini coefficients.

The entire paper is exploratory in nature, due both to the scarcity of data and to the dearth of earlier studies investigating in systematic fashion the spatial aspects of Fujian's economic growth.

2. Regional Development Strategies in Fujian

As many observers have noted, China has pursued development strategies with strong, and frequently explicit, regional components; the regions subject to such strategies are generally understood to be sets of provinces. In fact, the regional dimension of strategy is evident within individual provinces, as well as across the provinces of China as a whole.

Inland Strategy, 1957-78

Although no formal "Inland Development Strategy" was announced in Fujian province, the existence of such a strategy prior to the reform era can be inferred from various strands of announced development policy and from the substance of provincial plans and the manipulation of other policy instruments.

In the early 1950s, Fujian's very weak industrial base was distributed mainly in a few coastal cities. At the end of 1956, the Ying-Xia Railroad, the first rail line connecting the province with the rest of China, opened to traffic. The Wai-Fu Railroad opened to traffic in early 1959. These lines, originally built for the needs of coastal defense, made it possible to develop industries in interior Fujian. As soon as transport was available, the provincial government prepared to construct a chemical fertilizer plant and a steel plant at the small town of Sanming, located on the Ying-Xia line. Sanming was to become a major heavy industrial center and a focus of inland development.

In August 1958, forces of the People's Liberation Army bombarded the Nationalist base on Jinmen Island, near Xiamen. Bombardment, in both directions, continued intermittently for more than twenty years. With the continuing tensions in the Taiwan Strait, provincial decision-makers were more inclined to locate industrial projects inland—not just at Sanming, but also at other railroad towns such as Longyan, Yongan, and Nanping. As Fujian responded to the threat posed by the Nationalists by building industry in interior counties and towns, China's central leadership responded to a perceived international threat by constructing the so-called "Third Front" in interior provinces.[1] All large investment projects were to be located in these provinces, and many plants in the coastal provinces were to be relocated to the "Third Front" area. The "Third Front" strategy governed both the Third Five-Year Plan (1966-70) and the Fourth Five-Year Plan (1971-75). The central government endorsed the "small third front" already under construction in inland areas of Fujian, by requiring that every coastal province energetically develop its own interior.[2]

In April 1964, the provincial Party committee of Fujian resolved to set up a leading group in charge of industrial development and "small third front" construction.[3] Heavy industries and "front-supporting" industries were formally designated as the focus of provincial strategy, so as to serve the military and contribute to preparations for war. Under this strategy, many plants were located in the counties and towns of Sanming, Longyan, and Nanping prefectures (all in western Fujian).

Coastal Strategy

In July 1979, the central government authorized implementation of "special policies and flexible measures" in the foreign economic relations of Fujian and neighboring Guangdong. A Special Economic Zone was established at Xiamen in Fujian, along with three zones in Guangdong. The Xiamen Zone initially encompassed only 2.5 square kilometers, but in March 1984 it was expanded to include the whole of Xiamen Island plus Gulang Island—a total of 131 square kilometers. Fuzhou was included among the fourteen "open coastal cities" of 1984, and the Mawei Technology Zone was established in Fuzhou in the same year. An "Open Area" encompassing eleven counties and cities in the southeastern part of Fujian was established in 1985 and was later expanded to include thirty-three counties and cities. In early 1988 Zhao Ziyang, secretary general of the Chinese Communist Party, inspected Fujian; soon thereafter, Fujian's attempt to build a network of outward-oriented local economies along the coast was subsumed into an explicit "Coastal Development Strategy." Since 1988, application of this strategy within Fujian has been further refined and articulated, to include export-oriented agriculture, industrial "satellite" towns in the open area, and active pursuit of foreign and Taiwanese investment, especially in those districts with a history of overseas connections.

In Fujian, the coastal development strategy has been complemented by a concerted attack on rural poverty, which is concentrated largely in the northeastern part of the province (Ningde prefecture) and, to a lesser extent, in the southwest. Ningde, which has only two counties in the open area, is best viewed as a region unto itself, in that the constellation of policies impinging upon it differs significantly from that in either the inland areas farther west or the coastal districts from Fuzhou south.

Table 1. Gross Fixed Assets in Ten Counties and Cities

County or City	Amount[a]	Share[b]	Location
		1984	
Fuzhou	1171	13.37	coastal
Sanming	718	8.20	inland
Nanping	480	5.48	inland
Xiamen	440	5.02	coastal
Yongan	381	4.35	inland
Longyan	291	3.32	inland
Zhangzhou	248	2.83	coastal
Shaxian	186	2.12	inland
Shaowu	160	1.83	inland
Jianyang	154	1.76	inland
		1991	
Fuzhou	4499	15.57	coastal
Xiamen	4486	15.52	coastal
Nanping	1915	6.63	inland
Sanming	1805	6.23	inland
Yongan	1669	5.78	inland
Longyan	1024	3.54	inland
Zhangzhou	881	3.05	coastal
Putian	811	2.81	coastal
Quanzhou	776	2.69	coastal
Shunchang	648	2.24	inland

Note: The counties and cities included in each list are the top ten, in terms of gross fixed assets.

a. Gross value of fixed assets of all independent accounting firms in the industrial sector, in million yuan.
b. Share in provincial total.

Sources: Zhang Ruiyao and Lu Zengrong, *Fujian diqu jingji* (Fuzhou: Fujian renmin, 1986); Fujian sheng tongji ju, *Fujian tongji nianjian 1983* (Fuzhou: Fujian renmin, 1984); Fujian sheng tongji ju, *Fujian tongji nianjian 1992* (Beijing: Zhongguo tongji, 1992).

Investment under the Two Strategies

The key policy measures in realizing inland development prior to 1978 were a planned increase in the investment share going to interior regions and transplant of existing capacity from coastal regions (of both Fujian and other provinces). Sanming prefecture, for example, received less than 2 percent of Fujian's total investment in capital construction through 1957. This share jumped to over 25 percent during the Third and Fourth Five-Year Plans (1966-75) and peaked during the Fifth Plan (1976-80).[4] The government of Shanghai decided to move thirteen light industrial plants from Shanghai to Sanming during 1960-70, and additional plants were moved inland from coastal areas during Third Front construction.[5]

In realizing the subsequent coastal development strategy, Fujian relied to a significant extent upon inducements to potential investors—in the form of, e.g., reduced tax rates on foreign-invested firms, greater local latitude in approving foreign investment projects, remission of import duties on equipment and some current inputs, and incentives for export-oriented activities.

The available data do not permit our tracing in any detail the dynamics of realized capital investment over the entire period. By appeal to county data on fixed asset stocks in 1984 and 1991, however, we can gain some sense of the amount of investment that each locale has received. Table 1 collects these data, for the top ten cities and counties in each of the two years. In 1984, seven inland cities and counties had 27 percent of the gross value of fixed assets of the province, and three coastal cities had 21.2 percent (Table 1). By 1991, the share of the coastal group increased to 39.6 percent and that of the inland group fell to 24.4 percent—and the top ten cities and counties were evenly split between coastal and inland.

Migration under the Two Strategies

In China, there have been three sorts of large-scale migration since 1949: from one rural area to another, from urban to rural areas, and from rural to urban areas. The rural-rural migration includes some movement from coastal areas to thinly populated inland areas, for reclamation and cultivation of wasteland, and migration necessitated by construction of reservoirs. The urban-rural migration includes the "sending down" of urban youth and transfer of urban cadres into villages during recurrent campaigns. The rural-urban migration includes the return of sent-down youth and transferred cadres, and the provision of labor to newly built factories.

In the case of Fujian province, the available data do not permit isolation of those components of migration that are closely related to regional strategy. The coarser data we have at hand, however, do provide

Table 2. Net In-Migration in Ten Counties and Cities, 1953-88

County or City	Net In-Migration[a]	Rate of Net In-Migration[b]	Location
		1953-57	
Nanping	25,079	12.97	inland
Shunchang	7810	11.33	inland
Zhangzhou	8090	9.87	coastal
Shaowu	9919	9.10	inland
Nanjing	12,031	7.43	coastal
Yunxiao	10,877	6.84	coastal
Sanming	4756	6.23	inland
Zhouning	4702	6.21	coastal
Wuyishan	4944	6.01	inland
Zhangping	5956	5.98	inland
		1957-62	
Sanming	44,012	40.63	inland
Shaowu	40,578	28.35	inland
Zhangping	15,616	12.97	inland
Quanzhou	21,012	12.92	coastal
Nanping	31,125	12.83	inland
Guangze	7039	9.62	inland
Xiamen	32,225	9.56	coastal
Yongan	12,163	9.37	inland
Zhouning	7931	8.36	coastal
Wuyishan	7842	8.27	inland
		1962-65	
Jianning	12,820	16.94	inland
Sanming	20,411	13.11	inland
Wuyishan	3287	3.00	inland

Table 2, continued

County or City	Net In-Migration[a]	Rate of Net In-Migration[b]	Location
Yongan	3876	2.55	inland
Changtai	195	0.20	coastal
Zhangzhou	-321	-0.16	coastal
Yunxiao	-494	-0.24	coastal
Tongan	-794	-0.28	coastal
Huaan	-444	-0.51	coastal
Dehua	-748	-0.53	coastal
		1965-76	
Shunchang	49,896	25.27	inland
Sanming	37,758	16.97	inland
Taining	9577	11.44	inland
Yongan	22,578	11.23	inland
Jianou	30,249	8.65	inland
Tongan	26,041	7.29	coastal
Longyan	16,981	6.12	inland
Guangze	6234	6.12	inland
Changtai	7090	5.62	coastal
Quanzhou	15,189	5.11	coastal
		1976-82	
Fuzhou	94,629	8.99	coastal
Zhangzhou	15,720	5.66	coastal
Xiamen	26,441	5.48	coastal
Sanming	6857	2.43	inland
Wuyishan	3240	1.95	inland
Shunchang	3620	1.78	inland
Dongshan	2577	1.68	coastal

Table 2, continued

County or City	Net In-Migration[a]	Rate of Net In-Migration[b]	Location
Taining	1760	1.64	inland
Quanzhou	6101	1.56	coastal
Ningde	4185	1.38	coastal
1982-88			
Xiamen	36,779	6.76	coastal
Fuzhou	65,058	5.48	coastal
Putian	79,012	4.95	coastal
Zhangzhou	13,589	4.36	coastal
Sanming	13,278	4.25	inland
Longyan	14,890	3.94	inland
Quanzhou	16,970	3.89	coastal
Nanping	10,285	2.45	inland
Yongan	6217	2.31	inland
Nanan	26,713	2.29	coastal

Note: For each subperiod, the counties and cities included are the top ten, in terms of rate of net in-migration. Counties and cities are ranked by rate of net in-migration.

a. Total population in terminal year less total population in the initial year less the natural increase over the period.
b. Net in-migration as share of total population in the initial year, in percent.

Sources: Fujian sheng tongji ju and Fujian sheng gongan ting, *Fujian sheng renkou tongji ziliao huibian, 1949-1988* (Beijing: Zhongguo tongji, 1989).

some insights. Table 2 shows, for several subperiods, the ten counties and cities having the highest rates of net in-migration. Migration to inland areas clearly dominated during 1957-76. The direction of migration, however, changed dramatically after 1976. During 1976-1982, the coastal cities and counties claimed the top three positions and half of the top ten. During 1982-88, they claimed the top four positions and six of the top ten.

In short, an initial examination of both regional policy pronouncements and development patterns reveals substantial differences between the

Maoist and post-Mao periods—differences that we expect to see reflected in the patterns of regional growth examined later in this paper.

3. Growth Centers in Fujian

Method and Data

In the literature of regional economics, growth centers are defined as those places likely to attract investment and to provide significant employment opportunities in the future.[6] Growth centers may be spontaneous or induced. The former grow without benefit of special assistance, or at least without benefit of explicit policy; the latter are those where public policy tries to promote growth.[7] By these definitions, the growth centers in Fujian are of the induced variety, as demonstrated by the review of regional strategy in Section 2 above.

In the literature, growth centers have been identified by appeal to a number of different indicators. For purposes of this paper, we rely mainly upon the growth rate of real GVIAO (gross value of industrial and agricultural output) per capita. As explained below, this choice is based partly upon considerations of data availability. Concretely, suppose R_t is the growth rate of GVIAO in the province of Fujian during period t, and let $\alpha(t)$ be a parameter in period t. A county or city i is a possible growth center if

$$R_t^i > \alpha(t)R_t, \ \alpha(t) \geq 1,$$

where R_t^i is the growth rate of county or city i. We admit changes in the value of $\alpha(t)$ according to circumstances—higher when the average rate of growth in the province is low, and lower when the average rate is high.

Consider the possible situations where a county initially has a very low GVIAO per capita or contributes very little to the increment in GVIAO of the province as a whole, due to the county's small population. We will use two subsidiary criteria to weed out such cases, even if they display high growth rates. The first subsidiary criterion is that initial GVIAO per capita in a growth center must be higher than that of the province as a whole. The second is that a growth center's contribution to the increment in GVIAO of the province as a whole must be disproportionately large—i.e., larger than one sixty-seventh of the total increment, since there are sixty-seven counties and cities in Fujian, as explained below. Hence, a growth center is a city or county that has a growth rate of GVIAO per capita $\alpha(t)$ times that of the province, and has an initial GVIAO per capita higher than

Table 3. Growth Centers in Fujian, 1950-91

County or City	Initial GVIAO[a]	Terminal GVIAO[a]	Growth Rate[b]	Share[c]	Location
			1950-57		
Nanping	119.15	352.84	16.78	3.35	Inland
Xianyou	104.00	285.69	15.53	5.33	Coastal
Fuzhou	89.20	213.56	13.28	6.96	Coastal
Zhangzhou	141.40	337.25	13.22	2.45	Coastal
Xiamen	127.68	291.67	12.53	3.69	Coastal
Jianou	190.87	421.28	11.97	3.85	Inland
Lianjiang	103.65	217.82	11.19	2.30	Coastal
Fujian	102.24	212.05	10.98	100.00	
			1957-65		
Xiamen	291.67	622.16	9.93	13.37	Coastal
Fuzhou	213.56	446.96	9.67	22.13	Coastal
Zhangzhou	337.25	641.14	8.36	7.32	Coastal
Sanming	340.15	633.27	8.08	4.92	Inland
Shunchang	221.61	386.48	7.20	2.76	Inland
Yongan	230.09	359.15	5.72	2.71	Inland
Quanzhou	264.02	395.78	5.19	4.69	Coastal
Nanping	352.84	465.55	3.53	4.44	Inland
Fujian	212.05	244.98	1.82	100.00	
			1965-78		
Sanming	633.27	2860.54	14.69	6.90	Inland
Yongan	359.15	1211.20	11.68	3.61	Inland
Shaxian	259.66	812.24	10.92	1.97	Inland
Fuzhou	446.96	1301.52	10.20	13.89	Coastal
Longyan	277.50	743.98	9.38	2.79	Inland
Xiamen	622.16	1630.62	9.15	7.93	Coastal

Table 3, continued

County or City	Initial GVIAO[a]	Terminal GVIAO[a]	Growth Rate[b]	Share[c]	Location
Shaowu	311.71	787.12	8.79	2.11	Inland
Nanping	465.55	1060.52	7.77	4.24	Inland
Fujian	244.98	434.71	4.51	100.00	
			1978-84		
Fuzhou	1301.52	2669.20	12.72	19.61	Coastal
Xiamen	1630.62	2862.94	9.84	8.33	Coastal
Fujian	434.71	733.61	9.11	100.00	
			1984-91		
Xiamen	2862.94	11095.36	21.35	13.40	Coastal
Jinjiang	694.04	2334.95	18.92	5.30	Coastal
Yongan	1852.47	5134.32	15.68	2.64	Inland
Zhangzhou	1719.34	4569.41	14.99	2.67	Coastal
Fujian	733.61	1948.56	14.98	100.00	

Note: $\alpha(t)$ as follows: 1, for 1950-57, 1978-84, and 1984-91; 1.5, for 1957-65 and 1965-78; see text. For each subperiod, growth centers are ranked by average annual growth rate.

a. GVIAO per capita, in 1980 constant yuan.
b. Percent per annum, average.
c. Share in total increment, in percent.

Sources: Zhang and Lu, *Fujian diqu jingji*; *Fujian tongji nianjian 1992*.

that of the province, and contributes more than one sixty-seventh of the increment in GVIAO of the province as a whole.

The government of Fujian began regular publication of annual county-level data only in the 1980s. But for some important indicators, such as population, GVIAO, GVIO, and GVAO, complete sets of county data are available for earlier years. Unfortunately, there are several problems with these earlier data: (1) data are available only for certain benchmark years, typically in index form; (2) for 15 counties and cities (out of 67), the pricing basis differs from the 1980 constant price convention used for the other locales; and (3) some county and city boundaries have changed over time. Nothing can be done about the first problem. To deal with the second problem, we use the provincial deflator to convert to 1980 constant prices (introducing some errors, if the true local deflators differ significantly from that of the province as a whole). To deal with the third problem, we adjust for boundary changes where possible. In particular, when one county-level unit splits into two, we continue to treat the two as a single composite unit throughout. There are sixty-seven such units throughout the 1950-91 period; we will frequently refer to them collectively as "counties," although a few are in fact cities and a few are composite units.

Results

Table 3 lists all of Fujian's growth centers during each of five subperiods, 1950-91. Using the table, we can trace out the spatial evolution of Fujian's growth centers over time. During 1950-57, five of the seven centers are coastal, and they account for a substantial portion of the province's total increment in GVIAO. This pattern begins to change during 1957-65, when only four growth centers are coastal and four are inland. Although Xiamen and Fuzhou account for some 35 percent of the total increment in GVIAO, the new railroad city of Sanming in the interior moves up to fourth place, in terms of both growth rate and share in total increment. By 1965-78, the inland centers have taken the lead in terms of growth rate and have greatly enlarged their share in the total increment.

Each of the first three subperiods shows at least seven growth centers. After 1978, however, the number of centers drops off sharply. Furthermore, there is a conspicuous shift from inland areas to the coast. In 1978-84, only the major coastal cities, Fuzhou and Xiamen, qualify as growth centers. The two account for 28 percent of the total increment in GVIAO, as compared to their 35 percent share twenty years earlier. And in 1984-91, Xiamen again qualifies, along with coastal Jinjiang (inclusive of Shishi city) and Zhangzhou, but Fuzhou does not. The only inland growth center is Yongan, accounting for only 2.6 percent of the total GVIAO increment.

In brief, the regional economic development of Fujian clearly underwent a process of transition, with centers of growth shifting first from the coast to inland areas and then back to the coast. This realized pattern is, of course, consistent with the main thrust of development strategy, as surveyed in Section 2.

4. Sectoral Origins of Growth-Center Development

Method and Data

In this section, we use the shift-share method to examine structural changes associated with the spatial movement of growth centers in Fujian. As applied to our GVIAO data, the shift-share model is as follows.[8]

$$\Delta Y_{ij} = R_{00}Y_{ij} + (R_{i0} - R_{00})Y_{ij} + (R_{ij} - R_{i0})Y_{ij}.$$

Y_{ij} is GVIAO from the ith sector in county (or city) j in the base year,

ΔY_{ij} is the change in GVIAO from the ith sector in county j, between the base and terminal years,

R_{00} is the provincial growth rate of GVIAO (i.e., the change in GVIAO over the entire period divided by the initial level),

R_{i0} is, similarly, the provincial growth rate of GVIAO from sector i, and

R_{ij} is the growth rate of GVIAO from sector i in county j.

The increment in GVIAO from sector i in county j consists of three components. The first, $R_{00}Y_{ij}$, is the provincial growth component—the increment that would have occurred had the ith sector in county j grown at the same rate as provincial GVIAO. The second, $(R_{i0} - R_{00})Y_{ij}$, is the sector-mix component, which captures the differential growth of the ith sector in the province as a whole (R_{i0}) as compared to provincial GVIAO (R_{00}). The third, $(R_{ij} - R_{i0})Y_{ij}$, is the residual component, which captures the differential growth of the ith sector in the county (R_{ij}), as compared to provincial GVIAO from that sector (R_{i0}).

Rewriting the shift-share equation as

$$\Delta Y_{ij} - R_{00}Y_{ij} = (R_{i0} - R_{00})Y_{ij} + (R_{ij} - R_{i0})Y_{ij},$$

we see that the difference between the actual and expected change in output of sector i in county j, called the net relative change, is attributed to (1) sector strength (or weakness) in the province as a whole, as reflected in the sector-mix component, and (2) locational advantages (or disadvantages) of county j and the effects of regional development strategies, as reflected in

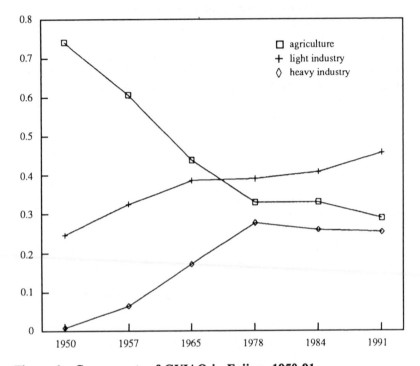

Figure 1. Components of GVIAO in Fujian, 1950-91

Source: Fujian sheng tongji ju, *Fujian tongji nianjian 1992* (Beijing: Zhongguo tongji, 1992).

the residual component. The sum of these two—i.e., the net relative change—measures the relative economic performance of the county, in the sector in question.

In the case of Fujian, data availability limits us to examination of only three sectors: light industry, heavy industry, and agriculture. Y_i (i = 1, 2, 3) are, therefore, Gross Value of Light Industrial Output (GVLIO), Gross Value of Heavy Industrial Output (GVHIO), and Gross Value of Agriculture Output (GVAO), respectively. In Figure 1, the time paths of these sectors for the province as a whole are shown (as shares in GVIAO), for 1950-91.

Results

The remainder of this section applies shift-share analysis to Fujian's growth centers. This analysis will point to the sources of growth in each center during various subperiods and, hence, contribute to an understanding of the spatial evolution of growth centers since the 1950s. The results summarized in this subsection are based upon the detailed report in Tables A1 through A5 of the Appendix; the summary comments here focus primarily upon the residual components (explained in the preceding subsection). Note that it is possible for a growth center to exhibit negative residual components in all three sectors; this might occur if the growth rate of population in that center is below average, even if output per capita is increasing.

1950-57 (Table A1). In the inland growth centers, heavy industry dominates—i.e., exhibits larger residuals than light industry and agriculture, and the locational factors captured in these residuals account for almost all of the increment in heavy-industrial growth. In part, this is a statistical artifact, given the initial near-zero base; in part, however, it reflects the locational pattern of investment—and, in particular, the construction of chemical, cement, and electric power plants in such inland areas as Nanping. (Nanping is one of only two growth centers with positive residuals in all three sectors.) By contrast, with the exception of Lianjiang, the coastal growth centers show negative residuals in heavy industry; light industry dominates in Xianyou and Fuzhou (and probably Zhangzhou), and agriculture dominates in Xiamen and Lianjiang. Fuzhou is the only coastal growth center in which the bulk of the increment in light industrial output is attributable to locational factors captured in the residual.

1957-65 (Table A2). This subperiod includes the Great Leap Forward of 1958 and the post-Leap depression and famine. During the Leap, the central and provincial authorities called for "taking steel as the key link" and, more generally, for emphasizing development of heavy industries. The subsequent collapse forced a shift into agriculture, but with continuing development of heavy industries serving agriculture—industries such as chemicals, cement, and machine-building.

Two of the four inland growth centers in Fujian exhibit the expected dominance of heavy industry. But Nanping shows a large negative residual in heavy industry and a pronounced lurch toward light industry (possibly paper-making); agriculture probably dominates in Shunchang. The pattern in the coastal centers is similar to that of the 1950s, but with Xiamen now exhibiting dominance of light industry rather than agriculture. Overall, the 1957-65 data show a conspicuous pattern of positive residuals across centers and sectors, with negative residuals only in Sanming's agriculture and Nanping's heavy industry. (Four of the 24 residuals cannot be calculated with the data available; see Table A2.) Interestingly, although agricultural output actually fell in the province as a whole, all but one of the growth centers show increases in agricultural output.

1965-78 (Table A3). The inland growth centers, notably Sanming, Yongan, and now Longyan, no longer exhibit dominance of heavy industry, in terms of residuals. These areas, however, benefit immensely from the provincewide drive to develop heavy industry, as shown by the large industry-mix components. The coastal growth centers, Fuzhou and Xiamen, no longer exhibit any strong residuals at all; indeed, in the case of Fuzhou, all three residuals are negative.

1978-84 (Table A4). In this subperiod, the strategic sectors in Fujian were light industry and agriculture. Fuzhou shows large residuals in both of these sectors, but Xiamen for the first time sees dominance of heavy industry. This appears to be very much a transitional subperiod, from the Maoist patterns of the 1950s, 60s, and 70s, to a new pattern (hints of which are evident in the 1980s, below).

1984-91 (Table A5). During this subperiod, the transition from planning and autarky to markets and outward orientation took hold throughout most of the province. At the provincial level, there were no sharply defined strategic sectors and industries, as there had been in past subperiods.

The only inland growth center, Yongan, shows a large positive residual in light industry—and now has a negative residual in heavy industry. Coastal Jinjiang (including Shishi city) experienced very rapid industrial growth, driven by both light and heavy industries; Jinjiang also posted a dramatic negative residual in agriculture and a 50 percent drop in agricultural output. Xiamen shows positive residuals in all three sectors, with a shift back to light industry as the clearly dominant sector. Zhangzhou now posts negative residuals in all three sectors, as did Fuzhou in 1965-78. Fuzhou is no longer a growth center.

Summary. The overall pattern of county-level components, described by subperiod here and laid out in detail in Tables A1-A5, reflects both the general impact of provincewide development strategy (in the industry-mix components) and much variation across regions in location-specific effects, as captured by the residual components. Over time, there is considerable volatility in these residuals, suggesting that local development policies have varied considerably around the provincial norm.

5. Growth Centers and Regional Disparities

In this section, we try to uncover the distributional implications of the spatial transition already examined. Specifically, how did the movement of growth centers affect the distribution of productive capacity and living

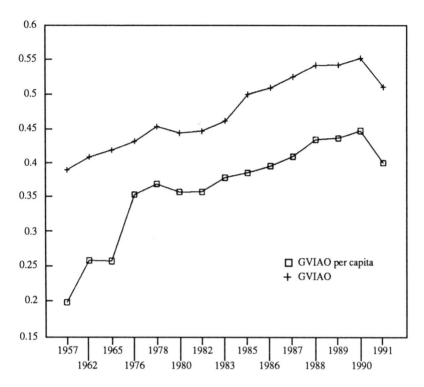

Figure 2. Gini Coefficients, County GVIAO and County GVIAO per Capita, 1957-91

Sources: Zhang Ruiyao and Lu Zengrong, *Fujian diqu jingji* (Fuzhou: Fujian renmin, 1986); Fujian sheng tongji ju, *Fujian tongji nianjian* (see Table A1).

standards across counties provincewide and between the major regions of the province?

Method and Data

For purposes of this section, the counties of Fujian are grouped into regions according to the development strategy to which they were subject. The inland region includes counties in Nanping, Sanming, and Longyan prefectures—counties which have been consistently targeted by the sorts of inland strategy outlined in Section 2, above. Similarly, the coastal region includes counties in Fuzhou, Xiamen, Putian, Jinjiang (now Quanzhou), and Longxi (now Zhangzhou) prefectures. The northeastern region includes the counties of Ningde prefecture, which have not benefitted to any great extent

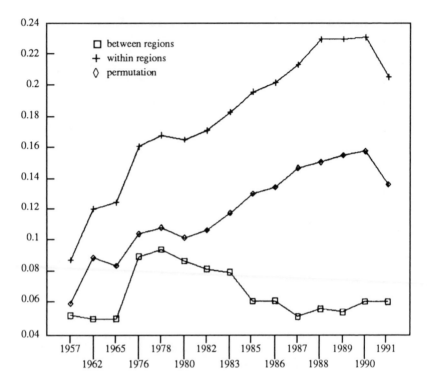

Figure 3. Decomposition of Gini Coefficient, County GVIAO per Capita, 1957-91

Sources: See Figure 2.

from either of the regional strategies—but which have received special assistance targeted at the large pockets of poverty within the prefecture. No county in this third region has ever been a growth center.

We use the Gini coefficient as a measure of intercounty disparities and a decomposition of the Gini coefficient into intra- and interregional components as a tool for tracing the relationship between the evolution of growth centers and changes in disparities. County GVIAO is used as a measure of productive capacity, and county GVIAO per capita as a measure of living standards.

107

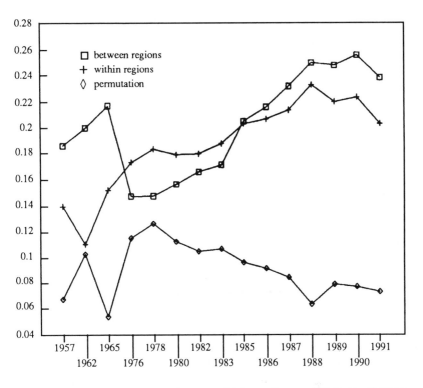

Figure 4. Decomposition of Gini Coefficient, County GVIAO, 1957-91
Sources: See Figure 2.

Results

Figure 2 shows the time paths of Ginis for both county GVIAO and county GVIAO per capita. The Gini for county GVIAO grew from 0.39 in 1957 to 0.51 in 1991, with slight downturns in the late 1970s and in 1991. The Gini for county GVIAO per capita shows a more pronounced increase during the Maoist era (to 1978) than in the post-Mao era. This increase is also large relative to that shown by the first time path (for GVIAO). Comparing the two curves in Figure 2, we also find that (1) the Gini for GVIAO per capita is always lower than that for GVIAO, and (2) the gap between the two curves is very large before 1976 but remains virtually constant thereafter. The latter observation is consistent with the spread of productive capacity into counties with relatively small populations, driving their standards of living sharply higher.

108

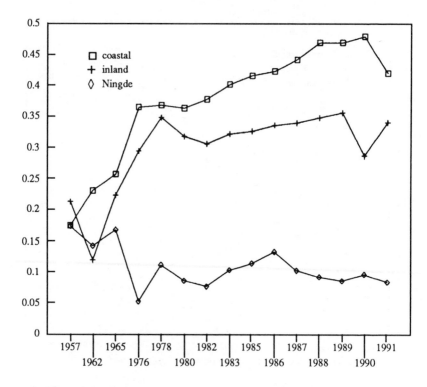

Figure 5. Gini Coefficients, County GVIAO per Capita within Regions, 1957-91

Sources: See Figure 2.

Decomposition of intercounty disparities. To illuminate the sources of inequality and link them to the evolution of growth centers, we decompose the intercounty Gini coefficients into three components: the contribution of interregional disparities, that of intercounty disparities within regions, and a "permutation" term.[9]

Figure 3 shows the decomposition of the Gini for county GVIAO per capita. The interregional component is always the smallest of the three—and, indeed, contributes a very small portion of the intercounty disparities in 1957-65 and in the late 1980s. During the first of these two subperiods, the inland growth centers were emerging and beginning to catch up with those on the coast. With the transition to inland growth, the interregional component expanded, reaching its maximum in 1978.

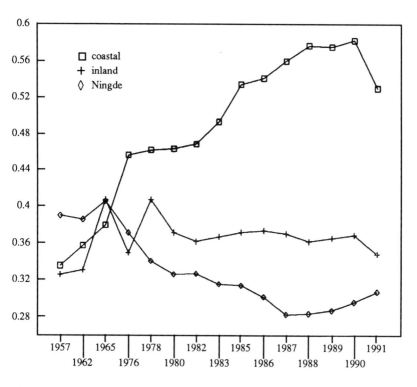

Figure 6. Gini Coefficients, County GVIAO within Regions, 1957-91
Sources: See Figure 2.

Figure 4 shows the decomposition of the Gini for county GVIAO. Here, the between-region component is large and increasing in 1957-65, and falls sharply in 1965-76—just the opposite of the pattern in Figure 3.

In both Figure 3 and Figure 4, the within-region component is a large portion of overall inequality among counties. And the within-region components trend up in both figures until the reform era, displaying broadly similar time paths. In general, the recent transition of growth centers appears to entail an amelioration of increases in within-region disparity, in terms of both GVIAO per capita and GVIAO.

Inter-county disparities within regions. Figures 5 and 6 present Gini coefficients showing disparities within each of the three regions. Again, Ginis for both county GVIAO and county GVIAO per capita are included. Both Figure 5 and Figure 6 suggest a strong association between the location of growth centers and intraregional disparities. The Gini coefficients in the three regions were similar, as of 1957-65. After that, the gaps widened. Ningde has never had a growth center—and Ningde shows a very low, and decreasing, Gini in both figures. In the inland region during 1965-91, there were six growth centers (out of 28 counties), and the largest share of a single center in the total GVIAO increment is 7 percent (Sanming, 1965-1978). The inland region ranks second in inequality among counties, and exhibits stability in both Ginis. In the coastal region during 1965-91, there were only four growth centers (out of 30 counties), but the largest share of a single center in the total GVIAO increment is 14 percent (Fuzhou, 1965-1978). The more concentrated spatial pattern of growth centers in the coastal region seems to be associated with more inequality within the region, and with growth of this inequality.

7. Conclusions

This paper suggests quite clearly that the strategies of the central and provincial governments have had profound effects upon the actual pattern of development in Fujian, in terms of the location of growth centers, the sectoral structure of those centers (and, presumably, of other counties and cities as well) and the pattern of disparities in productive capacity and living standards across regions. Given the evident impact of government decision-making on the pattern of development, a more careful investigation of government decisions and their economic implications will be of considerable interest—and the approach explored in this paper is likely to be of some use in framing such an investigation. The possibility that, e.g., government seriously distorted the economy of Fujian by forcing regions into growth patterns inconsistent with their endowments is clearly susceptible to study within the framework sketched here. Further progress along these lines will depend, however, on a more refined identification of growth centers, the construction of a spatial hierarchy of growth centers (rather than simply a listing of centers, as in this paper), and a more thorough understanding of the nature of growth in each. All of this awaits the release of more complete county-level data.

The approach suggested in this paper also extends the larger attempt to base our understanding of China's overall economic development more firmly upon regional building blocks. Hence, this paper complements recent work by, among others, Penelope Prime, the World Bank, Thomas Lyons, and Ezra Vogel.[10] The province of Fujian is in all likelihood a growth center for China as a whole, and our study of Fujian suggests how local growth centers are nested within a provincial one.

Notes

1. Barry Naughton, "The Third Front: Defence Industrialization in the Chinese Interior," *China Quarterly*, no. 115, October 1989.

2. Zhao Dexin, *Zhonghua renmin gongheguo jingjishi gangyao* (Wuhan: Hubei renmin, 1988), pp. 248-49 and 252-53.

3. He Shaochuan, *Dangdai zhongguo de fujian sheng* (Beijing: Dangdai zhongguo, 1991), p. 126.

4. Zhang Ruiyao and Lu Zengrong, *Fujian diqu jingji* (Fuzhou: Fujian renmin, 1986), p. 225.

5. He, *Dangdai zhongguo de fujian sheng*, p. 436.

6. Brian J. L. Berry, *Growth Centers in the American Urban System*, vol. 1 (Cambridge, MA: Ballinger, 1973), p. 56.

7. William Alonso and Elliott Medrick, "Spontaneous Growth Centers in Twentieth-Century American Urbanization," in Niles M. Hanson (ed.), *Growth Centers in Regional Economic Development* (New York: The Free Press, 1972).

8. This model is adapted from A. Andrikopoulas, J. Brox, and E. Carvalko, "Shift-Share Analysis and the Potential for Predicting Regional Growth Patterns: Some Evidence for the Region of Quebec, Canada," *Growth and Change*, 21(1), 1990.

9. This decomposition follows N. Bhattacharya and B. Mahalanobis, "Regional Disparities in Household Consumption in India," *Journal of the American Statistical Association*, 62(317), 1967, as summarized in F. Nygard and A. Sandstrom, *Measuring Income Inequality* (Stockholm: Alonqvist & Wiksell, 1981), and developed in Jacques Silber, "Factor Components, Population Subgroups and the Computation of the Gini Index of Inequality," *Review of Economics and Statistics*, 71(1), 1989.

10. Penelope Prime, "Industry's Response to Market Liberalization in China: Evidence from Jiangsu Province," *Economic Development and Cultural Change*, 41(1), 1992; World Bank, *China: Growth and Development in Gansu Province* (Washington: World Bank, 1990); Thomas P. Lyons, "Grain in Fujian: Intraprovincial Patterns of Production and Trade, 1952-90," *China Quarterly*,

no. 129, March 1992; Ezra Vogel, *One Step Ahead in China* (Cambridge, MA: Harvard University Press, 1989).

Appendix. Shift-Share Analysis of Growth Centers in Fujian

Table A1. 1950-57

	Actual Change	Provincial Growth	Sector Mix	Residual	Net Relative Change
Nanping					
Light Industry	1632.84	65.49	36.62	1530.73	1567.35
Heavy Industry	1829.79	10.42	97.38	1721.99	1819.37
Agriculture	2149.42	2577.23	-821.89	394.08	-427.81
Xianyou					
Light Industry	3744.00	1594.63	891.62	1257.75	2149.37
Heavy Industry	33.00	282.92	2643.19	-2893.11	-249.92
Agriculture	3158.00	5658.41	-1804.48	-695.93	-2500.41
Fuzhou					
Light Industry	7458.59	1617.06	904.17	4937.36	5841.53
Heavy Industry	1585.62	1034.54	9665.21	-9114.13	551.08
Agriculture	2195.92	4398.52	-1402.70	-799.90	-2202.60
Zhangzhou					
Light Industry	N.a.				
Heavy Industry	N.a.				
Agriculture	884.00	1836.26	-458.03	-94.23	-552.26
Xiamen					
Light Industry	4284.50	2796.60	1563.69	-75.80	1487.90
Heavy Industry	522.30	197.21	1842.39	-1517.29	325.09
Agriculture	1376.31	1371.38	-437.34	442.27	4.93
Jianou					
Light Industry	1036.83	497.57	278.21	261.05	539.26
Heavy Industry	3246.20	1.91	17.83	3226.46	3244.29
Agriculture	2163.48	4717.23	-1504.34	-1049.41	-2553.75

Table A1, continued

	Actual Change	Provincial Growth	Sector Mix	Residual	Net Relative Change
Lianjiang					
Light Industry	587.47	248.71	139.06	199.69	338.76
Heavy Industry	190.82	3.28	30.61	156.94	187.54
Agriculture	3076.16	3060.69	-976.06	991.54	15.47

Note: All data in 1980 yuan, × 10,000. See text for explanation.

Sources: Zhang and Lu, *Fujian diqu jingji*; Fujian sheng tongji ju, *Fujian tongji nianjian 1983* (Fuzhou: Fujian renmin, 1984); Fujian sheng tongji ju, *Fujian tongji nianjian 1984* (Fuzhou: Fujian renmin, 1985); Fujian sheng tongji ju, *Fujian tongji nianjian 1986* (Fuzhou: Fujian renmin, 1986); Fujian sheng tongji ju, *Fujian tongji nianjian 1987* (Beijing: Zhongguo tongji, 1987); Fujian sheng tongji ju, *Fujian tongji nianjian 1988* (Beijing: Zhongguo tongji, 1988); Fujian sheng tongji ju, *Fujian tongji nianjian 1989* (Beijing: Zhongguo tongji, 1989); Fujian sheng tongji ju, *Fujian tongji nianjian 1990* (Beijing: Zhongguo tongji, 1990); Fujian sheng tongji ju, *Fujian tongji nianjian 1991* (Beijing: Zhongguo tongji, 1991); Fujian sheng tongji ju, *Fujian tongji nianjian 1992* (Beijing: Zhongguo tongji, 1992).

Table A2. 1957-65

	Actual Change	Provincial Growth	Sector Mix	Residual	Net Relative Change
Xiamen					
Light Industry	10672.36	2458.97	21140.07	6099.32	8213.39
Heavy Industry	3326.21	258.65	1594.17	1473.38	3067.56
Agriculture	1092.28	925.20	-982.26	1149.34	167.08
Fuzhou					
Light Industry	16285.54	3350.62	2880.65	10054.27	12934.92
Heavy Industry	7477.24	909.90	5608.07	959.28	6567.34
Agriculture	1195.68	2108.46	-2238.50	1325.72	-912.78
Zhangzhou					
Light Industry	N.a.				
Heavy Industry	N.a.				
Agriculture	745.00	753.13	-799.58	791.45	-8.13

Table A2, continued

	Actual Change	Provincial Growth	Sector Mix	Residual	Net Relative Change
Sanming					
Light Industry	1172.71	21.53	18.51	1132.67	1151.18
Heavy Industry	4459.92	20.62	127.08	4312.22	4439.30
Agriculture	-88.18	559.77	-594.29	-53.66	-647.95
Shunchang					
Light Industry	N.a.				
Heavy Industry	N.a.				
Agriculture	974.41	688.59	-731.06	1016.88	285.82
Yongan					
Light Industry	286.27	1366.62	117.46	32.19	149.65
Heavy Industry	2304.03	137.94	850.19	1315.90	2166.09
Agriculture	470.60	807.02	-856.79	520.37	-336.42
Quanzhou					
Light Industry	3619.00	1216.62	1045.98	1356.40	2402.38
Heavy Industry	608.00	54.21	334.12	219.67	553.79
Agriculture	1059.00	1295.22	-1375.11	1138.88	-236.23
Nanping					
Light Industry	3799.24	650.99	559.68	2588.57	3148.25
Heavy Industry	814.55	711.50	4385.27	-4282.22	103.05
Agriculture	398.61	1569.48	-1666.28	495.41	-1170.87

Note: All data in 1980 yuan, × 10,000. See text for explanation.

Sources: See Table A1.

Table A3. 1965-78

	Actual Change	Provincial Growth	Sector Mix	Residual	Net Relative Change
Sanming					
Light Industry	17589.67	2020.23	740.15	14829.29	15569.44
Heavy Industry	22523.62	7422.90	10183.05	4917.66	15100.72
Agriculture	3177.85	2232.63	-1538.03	2423.26	885.23
Yongan					
Light Industry	6108.67	1051.14	385.11	4672.42	5057.53
Heavy Industry	15039.45	4375.40	6002.36	4661.69	10664.05
Agriculture	2372.76	4201.90	-2894.64	1065.50	-1829.14
Shaxian					
Light Industry	1255.13	626.92	229.68	398.53	628.21
Heavy Industry	1921.19	450.83	618.47	851.88	1470.36
Agriculture	2124.72	4770.15	-3286.10	640.67	-2645.43
Fuzhou					
Light Industry	53403.51	41017.18	15027.49	-2641.16	12386.33
Heavy Industry	36556.45	16162.83	22172.86	-1779.24	20393.62
Agriculture	-3087.67	10922.41	-7524.32	-6485.75	-14010.07
Longyan					
Light Industry	11123.00	2776.29	1017.15	7929.56	8346.71
Heavy Industry	11722.00	1842.09	2527.05	7352.86	9879.91
Agriculture	1800.00	5264.75	-3626.83	162.08	-3464.75
Xiamen					
Light Industry	29338.13	27997.73	10257.54	-8917.14	1340.40
Heavy Industry	16560.70	6569.32	9012.08	979.29	9991.38
Agriculture	3600.02	5726.36	-3944.82	1818.48	-2126.34
Shaowu					
Light Industry	4174.93	975.99	357.58	2841.36	3198.94
Heavy Industry	7613.91	2188.33	2906.02	2589.55	5495.58
Agriculture	2232.22	5805.73	-3999.50	425.99	-3573.51

Table A3, continued

	Actual Change	Provincial Growth	Sector Mix	Residual	Net Relative Change
Nanping					
Light Industry	9328.74	9013.82	3302.40	-2987.48	314.92
Heavy Industry	12658.42	4361.86	5983.79	2312.76	8296.56
Agriculture	2879.52	7322.11	-5044.12	601.52	-4442.59

Note: All data in 1980 yuan, × 10,000. See text for explanation.

Sources: See Table A1.

Table A4. 1978-84

	Actual Change	Provincial Growth	Sector Mix	Residual	Net Relative Change
Fuzhou					
Light Industry	119407.79	66230.13	21273.80	31903.87	53177.66
Heavy Industry	40284.45	39212.43	2052.59	-980.57	1072.02
Agriculture	22937.78	3003.88	-988.74	20922.64	19933.90
Xiamen					
Light Industry	47480.48	39193.30	12589.29	-4302.11	8287.18
Heavy Industry	28836.60	17377.00	909.61	10549.99	11459.60
Agriculture	5473.56	5986.81	-1970.60	1457.34	-513.25

Note: All data in 1980 yuan, × 10,000. See text for explanation.

Sources: See Table A1.

Table A5. 1984-91

	Actual Change	Provincial Growth	Sector Mix	Residual	Net Relative Change
Xiamen					
Light Industry	450812.15	187945.56	103929.34	158937.24	262866.59
Heavy Industry	175507.74	98921.91	12471.40	64114.44	76585.84
Agriculture	4159.78	25145.79	-21238.13	252.12	-20986.01

Table A5, continued

	Actual Change	Provincial Growth	Sector Mix	Residual	Net Relative Change
Jinjiang					
Light Industry	212127.80	23106.30	12777.23	176244.27	189021.50
Heavy Industry	47879.64	4904.89	618.37	42356.38	42974.75
Agriculture	-31224.26	114691.53	-96868.43	-49047.36	-145900.00
Yongan					
Light Industry	60190.86	27057.39	14962.08	18171.39	33133.48
Heavy Industry	49698.37	56647.46	7141.73	-14090.81	-6949.09
Agriculture	4291.21	13776.53	-11635.65	2150.34	-9485.31
Zhangzhou					
Light Industry	104289.13	72048.73	39841.21	-7600.80	32240.40
Heavy Industry	22430.50	21566.28	2719.29	-1855.07	864.22
Agriculture	914.20	11239.79	-9493.12	-832.47	-10325.59

Note: All data in 1980 yuan, × 10,000. See text for explanation.

Sources: See Table A1.

Rural Industrialization in Fujian and Taiwan

William L. Parish

1. Introduction

In China, as elsewhere, rural industrialization and small town growth are commonly promoted as alternatives to rapid urbanization and the increased economic and social costs that rapid urbanization often entails. This modest paper provides an exploratory comparison of rural industrialization in China's Fujian Province and its sister "province" across the Taiwan Straits, where rural industrialization did indeed help soften the pace and social costs of rapid urbanization. Limited comparisons to South Korea, where lagging rural industrialization helped accelerate the rush to cities and subsequent employment problems, help further contextualize the situation in Fujian.

Many countries hope to use alternative forms of employment in or near villages to slow the flow of rural migrants into cities and reduce the demands upon government for new city services.[1] The path to realizing this hope, however, is fraught with difficulties. Frequently, the roads, electric power, education, and other conditions needed for dispersed production are absent. Or, byproducts of other policies, ranging from taxation, foreign exchange, and import duties to marketing boards, housing subsidies, and urban preferences undermine attempts at rural and small town development.[2] Several studies examine nonfarm employment and the closely related topic of industrial dispersion.[3] From case studies of societies such as Brazil, South Korea, and Taiwan and from cross-country comparisons, several features emerge as favoring rural nonfarm employment. These features include: (1) dispersed urbanization, providing many nodes of demand for rural goods; (2) developed infrastructure, including cheap and ample transport for getting goods to and from markets as well as cheap and ample electricity to power dispersed production facilities; (3) human capital, including not only a skilled labor force but also educational facilities for the children of employees and managers; and (4) rising rural incomes, which rapidly create a demand for non-agricultural products to be

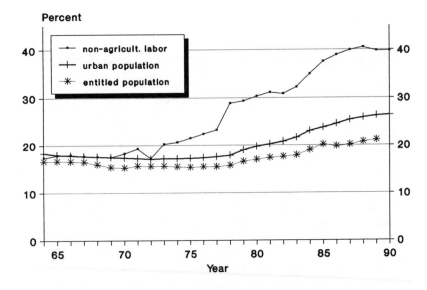

Figure 1. China's Urban and Rural Labor Force, 1964-90

Note: Shares, in percent, in total labor force or total population.

Sources: Grant Blank and William Parish, "Rural Industry and Nonfarm Employment," in Reginald Kwok, William L. Parish, and Anthony Yeh (eds.), *Chinese Urban Reform* (Armonk, N.Y.: M. E. Sharpe, 1990), p. 7; Guojia tongji ju, *Zhongguo tongji nianjian 1990 [Statistical Yearbook of China 1990]* (Beijing: Zhongguo tongji, 1990), pp. 570-71; Guojia tongji ju, *Zhongguo tongji nianjian 1991 [Statistical Yearbook of China 1991]* (Beijing: Zhongguo tongji, 1991), pp. 79, 99.

consumed locally, even without access to urban markets.[4] Features that seem to inhibit rural industrialization include: (1) large urban-rural gaps in both incomes and amenities, which encourage rural residents to abandon the countryside; and (2) centralized government control, which favors both enterprises that locate near the capital so as to have the bureaucrat's ear and extensive regulation of labor and supplies, creating red tape for small producers.[5]

As one would expect, in China rural industrialization is favored by some conditions—e.g., human capital, and rising rural incomes in the 1980s—and disfavored by others—poor transport and energy infrastructure, centralized government control. Perkins argues that much of the apparent growth in rural industry through the middle 1980s was artifactual, depending on tight controls over urban land and labor markets in ways that encouraged urban producers to engage in extensive subcontracting with rural industries in the immediate suburbs of cities.[6] Should new reform measures lead to urban land and labor markets being liberated, much of the artificial market for subcontracts would disappear. And, even without reform, there is little optimism for rural industry spreading much beyond the immediate hinterland of cities and ready access to urban subcontractors. Similarly, comparing international and interprovincial patterns, Blank and Parish argue that further rural industrialization is severely hampered by China's inadequate transportation system.[7] This paper delves further into these issues by examining, first, current national tendencies in urbanization and, then, patterns of rural nonfarm change in the paired locales of Fujian and Taiwan.

2. National Trends

Despite many definitional problems, it is possible to gain a clear sense of recent urbanization trends based on three separate indices of urban growth and labor market shifts (Figure 1). Our data for "urban population" is, by and large, that population living in contiguously populated urban neighborhoods. Because Chinese cities and towns are overbounded, often including much of the surrounding rural hinterland and even administratively subordinate rural counties, one must restrict the urban population data to urban neighborhoods. This restriction is particularly important in the 1980s, when including the broad administrative definition of urban would lead to a figure twice that in Figure 1. The 26 percent urban share for 1990 in Figure 1 seems close to reality, though it may be understated because of a large informal, floating population in many major cities that is not captured by official statistics. Including that "informal" urban population would raise the 1990 urban share to around 30 percent of the total population. It is the 30 percent share that we will assume is the best approximation for the purposes of this paper.

The adjusted urban share reflects distinct changes since the early 1980s. Following the exceptional curtailment of urban growth in the 1960s and 1970s, urban growth began to accelerate in the 1980s (Figure 1). Even in this most recent period, however, not everyone has been entitled to full urban benefits, which is our second indicator of urbanization trends. Starting in the early 1950s, every family got a household registration, which labeled the members of the family as either entitled (non-agricultural) or non-entitled (agricultural). The entitled were first in line for highly subsidized housing, subsidized food, and state sector jobs with many fringe benefits, including health care, disability, and pension payments. The non-entitled enjoyed almost none of these benefits. Thus formal entry into the entitled, urban sector was extremely attractive, leading on average to consumption levels 2.5 to 3 times higher than in the countryside. While attractive to individuals, urban entitlement was very unattractive to state planners, who by the middle 1950s found highly subsidized urban living standards increasingly difficult to support. As a result, by the early 1960s, central planners imposed a bamboo curtain between city and countryside, effectively walling off urban entitlements from most of the rural population. Many who had slipped illegally into cities in the late 1950s were driven back into the countryside in the early 1960s. With a relaxation of the rationing of food and other items in the 1980s, the attempt to exclude people from towns and cities weakened. But even as the numbers in towns and cities began to grow again, full entitlement through urban household registration was given only rarely. This promoted a two-class system. While perhaps as much as 30 percent of the population was in towns and cities by 1990, including the informal, "floating" population, only about two-thirds of this number were entitled to full urban benefits (Figure 1).[8]

A third index of trends potentially related to urbanization is the share of the labor force outside agriculture. For many years, urbanization and non-agricultural work moved in close parallel (Figure 1). However, by the 1980s the two trends began to diverge. One reason for this was the government policy that tried to limit urban expenses by promoting rural industry in place of urban industry. When new agricultural reforms freed farmers from field agriculture in the late 1970s and early 1980s, many of them flocked not to cities but to new enterprises in their home villages and in nearby market towns to which they could commute daily. Thus, the share working outside agriculture could rise to 40 percent by 1990, even while the share in cities and towns remained significantly lower (Figure 1).[9]

The overall conclusion that one draws from trends in both urbanization and the non-agricultural labor force is that, nationally, China has come to more closely approximate the urbanization patterns of several other large, low-income Asian nations. It is closest to Indonesia, which also has somewhat over 40 percent of its labor force outside agriculture and about 30 percent of its population resident in towns and cities.[10] Other large countries with similar levels of urbanization include India at 27 percent and Pakistan at 32 percent. Compared to many smaller countries and countries at slightly higher levels of development—e.g., the Philippines at 42 percent urban—China, of course, continued to have modest urbanization.

3. Fujian Province

In many ways, conditions in Fujian approximate the average for the nation as a whole. A rich coastal zone matched with a much larger, less developed hilly interior produces averages that are similar to those for all of China. For example, changes in the labor force and entitled population have tracked national trends over the last decade. By 1990, the 42 percent of the labor force working outside agriculture and the 17 percent entitled to full urban benefits were similar to the national figures. Though we don't have the appropriate estimate for urban population, it would probably be similar to the national figure as well.[11] Rural enterprise trends also tended to mimic those for the whole nation. After rapid acceleration of profits and labor force in the middle 1980s, rural enterprises began to suffer both from increased competition as more enterprises emerged and from national policies to control inflation by severely restricting the supply of bank loans available to non-state enterprises.[12] The result was that, although profit recovered after a 1989 downturn, employment growth was much slower to recover (Figure 2). As a share of all rural (*xiangcun*) employment, Fujian non-agricultural or nonfarm employment stood at 22 percent in 1990. This was sharply below other coastal provinces such as Guangdong (32 percent), Zhejiang (34 percent), and Jiangsu (38 percent), but not too different from the national average of 24 percent.[13] Thus, while sharing some of the advantages of other coastal provinces, Fujian also suffers disadvantages of terrain and transport that inhibit extensive rural enterprise growth.

4. Taiwan and South Korea

The contrasting experiences of Taiwan and South Korea suggest that rural industrialization can moderate the pace of urbanization and the problems of urban unemployment when people flood into cities. This is only a slight moderation, for both societies urbanized very rapidly. And the set of conditions needed for effective rural industrialization is long, suggesting that this is a policy not easily implemented. The comparison is instructive, nevertheless.

Compared to South Korea, Taiwan emerged from World War II and colonial rule with a denser network of roads and railroads, which helped contribute to rural industrialization later on.[14] Despite rapid urbanization in both societies, dispersed rural industrialization in Taiwan and ready access to many smaller towns and cities helped moderate the flow of labor out of the countryside and channeled that flow to more intermediate cities.

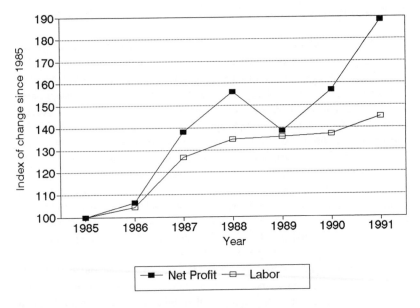

Figure 2. Fujian Rural Enterprises, 1985-91

Note: Indices, 1985 = 100. Includes all levels of ownership from township through individual.

Sources: Fujian sheng tongji ju, *Fujian tongji nianjian 1987 [Statistical Yearbook of Fujian 1987]* (Beijing: Zhongguo tongji, 1987); Fujian sheng tongji ju, *Fujian tongji nianjian 1991 [Statistical Yearbook of Fujian 1991]* (Beijing: Zhongguo tongji, 1991); Guojia tongji ju, *Zhongguo tongji nianjian 1992 [Statistical Yearbook of China 1992]* (Beijing: Zhongguo tongji, 1992); Taiwan Provincial Government, Department of Civil Affairs, *1967 Taiwan Demographic Fact Book* (Nantou, Taiwan: Taiwan Provincial Government, 1968); and Republic of China, Executive Yuan, Economic Planning Council, *Taiwan Statistical Data Book* (Taipei: Executive Yuan, 1977).

In South Korea, in contrast, rural industrialization was muted. Rural laborers flooded towards the larger cities. Rapid urbanization in primate cities in South Korea was combined with a pattern of larger enterprises, more male-employing heavy industry, and greater capital intensity in investment in ways that generated fewer jobs for everyone and, particularly, for women.[15]

Several conditions fed on one another. While Taiwan generated almost all investment funds from internal savings in ways that inhibited the growth of large enterprises, South Korea engaged in major external borrowing that was then funneled through the central government to a select set of large industrial conglomerates (*chaebol*). For this select set of conglomerates, government-subsidized loans cheapened the cost of capital. Simultaneously, for reasons having to do in part with efforts to tame

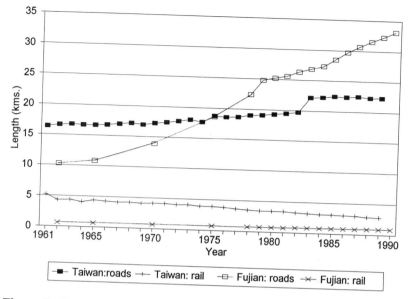

Figure 3. Roads and Railroads in Fujian and Taiwan, 1961-90

Note: All figures are densities, in kilometers per 100 square kilometers of cultivated area.

Sources: See Figure 2.

contentious labor and in part with the ability of larger enterprises to pay more, wage rates rose faster than explicable from demand and supply conditions alone. The net result was that Korean entrepreneurs engaged in capital deepening in ways that generated fewer jobs.[16] In Taiwan, in contrast, capital remained dear. Labor, often villagers who commuted to work, remained cheap. Thus, Taiwan's entrepreneurs continued to use labor-intensive methods in ways that pulled more men and women into the labor force.[17]

The net result of both less intense labor demand and the flooding of migrants into large cities was that urban unemployment remained a chronic problem in South Korea in the 1960s and 1970s, disappearing only in the 1980s.[18] Urban male unemployment hovered near 8 percent in the 1970s and remained at 5 percent even as late as 1985.[19] In Taiwan, in contrast, urban unemployment remained extremely low throughout these three decades. By 1968, the labor surplus was gone, by some accounts, and by the 1980s labor shortages were so severe that the hiring of illegal migrant laborers was a public policy issue of increasing concern.[20] Even in the

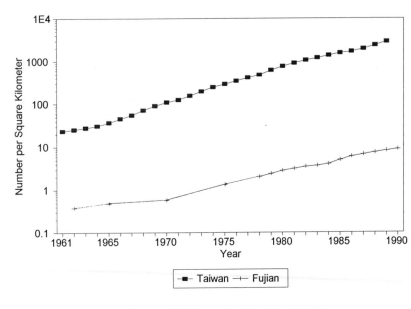

Figure 4. Motor Vehicles in Fujian and Taiwan, 1961-90

Note: Includes cars, trucks, and buses. All figures are densities, in vehicles per square kilometer of cultivated area.

Sources: See Figure 2.

largest Taiwan cities, male unemployment was only about 3 percent through the 1970s and often less than that in the 1980s.[21]

The issue is whether Fujian and other provinces in China will follow a course that is more similar to that of Taiwan or South Korea. Some of the old barriers to urban migration and residence will still encourage urban-based state industries to engage in extensive subcontracting of their labor-intensive processes in ways that encourage rural industry in the immediate hinterland of cities. Taiwan entrepreneurs, searching for cheap labor to solve the problems of labor-intensive production in labor-short Taiwan, may also encourage this process. However, transport constraints, government-subsidized capital for state industry, a continuing investment tilt toward heavy industry (which generates fewer jobs), and hidden bargaining in state enterprises in ways that drive up urban wages all suggest processes more similar to what happened historically in South Korea.

The comparative condition of transport provides one example. In simple length of roads, Fujian compared well with Taiwan (Figure 3). By the middle 1970s, including both paved and unpaved extra-urban highways (*gonglu*), road density achieved parity with Taiwan—at least in length, if not in quality.[22] This was even truer of the coastal regions of Fujian, which more closely approximated much of Taiwan. As expected, railway density continues to lag behind in Fujian, though for many light industrial goods produced in the countryside, it is probably road availability that is the more important factor in getting supplies and finished goods to and from urban markets (Figure 3). Despite the wide availability of roads, however, cars, trucks, and buses to use these roads remained scarce in Fujian (Figure 4). The earlier aversion to investing in trucks and other motorized vehicles continues to affect access to the means of transport. By 1990, whether standardized by population, total area or cultivated area, cars, trucks, and buses remained scarcer in Fujian than in Taiwan a full three decades earlier. Thus, for the average producer in the countryside, the difficulty and cost of getting goods to and from market remain significantly greater in Fujian than during the rural industry takeoff phase in Taiwan.

The gap between rural and urban incomes provides another example of conditions that may accelerate rural-to-urban migration in Fujian. On a per capita basis, in 1990 Fujian farmers had incomes only half those of non-farmers. On a household basis, because farmers have larger families, farm households had incomes about three-fourths those of nonfarm households.[23] This gap was narrower by 1990 than it had been a few years earlier; however, excluding as it does many hidden subsidies for urbanites, it remained considerable. By comparison, during the rapid urbanization phase in Taiwan and South Korea, the rural-urban gap was narrower, and it included fewer hidden subsidies for urbanites. In the Taiwan of the late 1960s and early 1970s, on a per capita basis farmers had about 60 percent as much income as nonfarmers.[24] In the middle 1970s, on a household basis, farm income rose from three-fourths to four-fifths that of non-farmers—and remained there through the 1980s.[25] In Korea, the gap was even narrower through the 1960s and 1970s, with farm households receiving four-fifths to nine-tenths as much as nonfarm households.[26] These observations suggest several conclusions. One is that even with narrow rural-urban income gaps, urbanization can be extremely rapid, particularly if government investment assistance is skewed toward large industries in cities, as in South Korea. Another is that, to the extent that income gaps promote migration, the pressures will be greater in Fujian than in either Taiwan or South Korea, particularly in more remote regions where incomes are lowest.

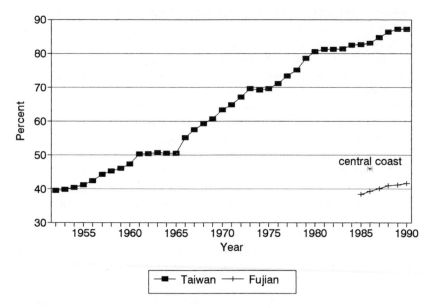

Figure 5. Non-Agricultural Labor Force in Fujian and Taiwan, 1952-90

Note: Shares in total labor force, in percent.

Sources: See Figure 2.

5. Taiwan—Fujian Comparisons

One issue in comparing Taiwan and Fujian is that of the appropriate time period. The rapid transition in Taiwan's economy, when rural industry began to blossom, started around 1960 with the shift toward export-led industrialization. A crude index of the shift in production is the share of the labor force working outside agriculture (Figure 5).[27] Once the transition began in Taiwan, it moved very rapidly, so that by 1990 only a very small minority of the labor force remained in village agriculture. Judged by labor force composition, Fujian lags about three decades behind Taiwan. For all of Fujian, the 1990 figure—42 percent of the total urban and rural labor force outside agriculture—was about the same as Taiwan's 1957 figure. Considering just the central coastal zone of Fujian between the two major cities of Xiamen and Fuzhou, the 1987 figure of 47 percent outside agriculture was about the same as Taiwan 1960 figure. Expressed as a share of gross domestic production value, Fujian's 68 percent produced outside agriculture in 1990 was about the same as Taiwan's share in 1960.

Thus, to compare Taiwan and Fujian at similar levels of industrial and urban development, one needs to use data from Taiwan for a period about three decades earlier.

I will not go back quite that far, but instead pick a date several years after the start of the modern, export-led stage of economic development in Taiwan. One easily available year, 1967, allows time for some of the effects of economic development to have begun to diffuse into the countryside, and it embraces a period when personal residence in Taiwan gave me impressions of what this development meant for the countryside. Thus, the emphasis in the more detailed county-level data will be on the situation in Taiwan as of 1967.

Though definitional differences plague all comparisons of rural employment in Taiwan and Fujian, we can still get some approximate answers. The strong similarity in basic patterns suggests some common dynamics. In Fujian, nonfarm employment figures are based on the distribution of work among laborers whose household registration remains at the village (*xiangcun*) level. In Taiwan, since there is no bamboo curtain between urban and village residents—people can move back and forth freely—there is no exact equivalent in labor force designations. The best we can do is to examine only the labor force that remains registered in rural townships (*xiang*). This excludes villagers whose village happens to be under the administration of an urban township (*zhen*) or city (*shi*). This means that the Taiwan figures are understated somewhat, since villages in rural townships, being more distant from urban markets, will have greater difficulty supporting rural industry compared to villages in urban townships.[28] This tendency to understate total nonfarm employment among villagers is offset by the fact that in Taiwan we use only the shares for male laborers, for whom employment data are more reliable. Females remained in agriculture longer, which would have pulled the Taiwan figure down somewhat.

The net result of these measurement decisions is that among villagers, as here defined, nonfarm employment was 29 percent in 1967 Taiwan and 24 percent in 1990 Fujian. These are reasonable figures. In the same years, measured by separate income surveys, Taiwan farmers got 42 percent of their income from nonfarm sources while Fujian farmers got 37 percent of their income from similar sources.[29] Thus, whether judged by labor force composition or income composition, Fujian rural nonfarm activities lagged behind Taiwan, even when it is 1967 Taiwan that is being compared.

These results are only averages for the total economy in each province. Within each there was considerable local variation, with the centrally located coastal counties in each place being much more similar to

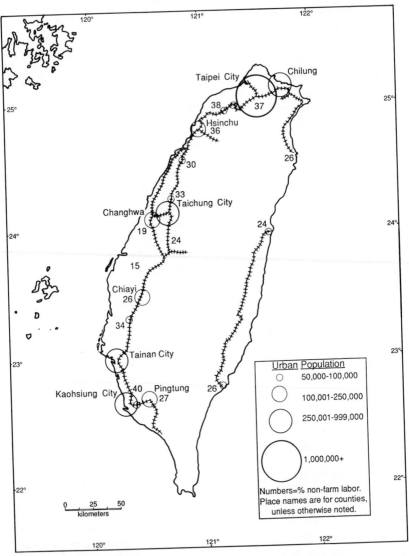

Map 1. Taiwan, 1967

one another. Proximity to an urban center was a strong promoter of rural nonfarm employment in both provinces. So as to make the Taiwan urban population figures more compatible with those on the mainland, the population of each town and city in Taiwan is prorated by the proportion of the male labor force working outside agriculture. Thus, the circles in Map 1 indicate the urban, non-agricultural population in each city (*shi*) and town (*zhen*) with more than 50,000 population.[30] The arabic numbers in Map 1 indicate the share of the rural labor force in nonfarm employment in each county. Near the major urban centers of Taipei in the north and Kaohsiung in the south, nonfarm employment approached 40 percent. It is only on the agriculturally rich plain south of Changhwa, centrally located and equally distant from the major urban centers, that nonfarm employment dropped below 20 percent. In the northern corridor between Taipei City and Taichung City, where there is little flat land, nonfarm employment was uniformly high even at some distance from major cities—e.g., in Miaoli, with 30 percent nonfarm employment. Thus with a widely dispersed network of urban centers and a well-developed transportation network, rural nonfarm employment was generally high throughout the countryside in 1967 Taiwan.[31]

In 1990, Fujian had a much wider range of nonfarm employment experiences in different counties (Map 2). Again, the circles indicate size of urban population and the numbers indicate share of nonfarm employment in each county and suburb. The inclusion of suburban villages sometimes leads to inflated figures—including, one suspects, many villagers who commute daily into the center of the city to work. Nevertheless, the patterns are much as one would expect. It is in the suburbs of cities and in counties abutting major cities that nonfarm employment rises to between one-third and one-half of the rural labor force.[32] At greater distances, counties not in the immediate suburbs but near cities were much like those in 1967 Taiwan. Indeed, in the central coastal corridor running from Xiamen in the south to Fuzhou in the north, rural nonfarm employment averaged 33 percent in 1990, similar to Taiwan's 1967 average of 29 percent nonfarm employment. Away from this central corridor, nonfarm employment dropped off steadily. Along the railway and major coastal roads, nonfarm employment was typically around 20 percent. In more remote counties, nonfarm employment often declined to 15 percent or lower, illustrating again the considerable effects of urban proximity and transport.

These effects appear as well in figures relating nonfarm employment to city and town size. In both Taiwan and Fujian, nonfarm employment was strongly related to the size of the county seat or nearest abutting city (Figure 6). The anomalous counties hint at some of the other conditions that were important determinants of nonfarm employment. In Taiwan, Taoyuan, Hsinchu and Miaoli counties, all located in the busy transportation corridor between Taipei and Taichung and all with terrain that inhibited

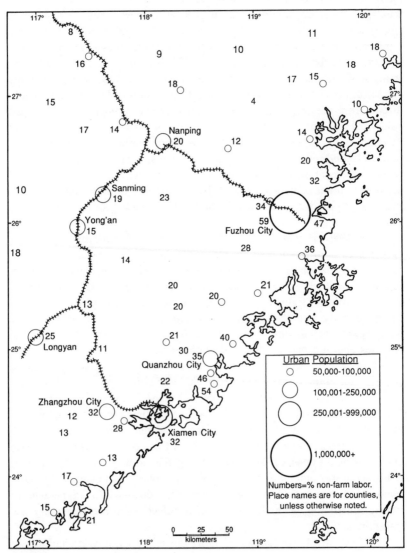

Map 2. Fujian, 1990

agriculture, had more nonfarm employment than one expects from the sizes
of their county seats alone.   Yunlin and Changhwa, between the major
centers of Taichung and Kaohsiung and with rich agricultural bases in a
well-irrigated plain, saw less rapid growth of nonfarm employment—

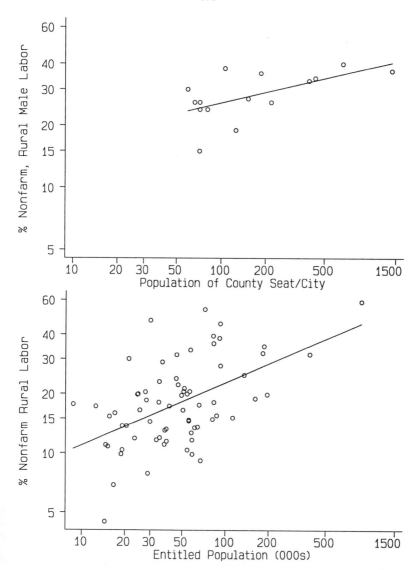

Figure 6. Nonfarm Employment by City Size, Taiwan 1967 and Fujian 1990

Note: For Taiwan (top), share of nonfarm labor in rural male labor force (in percent), plotted against population of the county seat/city (in thousands). For Fujian (bottom), share of nonfarm labor in rural labor force (in percent), plotted against entitled population of the county or city (in thousands).

Sources: See Figure 2.

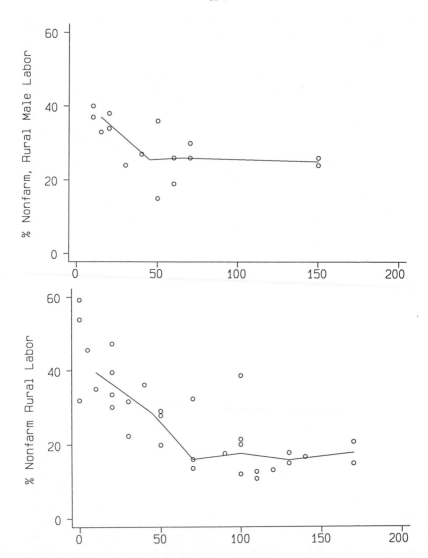

Figure 7. Nonfarm Employment by Distance from Major Cities, Taiwan 1967 and Fujian 1990

Note: For Taiwan (top), share of nonfarm labor in rural male labor force (in percent), plotted against distance from major city (in kilometers). For Fujian (bottom), share of nonfarm labor in rural labor force (in percent), plotted against distance from major city (in kilometers); includes only coastal counties and cities.

Sources: See Figure 2.

regardless of the size of the county seat. (In Figure 6, Taoyuan, Hsinchu, and Miaoli lie at the upper left, and Yunlin and Changhwa at the lower left.)

Distance had similarly strong effects (Figure 7). In Taiwan, with distance measured from the nearest major city (Taipei, Kaohsiung, Tainan, or Taichung), nonfarm employment declined steadily through a distance of about 70 kilometers. In Fujian, there were similar tendencies through the first 70 kilometers, measuring distance from the urban concentrations of Fuzhou, Xiamen, or Quanzhou. This suggests that in the central coastal corridor availability of roads and trucks may have begun to approximate that found in Taiwan in the middle 1960s. What is different about Fujian is that, with major cities distributed less densely, there were more counties 100 or more kilometers from a major city and thus less favored by urban market opportunities for nonfarm production. Even near the coast, in the more distant places nonfarm employment dropped below 20 percent (Figure 7, bottom half).

6. Conclusions

Comparing Fujian to Taiwan suggests several conclusions. One is that rural industrialization can be rapid. In 1957, Taiwan farmers had the same 36.7 percent from nonfarm sources as do Fujian villagers today. By 1972 the Taiwan figure had climbed to 60 percent and it remained high thereafter.[33] Dispersed industrialization, and the increasing flow of remittances from family members who had gone to cities, helped moderate the flood of farmers into cities. A second conclusion, however, is that rural industrialization only *moderated* that flow. Though rural industrialization in Taiwan helped avoid the urban employment problems that emerged in South Korean cities, the urban transition was extremely rapid nevertheless. Thus, while providing a model of how to moderate the transition experience, dispersed rural industrialization in Taiwan provides no model of how to avoid urbanization. Rapid urban growth and rural industrialization fed on one another. A third, related conclusion is that rural industrialization in Taiwan depended on a highly dispersed network of towns and cities. Given Taiwan's compact geographic structure and the earlier development of cities and towns throughout the island, few rural places were very distant from major urban centers. Even with an excellent transportation network, distance from cities and towns led to declining rural industrialization. This reinforces the view that urban growth and rural industrialization should not be seen as opposing one another. The argument must be for balanced growth of urban and rural rather than for promoting the growth of one over the other.

The comparison to South Korea suggests caution concerning the many additional conditions that may intervene to inhibit rural industrialization. Even with a narrow income gap between city and countryside, the concentration of government-supported investment funds, greater capital intensity, investment in heavy rather than light industry, larger enterprise sizes, and a less developed transportation network encouraged a flood of migrants to descend on major cities such as Seoul. Problems with unemployment and housing followed. The similarity between some of these background conditions and those in Fujian and other provinces suggests some pessimism about the continuing growth of rural industry, except in places near major cities.

Finally, the comparison of different counties within Fujian Province suggests that the central coast between Xiamen and Fuzhou may provide that very special environment that will promote continued rural and small town industrialization. Urban proximity, good transport, prosperous rural consumers, and foreign investment from Taiwan and elsewhere may produce an environment allowing this region to repeat Taiwan's rural experience of three decades ago. This is but a small part of the total province, however. Lagging development in other regions should continue to generate migration pressures that will not be easily dealt with under current policies.

Notes

1. I ignore for the moment debates about whether overurbanization is really a problem and the full range of determinants of urban migration. For an introduction to that literature, see Samuel H. Preston, "Urban Growth in Developing Countries: A Demographic Reappraisal," *Population and Development Review*, 5, 1979, pp. 195-216; Koichi Mera, *Income Distribution and Regional Development* (Tokyo: University of Tokyo Press, 1975); Lyn Squire, *Employment Policy in Developing Countries* (New York: Oxford University Press, 1981); Lorene Y. L. Yap, "The Attraction of Cities: A Review of the Migration Literature," *Journal of Development Economics*, 4, 1977, pp. 239-64; Allen Kelley and Jeffrey Williamson, "Population Growth, Industrial Revolutions, and the Urban Transition," *Population and Development Review*, 10(3), 1984, pp. 419-42; and George S. Tolley and Vinod Thomas (eds.), *The Economics of Urbanization and Urban Policies in Developing Countries* (Washington, D.C.: World Bank, 1987). Richard J. R. Kirkby, *Urbanization in China: Town and Country in a Developing Economy, 1949-2000 AD*

(London: Croom Helm, 1985), and Shuwei Sung, "On New Style Middle Level Urban Centers," *Chengshi guihua*, no. 1, 1990, pp. 3-9+, review the debates over some of these issues within China.

2. E.g., Johannes F. Linn, *Cities in the Developing World* (New York: Oxford University Press, 1983); Bertrand Renaud, *National Urbanization Policy in Developing Countries* (New York: Oxford University Press, 1981), pp. 102ff; and Michael Lipton, "Urban Bias Revisited," *Journal of Development Studies*, 20, 1984, pp. 139-66.

3. For non-farm employment, e.g., Dennis Anderson and Mark W. Leiserson, "Rural Nonfarm Employment in Developing Countries," *Economic Development and Cultural Change*, 28, 1980, pp. 227-48; Dennis Anderson, "Small Industry in Developing Countries" (Staff Working Papers, no. 518, World Bank, 1982); Samuel P. S. Ho, "Decentralized Industrialization and Rural Development: Evidence from Taiwan," *Economic Development and Cultural Change*, 28, 1979, pp. 77-96; Samuel P. S. Ho, "The Asian Experience in Rural Nonagricultural Development and Its Relevance for China" (Staff Working Papers, no. 757, World Bank, 1986). For industrial dispersion, e.g., John Vernon Henderson, "International Experience in Urbanization and Its Relevance for China" (Staff Working Papers, no. 758, World Bank, 1986); Richard Taub, *Entrepreneurship in India's Small-Scale Industries* (New Delhi: Manohar Publications, 1989).

4. Anderson, "Small Industry in Developing Countries."

5. Hernando DeSoto, *The Other Path* (New York: Harper and Row, 1989).

6. Dwight Perkins, "The Influence of Economic Reforms on China's Urbanization," in Reginald Kwok, William L. Parish, and Anthony Yeh (eds.), *Chinese Urban Reform* (Armonk, NY: M. E. Sharpe, 1990).

7. Grant Blank and William Parish, "Rural Industry and Nonfarm Employment," in Reginald Kwok, William L. Parish, and Anthony Yeh (eds.), *Chinese Urban Reform* (Armonk, NY: M. E. Sharpe, 1990).

8. Some of the "entitled population" live in the countryside—e.g. rural administrators and school teachers. This explains why the percent entitled exceeded the percent urban in the 1950s, and it suggests that two-thirds entitled among all urban may be a generous estimate for 1990.

9. The 1978-1979 uptick in percent non-agricultural labor includes a redefinition of non-agricultural to include villagers working outside agriculture. The pre-1979 figures are thus understated by a few percentage points. Note, also, that some villages, particularly on the outskirts of cities and towns, have become so industrialized that they might be more properly counted as urban. If so, the urban share would move up more towards 40 percent.

10. World Bank, *China: Reform and the Role of the Plan in the 1990s* (Washington, D.C.: World Bank, 1992).

11. Prior to definitional changes in the early 1980s, Fujian was 20 percent urban, which was about the same as for the nation.

12. Anthony J. Ody, "Rural Enterprise Development in China, 1986-90," (Discussion Papers, China and Mongolia Department Series, no. 162, World Bank, 1992).

13. Guojia tongji ju, *Zhongguo tongji nianjian 1991 [Statistical Yearbook of China 1991]* (Beijing: Zhongguo tongji, 1991), p. 312.

14. Norton Ginsburg, *Atlas of Economic Development* (Chicago: University of Chicago Press, 1961); Blank and Parish, "Rural Industry and Nonfarm Employment."

15. Alice H. Amsden, *Asia's Next Giant: South Korea and Late Industrialization* (New York: Oxford University Press, 1989).

16. Won-tack Hong, *Trade, Distortions and Employment Growth in Korea* (Seoul: Korea Development Institute, 1979); Edward S. Mason et al., *The Economic and Social Modernization of the Republic of Korea* (Cambridge: Harvard University Press, 1980); Amsden, *Asia's Next Giant*; Changsoo Kim, "Labor Market Developments of Korea in Macroeconomic Perspectives," (Working Papers, no. 8909, Korea Development Institute, 1989); and Ho Keun Song and Aage B. Sorensen, "The State and Economic Segmentation: Analysis of Effects of Export-Promotion Strategy on Wage Differentials in Korea's Manufacturing Industries," *Korea Journal of Population and Development*, 19, 1990, pp. 1-26.

17. Gustav Ranis, "Industrial Development," in Walter Galenson (ed.), *Economic Growth and Structural Change in Taiwan* (Ithaca: Cornell University Press, 1979); Erik Lundberg, "Fiscal and Monetary Policies," in Galenson, *Economic Growth and Structural Change*; Walter Galenson, "The Labor Force,

Wages, and Living Standards," in Galenson, *Economic Growth and Structural Change*.

18. Mason, *Economic and Social Modernization*; Amsden, *Asia's Next Giant*.

19. Korean Women's Development Institute, *Socioeconomic Indicators of Women's Position* (Seoul: Korean Women's Development Institute, 1986), p. 318.

20. Chang Ching-hsi, "Foreign Workers: A Preliminary Economic Analysis," in *Symposium on Social Sciences* (Taipei: Institute of the Three People's Principles, Academia Sinica, 1987), pp. 198-216 (in Chinese).

21. Alden Speare, Paul K. C. Liu, and Ching-lung Tsay, *Urbanization and Development* (Boulder: Westview Press, 1988); Republic of China, Executive Yuan, Directorate-General of Budget, Accounting, and Statistics, *Statistical Yearbook of the Republic of China, 1991* (Taipei: Executive Yuan, 1991).

22. In an attempt to correct for more hilly terrain in Fujian, Figures 3 and 4 use cultivated area as the basis for comparison. Recalculating the results using total land area produces similar results.

23. Calculated from *Zhongguo tongji nianjian 1991*, p. 34.

24. Simon Kuznets, "Growth and Structural Shifts," in Galenson, *Economic Growth and Structural Change* (note 17), p. 115.

25. Republic of China, Executive Yuan, Directorate-General of Budget, Accounting, and Statistics, *Social Indicators in Taiwan Area of the Republic of China 1990* (Taipei: Executive Yuan, 1991).

26. Mason, *Economic and Social Modernization*, p. 323.

27. The measure of labor force distribution is crude because it is based on the household register, where occupation data is updated slowly. This accounts for some of the jerkiness in the trend lines in Figure 5. However, since the data come from household registers both in Fujian and in Taiwan, the tardiness bias should be shared—and, therefore, should not seriously distort comparisons between the two locales.

28. In 1967, of males engaged in farm work, about one-third resided in cities (*shi*) and urban townships (*zhen*), and about two-thirds in the rural townships (*xiang*) that are used here.

29. Kuznets, "Growth and Structural Shifts," p. 109; Fujian sheng tongji ju, *Fujian tongji nianjian 1991 [Statistical Yearbook of Fujian 1991]* (Beijing: Zhongguo tongji, 1991), p. 433. Of the 37 percent of nonfarm income, two-thirds was earned income and one-third was unearned income, including mostly, it would seem, remittances from kinsmen working outside the village. Note that the 37 percent figure was what Taiwan farmers got from nonfarm sources in 1967, again suggesting the considerable lag in nonfarm employment in Fujian.

30. The Taipei County figure for nonfarm employment excludes the bedroom townships (*xiang*) of Chunglo, Musha, and Luchou, helping account for a slightly lower percentage here than one might expect.

31. There was, of course, considerable variation even within counties. For example, in Yunlin County on the south-central agricultural plain, a few coastal townships (*xiang*) that are distant from the main railroad, major roads, and ports dropped to only 8 or 9 percent nonfarm employment. Near the major towns in Yunlin, nonfarm employment rose to near 30 percent. Thus, even with good transport, proximity to cities and towns is necessary for considerable nonfarm employment.

32. Though we do not present the figures here, Taiwan suburban villages also had one-half or more of their labor force in nonfarm employment in the 1960s.

33. Kuznets, "Growth and Structural Shifts," p. 433.

Economic Reform in Fujian: Another View from the Villages

Thomas P. Lyons

1. Introduction

In 1979, Fujian was one of two provinces selected for "flexible" market-oriented policies, the most conspicuous being the establishment of a special economic zone at Xiamen. Since then, the province has remained a leader in reform. The authorities in Fujian have seized upon their favored status, actively promoting marketization and, in particular, development of a market-oriented agriculture and of rural enterprises in industry and services. The pervasiveness of these efforts is evident in the flourishing of entrepreneurship and market institutions and in the resultant restructuring of local economies. Some counties rapidly emerged as centers of commerce in such products as grain, mushrooms, fruits, and tea; others have experienced massive and sudden shifts into production of cash crops and other local specialties—asparagus in Dongshan, mushrooms in Gutian, oranges and litchi near Zhangzhou, shellfish in Zhaoan and Xiapu.

Given the preferential treatment Fujian has enjoyed, the vigor with which it has seized new opportunities, and the substantial progress it has made, the province may well serve as a harbinger of things yet to come in regions where reform is less advanced.[1] This paper examines how various components of a market-oriented system have actually worked in Fujian, revealing not only dramatic institutional changes during the first decade of reform, but also difficulties of doing business within the context of the new institutions and hazards that other regions may yet encounter as their reforms move forward. The bulk of the paper focuses on the period 1986-88, when Fujian's reform was in full swing, and on the rural economic institutions seen by individual farmers, small businessmen, and local officials.[2]

This paper is based almost entirely upon items drawn from the provincial press—local news items, letters to the editor, investigative reports, and interviews. In Fujian, and probably in other provinces as well, the press has taken an aggressive role in investigating complaints from farmers and small businessmen. As many of the cases described in this paper suggest, government officials frequently feel compelled to take the power of the press quite seriously. This in itself may constitute an important, and little noticed, dimension of the broader reform.

Throughout this paper, our informants (farmers, small businessmen, and local officials) tell their own stories: the cases to follow all hew very closely to the substance and tone of the original sources—at some points, quoting those sources verbatim. Of course, no sampling of individual cases can paint a complete picture of the larger institutional context. But the rich detail of the cases to be examined here, and the jolt of realism provided by first-hand testimony, add new texture to formal analyses of institutional change in rural China.[3]

All of the cases examined in this paper involve, in one way or another, property rights—protection of the individual's rights to use productive assets and to realize the lawful income generated in doing so; to transfer various property rights by bequest, lease, or sale; and to secure the compensation due in exchange for property surrendered. Section 2 concerns the security of property rights explicitly conveyed by contracts and the resolution of contract disputes, in both agriculture and small-scale local industry. Section 3 turns to farmers' efforts to secure current inputs, such as fertilizer, that they are entitled to purchase by virtue of contracts between themselves and the state. Section 4 takes up administrative barriers to commerce and, in particular, the inspection stations set up along highways to extract payments from traders transporting merchandise. Section 5 illustrates the looting and banditry that businesspeople have faced. Section 6 makes a brief concluding comment.

2. Contracts and Contract Disputes

Throughout Fujian (and throughout China), the rights to use land and to dispose of income earned through such use are assigned through "responsibility" contracts between farmers and village officials. In many areas, collectively owned non-farm enterprises are also contracted out to individuals and partnerships, much as farmland is. The cases in this section reveal not only various terms of contracts for land and other assets, but also attitudes toward contracting, the forms of recourse available to those whose rights are infringed upon, and the reactions of various government agencies in instances of such infringement.

The first four cases all involve fruit farms, where secure property rights are of special importance due to the substantial initial investment and long gestation times involved in fruit production. The last three cases involve factories, in different industries.

Case 1: Chen Jinzhang's longan orchard[4]

In November 1985 Mr. Chen, of Nanan county, entered into a contract (*guolin chengbao hetong*) with the village committee of Zengcuo, in Huian county. Under the terms of the contract, Chen leased a 40-mu orchard for ten years, for total payments of 47,000 yuan. The orchard, opened by the village during the 1970s, had 800 longan trees and over 100 litchi, pear, and guava trees. The longan trees produced a bumper crop in 1987.

On 3 September 1987, a group of Zengcuo villagers raided Chen's orchard, just as the longan were ready for harvest. As soon as local officials heard of the incident they rushed to the scene to intervene, but a large quantity of longan had already been stolen. Three factors reportedly precipitated the raid: villagers felt that the contractor's rent payments were out of line with the market price of longan and the quantity produced; the contractor was perceived to have brought in a large crop with little effort; and the contractor's payments to the village were not divided up among individual households.

Mr. Chen, in seeking compensation for the damages he suffered, found himself embroiled in a dispute with the village authorities. His case dragged on for months. In April 1988, county officials ruled that the contract between Mr. Chen and Zengcuo village was in accord with the law and that the behavior of those plundering the longan orchard was illegal; nevertheless, they decided that the two parties to the contract should renegotiate, because the village, when it leased out the orchard, set the rent too low. On 23 May, with township officials mediating, the two parties agreed to terminate the original contract. The village, accepting responsibility for the termination, undertook to repay 50 percent of the original contract amount (i.e., 23,500 yuan) and to return the original security deposit of 8,600 yuan to Mr. Chen.

After terminating its contract with Mr. Chen, the village leased the orchard to another farmer, for 66,660 yuan. The new tenant also assumed responsibility for the 23,500 yuan due Mr. Chen under the village's prior agreement with Chen. The new tenant agreed to undertake management of the orchard according to prevailing regulations and to divide the harvest 60/40 with the village (keeping the larger portion for himself). Over ten years, the village may well receive an additional 200,000 yuan.

Although Zengcuo village reneged on its contract with Mr. Chen so as to enter a more lucrative one, *Fujian Daily* concluded that the dispute had been smoothly resolved, with both parties to the original contract satisfied. *Fujian Daily* did not report punishment of the villagers who plundered Mr. Chen's property.

Case 2: Peng Yousheng's oranges[5]

Peng Yousheng's dreams were shattered on the morning of 27 October 1988. More than twenty villagers, led by Peng Jiaxiang and his three brothers, raided Peng Yousheng's orange grove and carried off over 5,200 kilograms, worth 4,000 or 5,000 yuan.

The orange grove, 175 trees on 3.5 mu, belonged to the Xinyang #2 small group (*cunmin xiaozu*) of Chishi village in Chongan county. The grove had yielded very poor harvests because no one took care of it, and had been virtually abandoned. Peng Yousheng leased the grove from the small group in 1982.

In February 1988, the four Peng brothers decided to reclaim the fruit trees and to divide them among households of the small group. When Peng Yousheng took the dispute to the county court, it decided in his favor: the contract would continue in force. After the prefectural court upheld the county's decision, the Peng brothers openly defied the courts, saying that their judgements were worthless pieces of paper and threatening to steal Peng Yousheng's oranges at harvest time. No one intervened to stop them.

At the end of the year, the county court ordered the Xinyang #2 small group to pay restitution in the amount of 1,200 yuan to Peng Yousheng. Participants in the plundering of his orange grove were to be fined 10 yuan each; those who had participated but failed to confess would be fined 100 yuan. Two leaders of the small group were taken into custody and fined 105 yuan each, for failure to enforce a decision having the force of law.

Fujian Daily examined four aspects of the case.

(1) When reporters inquired into the perpetrators' motives, they were shocked by the replies:

> Although the orchard's output had been low, everyone did get some oranges [when it was collectively operated]. After Peng Yousheng contracted the orchard, we didn't get to eat a single orange.

> Last year Peng Yousheng earned 7,000 or 8,000 yuan from the orchard, but he only paid 700 yuan in rent; he got too good a deal.

This is a collective orchard—it wasn't sold to Peng Yousheng; everybody gets to share in collective things.

Only six households did not participate in the plundering—because no one was home at the time. Villager Wang Pengfei told the reporters that, at the time of the raid, he happened to have gone into town to sell some radishes; otherwise, he would have gotten some oranges, too.

(2) For the great majority of villagers, contracts and court decisions are just pieces of paper. They supposed that, if everybody is unwilling to allow Peng Yousheng to continue leasing, they can simply stop him from doing so. They were amazed to learn that dissolving a contract requires legal procedures, and couldn't understand why this is so.

(3) After the incident, the county and prefectural courts repeatedly sent investigators into Chishi village, but no one would say who had instigated the incident or who had participated. One villager admitted that if he told the truth there would be reprisals later.

(4) Although this particular incident has been settled, the feudal mentality behind it lives on strong. The Xinyang small group sold off some public property in the village, using the proceeds to pay the fines and expenses, and make up the lost work time, of the instigators.

Case 3: Chen Pinshan's fruit farm[6]

The hill in front of Dongqi village, in Ningde county, had been used to grow only a few potatoes. When the county sent technicians to do soil surveys, however, they discovered that the land on the hill was well-suited for growing fruit. A young farmer named Chen Pinshan took the lead in bringing together five partners and seeking a contract for development of a fruit farm.

The village authorities convened a number of meetings, to revise and amend the proposed contract with Chen's group. When finalized, the contract document carried the seals of the village committees and 95 percent of the village's people, and was notarized by the judicial authorities. It stipulated a term of 40 years (beginning January 1988), payment to the village of fees (*shanchang peichang fei*) in the amount of 230,000 yuan, and reversion of the fruit trees to village ownership after the 40 years, without compensation. The village set up a working group to begin using the money for electric lines, roads, running water, and other collective undertakings.

But a turmoil was brewing. Chen Shaoshan (an elementary-school teacher, originally from Dongqi village) and his brother-in-law Ruan Hengsheng (a prefectural cadre, also from Dongqi) incited some of the villagers to oppose the contract with Chen Pinshan, by saying that the village's *fengshui* was being disrupted and that, as a consequence, the villagers would surely suffer. They also complained to higher authorities that, to plant fruit trees, the contractors were illegally destroying a forest. In fact, the forestry bureau determined that developing fruit production would have economic and ecological benefits and formally approved felling the pine trees on the hill.

A number of untoward incidents occurred after Chen and Ruan incited the villagers. (1) Two people in the village drowned after getting drunk. Some villagers, insisting that this was caused by disruption of the village's *fengshui*, brought in a sorcerer to conduct the appropriate rituals. (2) Surveyors hired by the contractors were threatened, and surveying markers on the hill were destroyed. (3) The wife of the village leader, who supported the contract, was beaten. (4) Those opposing the contract (mostly relatives of Chen Shaoshan and Ruan Hengsheng) fought with the contractors on a number of occasions, putting several people in the hospital. (5) Longan seedlings purchased by the contractors were stolen.

As of June 1988, nearly six months after the contract took effect, such incidents were still preventing Chen Pinshan and his group from going about their business. Several thousand longan seedlings were still unplanted; the contractors, losing money, told reporters that they now wished they had never entered the contract.

In June, the county government convened a meeting of county and township officials, aimed at resolving the dispute. The attendees believed that Chen Pinshan's contract was valid, that the contract was beneficial to the village's economic development, and that it should be enforced. The main reasons for the dispute were apparently a strong "small peasant mentality" and a weak appreciation of the commodity economy on the part of some villagers.[7] In addition, some villagers were envious, and some were motivated by superstition and clannishness. The county's public security bureau and the township police station initiated an investigation of the fights, taking three of the perpetrators into custody, fining five, and imposing restitution of the injured parties' medical bills.

The township Party Secretary led a team of officials into Dongqi, to convene village meetings and to discuss the matter with villagers in their homes. The fruit farmers signed an agreement with the township police station, providing for security and protection of their legal rights.

By July, the contractors were able to get to work developing their fruit farm.

Case 4: The Li family's fruit farm[8]

In July 1988, a contract dispute that had dragged on for nearly a year was resolved in Lianjing village, Xianyou county. This dispute centered upon the 875-mu Mashan Forest and Fruit Farm, which had been operated by Mr. Li Jinyao from 1979 until his death in April 1987. The forestry bureau placed the value of the farm at about 357,000 yuan.

After Mr. Li died, his daughter Li Meihe came forward to take over his contract, suggesting that the original contract terms be continued and that she assume the debt of 160,000 yuan her father had incurred. The village officials, however, proposed changing various terms of the original contract. Whereas the original had stipulated that the lease would be perpetual, the village now wanted a 50-year lease; whereas the original stipulated that all output from newly planted trees would belong to the contractor, the village now wanted 30 percent of gross output. Ms. Li agreed to changing the contract term to 50 years, but would not agree to paying the 30 percent, since the village had not invested in the fruit trees her father had planted. Ms. Li did recognize, however, that ownership of the land itself resided with the village, and would agree to paying 20 percent of her net income, after the fruit trees were in full production. At expiration of the contract term, if the fruit trees reverted to the village, it should repay the Li family's investment in planting.

When the village officials insisted on getting their own way, Ms. Li said she would return the farm to the village—and that the village must assume the 160,000-yuan debt and compensate her family for their years of hard work. The village officials would not agree to these terms, and the negotiations deadlocked.

County officials visited the village on numerous occasions, trying to reconcile the two parties. In late June 1988, they reached an agreement. The new contract term is 50 years. The original formula for dividing timber is unchanged; fruit output is divided 20/80 (20 percent to the village), beginning in the 11th year and running through the 40th year. The payments that the village forgoes during the last 10 years of the contract term will serve as compensation for the trees themselves. After the contract term expires, all of the trees revert, without further payment, to village ownership.

Investigators from *Fujian Daily* noted that, according to provincial regulations, "in cases of contracts for opening wasteland and planting fruit trees, the trees will be managed over the long term by the contractor, who can bequeath them or lease them." According to *Fujian Daily*, the legal rights of heirs to contracts must be protected, so that people will be willing to contract for forestry production, where the gestation period is long; if the contract signed by Li Jinyao and the village was not sufficiently precise, it could have been revised through negotiations by the two parties.

Case 5: Chen Qingtang and the cement plant[9]

On 6 September 1988, one day after its ribbon-cutting ceremony, the Dingjiao village cement plant, in Zhangping county, announced that it would close.

Because almost all of Dingjiao's arable land had been taken by the government, the villagers' livelihood depended upon the cement plant. Naturally, the question of who should manage the plant was everyone's number-one concern. The village authorities decided to publicly invite potential managers to submit contract proposals, stipulating rent payments of 3.08 million yuan over three years. At the end of June, Mr. Chen won out over two other contenders, by virtue of his superior plan, and got the contract. He successfully trial-produced a large quantity of cement, all of it up to standard; no one else in the village had the skill to do this.

Then an anonymous letter to the local authorities pointed out that Chen's assistant manager for purchasing and sales was not a native of Dingjiao village.[10] A village official went to the cement plant and the bank, ordering a halt to production and freezing the plant's accounts.

The county's vice-mayor in charge of industry sent a work team into the village to deal with the problem. After negotiations, the amount that Chen would pay the village was increased from 3.08 to 5.03 million yuan. At the time of the ribbon-cutting, however, a group of villagers burst into the plant grounds and posted banners that read "Resolutely oppose outsiders in our factories!" The assistant manager for purchasing and sales was driven out the plant gate. At this point, Mr. Chen, already exhausted by months of hard work and contention, had no choice but to request termination of the contract.

Case 6: Chen Shizhong's two enterprises[11]

On 7 December 1987, fire damaged a rice mill leased by Mr. Chen Shizhong of Zhuyu village in suburban Fuzhou. The village authorities sought 6,000 yuan in compensation. Mr. Chen objected, because losses from the fire, as reported by the village, totalled less than 3,000 yuan.

When the two sides couldn't reach agreement, the village Party branch seized 47 barrels of lye, worth over 20,000 yuan, from a caustic soda factory also contracted by Mr. Chen. The chief of the local police station stepped in to stop the seizure of Mr. Chen's property, but the village Party secretary was not to be dissuaded. After the lye had been moved, he delivered a document—without any official seal—stating that it would be held as security against the sum due from Mr. Chen.

On December 24th and 25th, the village committee placed announcements in the *Fuzhou Evening News*, claiming that Mr. Chen's contracts for the caustic soda factory and the rice mill had expired. On 29 December, the committee instructed that the soda factory's building and equipment be destroyed, to force Chen to cease operations.

By February 1988, the Fuzhou suburban court had agreed to hear the case brought by the village, and both sides had retained lawyers. The village authorities claimed that Chen had signed a contract for operation of the caustic soda factory on 15 March 1983, and a supplementary contract for the rice mill a year later. This later contract covered the period through 30 September 1987. Between March 1987 and August 1987, the village committee informed Chen Shizhong on five occasions that, if he wanted to continue operating the factories, he would have to negotiate and sign a new contract before his old one expired. But Chen paid no heed; when his old contract expired without his having signed a new one, he continued to operate the two factories.

The Fuzhou suburban court, after three open sessions, handed down its decision in August 1988. The court held that the contracts signed by Mr. Chen and the village should have expired on 30 September 1987; however, neither party had completed the documents terminating their relationship. Rather, when Chen continued to operate the two factories, the village voiced no objection and continued to collect a management fee. These actions must be interpreted as implicit consent to continuation of the contract.

The court ruled that Mr. Chen should be held responsible under civil law for economic losses of 10,836.37 yuan and that he should replace 14.2 tons of soda, which the village had stored in the factory and which Chen had sold. The court also ruled, however, that some of the lye seized by the village belonged to a third party. This lye was to be returned to the owner, with the village compensating him for any loss.

According to *Fujian Daily*, neither party was satisfied with the court's decision. Mr. Chen felt that it was unfair for him to pay a large sum on top of his own considerable losses, and claimed that people had given false testimony against him. Chen's lawyer pointed out that the cause of the fire was unclear, and that, by the terms of the contract, the contractor could not be held responsible for acts of God. The village leaders felt that all of the lye they had removed from the factory belonged to the village, and that they had acted so as to protect collective property. Both sides planned to appeal the rulings against them.

Case 7: Li Desheng's craft shop[12]

In September 1987, *Fujian Daily* carried the following letter from Mr. Li Desheng of Gushanzhou village, in Minhou county.

Dear Editor:

In keeping with the policy of opening up and reforming, on 11 December 1984 I established the Gushanzhou Craft Shop. I raised the funds, and I bought the equipment and the building. When I opened the workshop, I reached an agreement with the Gushanzhou village committee. I would operate under the sponsorship of the village collective (*guakao cun jiti*). If my factory encountered a problem with working capital, the village committee would guarantee a loan from the credit cooperative; I assumed responsibility for paying a certain management fee to the village committee each year.

Following some changes in the membership of the village committee, on 9 July 1987 the committee notified me that my factory's account at the credit cooperative must carry the village seal, and instructed the credit cooperative to implement this change. At the time, I thought this was improper, so I did not go to the credit co-op to deal with this matter. The credit co-op therefore froze my factory's account. Although I have discussed the matter several times with village leaders, we have not resolved the problem. They do not concede that my factory is simply under collective sponsorship, but rather insist that it is a village-run collective enterprise and demand that their seal be added to my account. Freezing my factory's account has seriously affected normal production and the livelihood of my employees; furthermore, there is no way to fulfill contract commitments, damaging the enterprise's good name.

In the case of this enterprise, funds were privately raised, the building and equipment privately purchased, workers privately recruited, and profits and losses borne by private parties—yet they say it is a village-run enterprise. Is this in accord with Party policy?

Fujian Daily confirmed the substance of Li's letter: according to the agreement between Li and the village, Li would act as sole manager of the factory and make operational decisions on his own, bearing all profits and losses and paying to the village each year a fixed management fee. If Mr.

Li needed to borrow money, the village collective would guarantee the loan. The newspaper found that, under Li's management, the workshop made steady progress for over two years, selling its products in 24 provinces and abroad and creating employment for over 100 villagers. Then, in May 1987, the membership of the village committee changed. In July, the committee notified nine local enterprises that each would have to add the village seal to its account at the local credit cooperative, and instructed the cooperative to implement this change. When Mr. Li sought out the village authorities to discuss this matter, they maintained that Li's workshop was a village-run collective enterprise, and that the village seal must be added to its account.

Li brought his problem to the attention of the county government and the provincial press. The vice-mayor of Minhou, who is responsible for overseeing rural enterprises, asserted that the Gushanzhou Craft Shop was in fact a privately operated enterprise under the sponsorship of the village collective and that the legal rights of private businessman Li Desheng were protected by law. The village authorities, however, pointing to the fact that the factory is officially licensed as a collective, continued to make trouble for Mr. Li. They proposed increasing the annual management fee from 8,000-odd yuan to 19,000 yuan; if Li did not pay the higher fee, the factory would be taken over by the village.

The county then sent a team to the village to investigate. Mayor Zhuo Binqing, after receiving the team's report, stated that a decision as to the ownership of an enterprise cannot be based upon the word "collective" appearing on a business license; rather, it is necessary to understand the history of the enterprise—who invested, who owns the fixed assets, how profits are distributed, and so on. But, on 25 August, a county official informed Li Desheng that the village collective would operate the enterprise jointly with Li, observing the principle of "equality and mutual benefit" and dividing up the profit.

3. Buying Inputs

When they seek to obtain current inputs, farmers and small businessmen face a byzantine and unreliable supply system. The cases examined in this section all pertain to chemical fertilizer, the most important purchased input for Fujian farmers. The basic organizational features of the fertilizer supply system, and the problems farmers encounter in dealing with it, are similar to those for other inputs.

Farmers in Fujian (circa 1987) buy fertilizer from the agricultural materials departments of their supply and marketing cooperatives (SMCs) at low "planned" prices, from SMCs at higher "negotiated" prices, and from other vendors at even higher "market" prices. (1) Some of the fertilizer from SMCs is supplied under the "three links" program (*san gua gou*), by which farmers are entitled to buy fertilizer at planned prices in exchange for their commitments to sell grain to the state. Some SMC fertilizer is also sold at planned prices under various other "special-use allocations" (*zhuanyong xiangmu zhibiao*) earmarked for purposes such as encouraging cultivation of particular crops. (2) Some SMC fertilizer is openly marketed at "negotiated" prices, rather than being earmarked for specific end uses and groups of buyers. (3) Fertilizer can be purchased from private merchants, and from government departments and enterprises other than the SMC, at market prices.

Local SMCs are the bottom tier of a large government-run supply system. Fertilizer enters this system from factories in Fujian, from factories elsewhere in China (via state allocations to Fujian and via purchases that the Fujian system arranges directly with suppliers), and from importers, mainly central and provincial foreign-trade companies. It is then allocated downward through the various tiers of the system until it reaches the materials departments of local SMCs. Private merchants buy fertilizer directly from factories and from the SMCs.

Farmers complain frequently about failures of the supply system. The SMCs do not deliver all of the planned-price fertilizer to which farmers are entitled (e.g., by virtue of having entered a contract to sell grain to the state); the fertilizer that is delivered is frequently late or of the wrong type. And when they deal with private merchants, farmers pay exorbitant prices or receive inferior—even completely worthless—fertilizer. The difficulties farmers report are due in part to shortages that occur despite the good efforts of local SMCs. But they are also due to the sheer complexity of the supply bureaucracy (Case 8) and to profiteering on the part of SMCs—diverting fertilizer intended for farmers to private merchants, at higher prices (Cases 9 and 10). Case 11 illustrates problems farmers encounter when they buy from private merchants.

Case 8: Fertilizer stockpiles in a certain county of central Fujian[13]

During the summer of 1988, farmers in Fujian were finding it difficult to buy fertilizer. At the same time, agricultural materials departments were stockpiling large amounts of fertilizer they couldn't sell. In a *Fujian Daily* article, provincial officials identified several factors contributing to this situation.

(1) Allocation plans wend their way down through the supply bureaucracy very slowly, causing delays in allocating and supplying fertilizer to farmers. For example, even after the spring plowing had begun, some prefectures still hadn't allocated their planned-price fertilizer, and some hadn't formally posted the negotiated prices for fertilizer, delaying sale of stocks on hand.

(2) As fertilizer allocations moved down through the bureaucracy, each level withheld something for itself. According to the provincial auditing bureau, provincial-level agencies retained 1.09 percent of all fertilizer allocated in 1987; prefectures (and municipalities), 1.1 percent; counties, 14.6 percent; towns and townships, 12.82 percent; and villages, 32.32 percent. Hence, only 38.07 percent was actually allocated to the farmers for whom it was intended. Pretty much the same thing occurred in 1988.

(3) Provincewide, planned-price fertilizer is divided into 50 or 60 different categories, according to intended "special uses." Even industrial, police, labor-reform, and tourism units get allocations. Some of these units have no real use for the fertilizer they are allocated, so they don't buy the fertilizer to which they are entitled—or they resell it so as to profit from the difference between negotiated and planned prices.

Upon investigating a farmer's complaint from a county in central Fujian, reporters from *Fujian Daily* found that the county's agricultural materials company held over 3,500 tons of planned-price fertilizer awaiting distribution. Over 1,900 tons could not be distributed because allocations had not yet been sent down from higher levels; the other 1,500-plus tons "slept soundly in a warehouse" as a result of complications at the county level.

The province had allocated a total of 4,817 tons to the county in question. But at least ten offices controlled bits of this total—the provincial agriculture bureau, the forestry bureau, the specialty-products company, and the medicinal products company, among others. Allocations from these higher-level offices were divided into 40-odd special-use items, such as "technology-demonstration fertilizer" and "aid-to-poverty fertilizer." The division among special-use items was so elaborate that the entire county got only a few tons for certain uses. There was no way to handle distribution of all these items down to the farm level, contributing to the materials company's excessive inventory.

Among the allocations for various special uses, those used in grain fields amounted to 26 percent of the total. Such allocations provided only a small share of the fertilizer actually needed; farmers had to buy the rest at high prices, with price differentials reaching 800 yuan per ton. For example, a Mr. He, who contracted 5 mu of grain fields, was allocated only 15 kilograms of urea and 130 kilograms of ammonium bicarbonate; he turned to private merchants for 75 kilograms of urea (at 1,320 yuan per ton) and for over 150 kilograms of ammonium bicarbonate (at 400 yuan per ton).

How is the remaining 74 percent of special-use fertilizer distributed? One township mayor referred to a "local reserve," formed by pooling special-use allocations. There is no distribution plan for this reserve; rather, the mayor distributes it in an *ad hoc* fashion. When reporters asked whether personal connections and favoritism played a role in this distribution, the mayor admitted, with some reluctance, that they did: "Village officials are farmers themselves; to maintain their enthusiasm, shouldn't we accord them preferential treatment?" Another mayor noted that, when township officials were sent into the countryside to work, they might demand a few bags of planned-price fertilizer—and the township would give it to them.

Delivery of reserve fertilizer to favored individuals was generally very informal. The local materials company might receive an instruction such as, "With the approval of the township mayor, supply XX kilograms of fertilizer to XX." After a while, even the person who handed out the fertilizer couldn't recall who really got it.

Nobody was satisfied with this supply system. Farmers had trouble buying the fertilizer to which they were entitled. Lower-level officials felt there were too many intermediate links in fertilizer supply and that intermediaries were raking off all the profits. People higher up in the supply system felt that they were being blamed unfairly; in fact, they only had authority to "supply," not to "allocate"—and if the fertilizer factories didn't deliver on time, there was nothing they could do.

Reports from other areas of Fujian suggest that the situation in this county is not unique. According to *Fujian Daily*, when the government of Quanzhou investigated distribution of special-use fertilizer at fifty units in the city, it found two sorts of abuses. First, some abuses arose from obvious misallocations. For example, a provincial bureau allocated 220 tons of urea to a tourism enterprise, at the planned price of 520 yuan per ton. The enterprise sold all of it to a group of private merchants, at the negotiated price of 670 yuan per ton. The merchants sold 136 tons to the two contractors of an SMC sales outlet in a neighboring county, at 780 yuan per ton. The contractors sold over 100 tons to other private merchants, at 1,050-1,100 yuan per ton. Those merchants then sold the fertilizer to farmers, at 1,250-1,300 yuan per ton—more than twice the original price. Second, some abuses arose when industrial enterprises received allocations of planned-price fertilizer, which they were supposed to exchange for the agricultural commodities they needed. The enterprises frequently sold their fertilizer allocations to agricultural materials departments at negotiated prices, realizing the difference between the negotiated and planned prices as cash. Sometimes industrial enterprises simply acted as fertilizer dealers themselves, marketing the fertilizer allocated to them.

Case 9: Profiteering in Putian[14]

During the summer of 1987, farmers complained of fertilizer shortages and rising prices in Putian municipality.[15] In fact, 37 percent more fertilizer was supplied in Putian municipality during the first six months of 1987, as compared to the first six months of 1986. *Fujian Daily* found that, apart from increases in demand for fertilizer and failures of factories to deliver fertilizer on time, the apparent shortage of fertilizer in 1987 was due to problems within the supply system itself.

An investigation conducted by the municipal government uncovered the following incidents.

(1) In late June, the SMC of Daji township, Xianyou county, illegally resold 18 tons of ammonium bicarbonate allocated by the county agricultural materials department. Without even moving the fertilizer into its warehouse, the SMC sold all of it to private merchants, from whom officials in the SMC had accepted bribes.

(2) In early July, a fertilizer depot in the town of Huating, Putian county, sold two truckloads of ammonium bicarbonate to an unlicensed merchant, making an illegal profit of 60 yuan. The depot later sold another truckload of ammonium bicarbonate to a merchant, making an illegal profit of 50 yuan.

(3) In July, four fertilizer depots in the town of Fengting, Xianyou county, sold 45 tons of urea and 20 tons of calcium superphosphate to Zhejiang province. These lots were seized by the local bureau of industry and commerce just as they were being loaded on a ship. A second ship, already loaded, escaped.

(4) In late May and early June, fertilizer depots in the town of Xitianwei, Putian county, sold imported potassium chloride to private merchants, who resold it to other provinces. The depots made illegal profits from the difference between the planned price they paid and the higher prices at which they sold.

(5) In late May and early June, fertilizer depots in the town of Wutang, Putian county, also sold imported potassium chloride to private merchants, who resold it to other provinces.

After these revelations, the Putian county SMC sent a circular throughout the county, demanding that all lower-level SMCs put an end to illegal activities. In Huating (incident #2, above), the SMC confiscated the 110 yuan of illegal personal profits from four clerks in the Xiahua fertilizer depot and imposed a fine of 250 yuan; the person responsible for the fertilizer depot was removed from office and placed on probation within the Party. The Xitianwei SMC (incident #4) was found to have improperly supplied potassium chloride to fruit growers and to have sold two lots, totalling 30 tons, to private merchants. The county SMC imposed a fine of 200 yuan, the county materials committee confiscated illegal profits of 1,980 yuan, and the chairman and vice-chairman of the Xitianwei SMC received administrative demerits. The fertilizer department of the Wutang SMC (incident #5) was found to have violated regulations governing fertilizer supply and to have illegally sold 57 tons of potassium chloride to private merchants for shipment out of the province. The county SMC imposed a fine of 100 yuan, the county materials department confiscated illegal profits of 960 yuan, the person responsible for the fertilizer department was dismissed, and three clerks received administrative demerits.

Case 10: Fertilizer merchants in Quanzhou[16]

In September 1987, *Fujian Daily* printed the following letter, from a Mr. Wang of Quanzhou.

> Dear Editor:
>
> Unlicensed fertilizer merchants are running rampant in Licheng district. At least 90 unlicensed private merchants have set up businesses, throughout Licheng; quite a few of them engage in both wholesale and retail trade. In Jiangnan township and the town of Fuqiao, there are over 20 private fertilizer merchants, of whom four deal in large quantities and can virtually control the local market. This area needs a total of over 3,000 tons of fertilizer a year, of which the SMC supplies less than 1/3, with most being in the hands of the merchants. They pay no attention to the government's various instructions that fertilizer is to be handled only by the SMC, and that individuals and units other than the SMC are not to trade in fertilizer without obtaining permission. The merchants are taking advantage of the fertilizer shortage—colluding with insiders [at the SMC], hoarding, driving up prices, adulterating fertilizer, and duping farmers. The

farmers demand that the government deal with these unlicensed merchants.

Case 11: Bogus fertilizer in Jinjiang[17]

In 1987, as the height of the spring plowing season approached and fertilizer was urgently needed, the "criminal element" in Jinjiang produced and sold bogus fertilizers. According to local people and government officials, fake phosphate, calcium superphosphate, and compound fertilizers were made by mixing clay, black earth, and powdered limestone. These mixtures, packaged in sacks bearing phoney trademarks, were passed off as products of the Xiamen Fertilizer Factory, Sanming Fertilizer Factory, and other state-owned factories. To attract customers, they were sold at 1/2 to 2/3 the prices of fertilizers from state plants.

To avoid being caught by the authorities, the producers and sellers of bogus fertilizer moved around, hiding in the hills at the Jinjiang-Nanan border, working in abandoned warehouses and barns, and putting up temporary structures where they could quickly whip up batches of fertilizer.

On the night of 9 March, officials of Neikeng township, accompanied by personnel from Jinjiang county's bureau of industry and commerce, cracked a bogus fertilizer case. On a hilltop in Neikeng, they nabbed Mr. Huang Jiayang and five accomplices and seized equipment used to mix bogus fertilizers and stamp phoney trademarks, as well as the fertilizer being mixed. Huang's group had hired 22 people from among the criminal element in the towns of Anhai (in Jinjiang) and Guanqiao (in Nanan) and had made 31.5 tons of bogus compound fertilizer between March 4th and 9th. They sold this fertilizer for 7,000 yuan.

On 11 March, the Jinjiang bureau of industrial and commercial administration cracked two more cases involving bogus fertilizers. The Xiamen Fertilizer Factory, when it analyzed some of the "calcium superphosphate" seized in these cases, found that the phosphorus content was only 0.09 percent.

Postscript[18]

On 28 September 1988, the State Council issued a decision, to take effect as of 1 January 1989, giving the SMC bureaucracy a nationwide monopoly in fertilizer, pesticides and plastic sheeting for agricultural use, and prohibiting all others—government departments, work units, and individuals—from dealing in these goods. All large and medium fertilizer plants were explicitly instructed to sell only to SMCs; small plants could sell to SMCs and, if commissioned by their local governments to do so, sell directly to farmers. Imports of fertilizer would be arranged only by foreign trade companies under the Ministry of Foreign Economic Relations and Trade, with the imported fertilizer distributed by the SMC system.

The State Council's decision was reportedly intended to protect farmers from profiteering and price gouging. According to a *Xinhua* item from Beijing, audits revealed that, over the past several years, over 60 percent of the fertilizer allocated for farmers' use nationwide had been diverted by various levels of the supply bureaucracy, to be sold at higher negotiated prices, exchanged for other goods, or distributed to employees. *Xinhua* cited in particular the abuses in Fujian province.

The Fujian provincial SMC publicized a number of measures for implementing the fertilizer monopoly. Most special-use allocations of fertilizer unrelated to grain production were to be discontinued; except for disaster relief, support for poverty counties, and agricultural research, 90 percent of the high-quality fertilizer under state allocation was to be used for grain production. The practice of retaining fertilizer reserves at each level of the bureaucracy was prohibited. Offices dealing in fertilizer were to make public their plans—quantities, varieties, prices, and schedules. Market regulation was to be strengthened, to end fertilizer dealings by individuals and departments other than those authorized. The provincial government also initiated a provincewide inspection of prices for agricultural inputs (covering fertilizers, pesticides, plastic sheeting, and diesel fuel).

These measures were not entirely successful, as evidenced by numerous reports of private merchants who continued to trade in fertilizer long after the SMC monopoly went into effect. As of April 1990, for example, there were still four private merchants dealing substantial quantities of urea in the single village of Meishan, in Longyan municipality.

4. Administrative Barriers to Trade

Once a farmer or businessman manages to secure his right to use land and other fixed assets and obtains the necessary current inputs, he faces a bewildering array of taxes and fees (Case 12). And apart from legitimate levies, businessmen must deal with numerous illegal barriers to trade—notably, inspection stations that stop trucks and demand payments, frequently in the form of an arbitrary "traffic fee" (Cases 13 through 15). These payments (reminiscent of the *likin* in late imperial China) sometimes benefit the local community, sometimes only the individuals imposing them.

Case 12: Bamboo in Boyang[19]

The following letter, from a Mr. Yu Canbiao, appeared in *Fujian Daily* in October 1986.

Dear Editor:

In mid July, I visited Boyang township in Xiapu county. The local farmers were complaining left and right that, having worked hard over the years to grow bamboo, when they sell a stalk of it now they earn only enough to buy a pack of cigarettes, after deducting taxes and fees.

As I understand it, when Boyang farmers bring bamboo into town for sale, they must pay eight levies:

> afforestation fund, 8 yuan per 100 stalks;
> development fund, 10 yuan per 100 stalks;
> special products tax, 8 percent;
> commodity tax, 5 percent;
> management fee, 3 percent;
> industrial and commercial fee, 1 percent;
> fee for inspection of weights and measures;
> fee for a vendor's stall.[20]

On average, these total 70 cents per stalk; if any of the taxes or fees are not paid, the bamboo cannot be sold. Even before the farmers have sold any bamboo, then, they have to raise money to pay taxes and fees. If, having raised this money, they carry the bamboo to market, and supposing each stalk sells for 2 yuan, they have left only about 60 cents per stalk after deducting the various taxes and fees as well as the costs of felling, processing, transporting, and so on. Because growing bamboo isn't worth the effort, this spring the farmers of Shenyang village in Boyang are digging up and selling the bamboo shoots as soon as they appear.

Case 13: Xue Heshun, the scrap dealer[21]

On the afternoon of 15 April 1988, three reporters from *Fujian Daily* observed vehicles being stopped for inspection at Baihuting, in suburban Fuzhou. In each case, the inspection station fined a scrap dealer and either confiscated his goods or procured them for a token sum. For example, Mr. Lin Wenwei had spent 2,000 yuan to buy a ton of scrap plastic from Lianjiang. He ended up paying a fine of 90 yuan and surrendering his plastic for 300 yuan. When Lin complained, he was told that the inspectors were following orders and there was nothing he could do about it.

A peasant by the name of Xue Heshun had purchased 6,000 kilograms of scrap wire with borrowed money. At about 6 p.m. on 15 April, Xue's scrap wire lay on a table in the Baihuting inspection station, with a tax receipt still attached. Xue, having learned that the station was going to procure the wire, was weeping and pleading. Bystanders sympathized, saying that since he hadn't violated any policies he should be allowed to go. In the end, he was fined 300 yuan. But Xue, even with the help of his driver, could come up with only 80 yuan, which the inspectors refused to accept.

When the *Fujian Daily* reporters tried to intercede on Xue's behalf, the inspectors called the police, and the reporters were taken to the local police station. They had no choice but to reveal their identities and explain that they were conducting an investigation. The attitude of the police then changed dramatically: claiming that it had all been a misunderstanding, the police offered the reporters refreshments and cigarettes.

By visiting the Fuzhou public security bureau, bureau of industry and commerce, and traffic police, the reporters determined that the inspections they had witnessed were illegal. The relevant regulations state:

> the market sections of supply and marketing cooperatives, the bureaus responsible for the metals industries, and recycling departments are all to assist the Public Security organs in seeing that those doing business in their respective trades observe the regulations pertaining to procurement, and they are to deal with illegal behavior. They are not allowed, however, to set up their own inspection stations, to inspect businesses outside their own trades, or to overstep their authority in procuring, confiscating, or imposing fines.

Fujian Daily's report on the Baihuting incident precipitated a flurry of activity in the Fuzhou government. Mayor Hong Yongshi circulated a memorandum expressing his concern that the prohibition of local inspection stations was not being enforced. Municipal agencies were instructed to crack down on inspection stations and to see that the fines illegally collected by such stations were returned to the injured parties. Investigators from the municipal auditing bureau confirmed that, on April 11th, 14th, and 15th, a total of fifteen vehicles were inspected at Baihuting. In nine cases, goods were seized; seven people were fined. Most of these vehicles were carrying proper documents at the time they were stopped.

By July, the people engaged in illegal inspections at Baihuting had moved on to Mawei, Hongshan, and Gushan, where they continued to stop vehicles and impose fines.

Case 14: Bamboo shoots in Sanming[22]

On 4 April 1987, Wang Chengxing and Deng Shizhang of Yanqian township, in Sanming, bought 6,350 kilograms of bamboo shoots and hired a truck to transport them to Shanghai. Between Sanming and Tongxiang county in Zhejiang, Wang and Deng paid thirteen taxes and fees—a total of 546.4 yuan on a cargo worth 1,524 yuan. With several hundred kilometers still to go, Wang and Deng had no idea how many more inspection stations they would encounter or how much more they would have to pay, so they decided to sell the bamboo shoots in Tongxiang.

Fujian Daily interviewed the director of the tax bureau in Sanming. According to the director, before departing their township, Wang and Deng had obtained permission to transport the bamboo shoots and had paid the township specialty-products tax, the village tax for supporting afforestation, the development tax, and the industrial/commercial tax. These five items cost them a total of 108 yuan. All of these were proper, with the exception of the industrial/commercial tax; that tax (18 yuan) should have been collected later, at the point of sale. Wang Chengxing, himself a tax collector in Yanqian, paid the industrial/commercial tax in advance and made out a receipt, so as to avoid problems en route.

After the truck got underway, it paid eight more taxes along the road; according to the director of the tax bureau, seven of these were improper. An SMC in Sha County collected a 70-yuan "supplementary fee for bamboo shoots" (which included a penalty for overloading the truck); an inspection station in Jianou county collected a 15-yuan fee for support of education; an inspection station in Pucheng county collected a 40-yuan "fee for supporting forestry" and 50 yuan for a "forestry fund." All four of these fees had already been paid when Wang and Deng purchased the bamboo shoots. Besides the overload penalty included in Sha county's assessment, a bureau of industry and commerce in Jianou county collected a 5-yuan penalty, and the Pucheng traffic bureau collected a 50-yuan penalty; these two constituted redundant charges. The Tongxiang bureau of industry and commerce initially assessed a 100-yuan penalty for improper documentation, but reduced the fine to 50-yuan upon learning that Wang Chengxing was a member of the prefectural People's Congress. (Wang presented his transport permit and receipts for all the taxes paid in Yanqian before departure; his documentation was actually complete.) The only legitimate assessment was a 148.4-yuan business tax collected by the Tongxiang county tax bureau.

Case 15: Hogs from Shanghang[23]

During 1985 and 1986, vehicles carrying live hogs from the Lufeng foodstuffs depot in Shanghang county were stopped six times by inspection stations. On 5 March 1986, the depot was transporting hogs to Guangdong. On the way, their truck was stopped by an inspection station in Yongding county. The station demanded a traffic fee (*fanyun fei*) of 165 yuan. The depot's man, fearing that the hogs would die if detained, forked over his own expense money—but was still 16 yuan short, so he had to leave his wristwatch as security.

Officials of the foodstuffs depot felt that, having paid the commodity sales tax, they were not required under the relevant regulations to pay a "traffic fee" as well. They complained to the prefectural finance commission and the prefectural bureau of industry and commerce. But the prefecture handed the matter down to the bureau of industry and commerce in Yongding county, which handed it down to its own market-management section. The section leader claimed that the traffic fee was in compliance with regulations from higher levels and refused to refund it.

Postscript[24]

On 9 January 1988, Cheng Xu, chairman of the standing committee of the Provincial People's Congress, discussed with reporters the problem of inspection stations and illegal fines.

> In the process of developing a market economy, the government must strengthen its management....The basic purpose of such management, however, is to promote rapid and healthy development of the market economy, not to obstruct its development. Hence, the problem of setting up inspection stations and of arbitrarily inspecting and fining must be viewed with concern.
>
> The province is known to have at least 578 inspection stations of various sorts—counting only fixed stations, not roving or temporary ones. Of these stations, only 107 have received official approval from the provincial government. One stretch of 9 kilometers has 4 inspection stations; when vehicles pass through this stretch, they must stop for inspection every four or five minutes. How can we develop a market economy in this manner?

At some stations, the scope of inspection is not specified, and there are no standards for imposing fines. This does not accord with the principles of socialist law....We should increase the transparency of law and strengthen public oversight. If the relevant laws and regulations are the monopoly of a few people, it does not make for observance of the law by the public and it permits abuse of law for private benefit of the few.

A *Fujian Daily* editorial notes, however, that attempts to address the problem of barriers to trade date back at least to 1984, and that such barriers have proven extremely resilient. Privately operated inspection stations, once shut down, simply reopen in a new location. Barriers thrown up by local governments reflect deep-seated fears that local factories will be starved of inputs if materials are allowed to flow out of the locale, coupled with an inclination to seek administrative solutions to economic problems. And local governments depend upon the income from inspection stations, without which they would be unable to meet the revenue targets handed down to them.

5. Banditry

Apart from the threat of violence associated with contract disputes and collection of various fees (legitimate and otherwise), businesspeople risk attack by bandits, urban gangs, and mobs of villagers.

Case 16: The Lius from Jiangxi[25]

The following letter, from Liu Huaiyang and Liu Xiaoming of Yugan county, Jiangxi, appeared in *Fujian Daily* in September 1988.

Dear Editor:

We are reporting with gratitude the actions of the police station at the Songxia border crossing in Changle county. The police of Songxia protected the legal rights of people from outside your province.

On 8 June, we bought 11,500 kilograms of kelp in Pingtan county and transported it to the town of Songxia in Changle. As we were loading the kelp onto trucks for the trip home, 20 or 30 local hoodlums saw that we were outsiders;

they swarmed around us, stole over 500 kilograms of kelp, and attacked us. One of us was seriously injured.

After the incident, we went to the police station at the Songxia border crossing to file a report. The station chief, Chen Guoping, immediately led five officers in an investigation and, within three hours, found out what had happened and rounded up the leader of the mob and four others. At 6:30 that evening, Chen worked out a settlement with us: the perpetrators would pay our medical expenses of 1,500 yuan, plus restitution for loss of the kelp in the amount of 700 yuan. Chen let us return to Jiangxi, seek treatment in the hospital of our own county, and report the facts of the treatment to him in writing. His police station would take responsibility for remitting the money to us.

After we returned home, we supposed that, as outsiders, we would not recover the money for our medical treatment. But we decided to give it a try, so on 14 July we sent the documents from the hospital by registered mail. By the end of the month we received the money from Mr. Chen—and not a penny short.

Case 17: The Dongshi fishfarms[26]

In October 1988, the plundering of two fishfarms in Jinjiang county caused total losses of 290,360 yuan. One of the farms, the Dongshi Shellfish Farm, was established in 1981 with an allocation of 200,000 yuan from the provincial finance bureau. It produces 150,000 kilograms of clams per year. The other farm, owned by the Dongshi Saltworks, was leased out to contractors who borrowed 510,000 yuan and developed 250 mu of prawn and over 50 mu of clams. It has been cited by the province as a model work unit.

Guoling village is located near the two fishfarms. Early on 16 October, the secretary of the village Party branch, along with several other local officials, led over 500 people in a raid on the two farms. They made off with over 32,000 kilograms of clams from the shellfish farm. Two military policemen, who happened to be studying fish-raising technology at the saltworks' farm, demanded that the mob immediately cease their criminal behavior. But the village officials were not to be dissuaded, and threatened to "cut the policemen to bits" if they got in the way. With no hope of stopping such a large mob, the policemen retreated, reporting the incident to the authorities. By noon or so, the saltworks' fishfarm had been stripped bare.

The village leaders incited over 200 people to plunder the fishfarms again on the 22nd and 27th, causing further damage and disrupting supply of clams to the Minnan region. The fishfarm contractors, after their heavy loss, were unable to repay the money they had borrowed from the government.

Two months after the raids, the perpetrators were still at large.

6. Concluding Comment

There are, of course, methodological shortcomings inherent in any examination of individual cases. But the farmers and small businessmen of Fujian do point quite clearly, in describing their personal encounters with market-oriented reform, to larger problems in the Chinese economic system. Indeed, some of their problems—in enforcing contracts, in buying inputs, in transporting and marketing products—are so serious as to have elicited repeated pronouncements of concern on the part of prefectural and provincial leaders, investigations by various levels of government, and attempts to impose corrective measures. And many of the problems discussed in the Fujian provincial press in the mid 1980s are reappearing as national issues in the 1990s.[27]

It is tempting to dismiss the problems described in this paper as transitional—or as inevitable products of a headlong rush toward the market, and, therefore, as part and parcel of Fujian's success. Some of the observed problems may indeed arise from the coexistence of a market-oriented allocational regime and remnants of the old planning bureaucracy; these are destined to fade away as the market eventually squeezes out planners. Other problems may reflect the absence of particular markets—markets that can be expected to emerge as reform proceeds. But it is difficult to see how, for example, local barriers to trade can be viewed in this light. Even in a totally marketized economy, local jurisdictions will frequently find it to their advantage to pursue policies that benefit themselves at the expense of others (and which reduce the welfare of the province, or country, as a whole).

Some of the problems noted in this paper, then, may point to constitutional deficiencies of the Chinese system, rather than to transitory features of the reform period. In particular, as the Chinese system is now constituted, the will of the central government is transmitted primarily through provincial and local governments, rather than being projected directly by central enforcement mechanisms. The Chinese government cannot directly enforce even the most basic underpinning of a market economy—access to markets themselves (as reflected in, for example, the "commerce clause" in the United States)—if such access is perceived by the provinces and/or locales as inimical to their own interests. Similarly, it cannot enforce the property rights conveyed by legally valid contracts and by legitimate ownership, and it cannot provide protection from unreasonable seizure. None of this will change as a result of market-oriented reform *per se*: it is unreasonable to expect that bureaucrats will simply stop preying upon businesspeople for their own private gain, that unscrupulous entrepreneurs will cease to exist, that local governments will suffer budget shortfalls without resort to rapacious behavior. Paradoxically, as China rushes toward the market, it needs more government regulation, not less—but more regulation in the constitutional sense of laying out the rules of the game and demonstrating a will and a capacity to enforce them.

In the language of institutional economics, *transactions costs* in rural China remain excessive.[28] As already suggested, they are excessive not only because communications and transportation are often primitive and because markets and commercial services are still new, but also because the prevailing constitutional framework makes property rights difficult to secure. In the early stages of reform, the potential benefits inherent in shifting away from collectivism and planning loom very large. As these initial benefits are realized, however, reaping further benefits from institutional change will require greater attention to fine-tuning of the new market-oriented regime itself.[29]

Notes

1. Articles in the Chinese press suggest a similar interpretation; for example, an item in *China Daily*, 7 August 1992, p. 4, is entitled "Reforms Spread Inland from Coastal Provinces."

2. Market-oriented reforms experienced a lull during 1989-91, due to (1) the central government's decision, in late 1988, to initiate an economic retrenchment, intended to address various reform-related problems (such as inflation); and (2) the demonstrations of spring 1989, the Tiananmen disaster of early June, and the subsequent removal of many reform-oriented government leaders and their advisors.

3. See in particular Victor Nee and Su Sijin, "Institutional Change and Economic Growth in China: The View from the Villages," *Journal of Asian Studies*, 49(1), February 1990, pp. 3-25; and Victor Nee, "Between Redistribu-

tion and Markets in China," *American Sociological Review*, 56(3), June 1991, pp. 267-82. As the title suggests, this paper examines issues taken up in Nee's work—but from a different point of view and with a different set of sources.

4. *Fujian ribao* (*FJRB*), 30 September 1987, p. 3; *FJRB*, 7 August 1988, p. 2.

5. *FJRB*, 29 November 1988, p. 3; *FJRB*, 24 January 1989, p. 4.

6. *FJRB*, 11 June 1988, p. 2; *FJRB*, 2 July 1988, p. 2.

7. "Small peasant mentality" means adherence to the values of a subsistence rural economy, in which goods are produced for on-farm consumption and commerce is relatively unimportant. A "commodity economy" is commercialized: goods are produced for sale, and much of what the household consumes is acquired by purchase.

8. *FJRB*, 8 July 1988, p. 2.

9. *FJRB*, 8 November 1988, p. 2.

10. "One should not allow fertilizer and water to run off onto someone else's fields" (*fei shui bu liu wairen tian*).

11. *Fuzhou wanbao*, 24 December 1987, p. 4; *Fuzhou wanbao*, 25 December 1987, p. 4; *FJRB*, 6 February 1988, p. 2; *FJRB*, 13 February 1988, p. 2; *FJRB*, 20 August 1988, p. 2.

12. *FJRB*, 7 September 1987, p. 2.

13. *FJRB*, 12 August 1988, p. 1; *FJRB*, 28 August 1988, p. 1; *FJRB*, 19 September 1988, p. 1.

14. *FJRB*, 22 September 1987, p. 2; *FJRB*, 7 October 1987, p. 2.

15. Putian municipality is a prefecture-level administrative region, which includes Putian county, Xianyou county, and the city of Putian.

16. *FJRB*, 22 September 1987, p. 2.

17. *FJRB*, 17 March 1987, p. 1; see also *FJRB*, 1 April 1987, p. 1, for mention of this problem in a telephone conference concerning spring plowing, convened by the provincial government.

18. Zhongguo nongye nianjian bianji weiyuanhui, *Zhongguo nongye nianjian 1989* (Beijing: Nongye, 1989), pp. 562-63; *FJRB*, 5 December 1988, p. 1; *FJRB*, 25 January 1989, p. 1; *FJRB*, 28 February 1989, p. 1; *FJRB*, 9 March 1989, p. 2; *FJRB*, 16 April 1990, p. 4.

19. *FJRB*, 3 October 1986, p. 1.

20. The eight levies are (in order): *yu lin jin, kaifa jin, te chan shui, chanpin shui, daiban jin, gongshang guanli fei, jian chi fei, tanwei fei.*

21. *FJRB*, 12 July 1988, p. 1; *FJRB*, 1 August 1988, p. 1.

22. *FJRB*, 14 June 1987, p. 1.

23. *FJRB*, 2 December 1986, p. 1.

24. *FJRB*, 11 January 1988, p. 1; *FJRB*, 28 June 1988, p. 1.

25. *FJRB*, 15 July 1988, p. 2.

26. *FJRB*, 19 December 1988, p. 2.

27. See, for example, an interesting series concerning illegal levies on farmers, illegal inspection stations, and the "jungle" of rural contracting, in *China Daily*, 1992, especially: 30 January, p. 2; 14 May, p. 3; 20 August, p. 1; 14 September, p. 4; and 16 September, p. 4.

28. Concerning institutional economics and transaction costs, see, e.g., Douglass C. North, *Institutions, Institutional Change, and Economic Performance* (Cambridge: Cambridge University Press, 1990), pp. 3-69.

29. This, of course, could open a Pandora's box. Even if the regime were to contemplate protection of individual rights purely in terms of property and contracts, unwanted demands for broader protections might well be rekindled.

Contractual Arrangements and Labor Incentives in Rural China: A Case Study of Northern Jiangsu

Echo Heng Liang

1. Introduction

Implementation of the "Financial Responsibility System" (FRS), beginning in 1985, has been a crucial component of rural economic reform in China. The FRS requires localities to submit only a portion of their revenues to higher levels and allows them to retain all, or at least most, of the remainder. The main aims of the FRS program have been to make localities fiscally self-sufficient, to reduce the government's fiscal burden, and to provide incentives for local authorities to promote economic development.[1] These reforms have greatly stimulated the growth of local industries.[2]

In the agricultural sector, a new contract purchase program was initiated as part of the FRS. Aimed at reducing grain subsidies, the program established a new price regime that in fact lowered marginal prices for grain.[3] The new pricing policy was a major factor contributing to the significant reduction in grain supplies in late 1985 and 1986; therefore, in addition to reducing its fiscal burden, another objective of the government in the later 1980s and the early 1990s has been to ensure fulfillment of grain quotas.

The Chinese state has pursued its objectives by decentralizing decision-making. The state enforces the fulfillment of fiscal contracts signed between government levels; authority over detailed economic planning and management has been given to localities. As a result, within the agricultural contract system, the former grain contracts between the state and farmers have evolved to become arrangements between the state and localities, between localities and their subordinates and, finally, between village leaders and farm households. To strengthen grain production incentives, the state also linked quota deliveries to credit, subsidized fertilizers, and other agricultural inputs. Hence, through decentralization, localities have not only gained decision-making power but have also accepted responsibility for fulfilling their obligations. These fiscal contracts have been enforced by the state's administrative control over its subordinates and regulations over labor migration and markets.

Due to the continual rapid growth of rural industries, the share of household income from off-farm work has been increasing. This raises the question of the effectiveness of these policy modifications in ensuring grain quota fulfillment. The purpose of this paper is to investigate contractual arrangements at the village level and to analyze empirically the impact of locally designed incentives on contract participation and grain quota fulfillment. It is argued that, in response to decentralization and the growth of rural industries, local institutions have evolved to cope with the hybrid system combining markets and state planning. In pursuing overall balanced local economic development, local leaders—in particular, village leaders—have devised an array of performance-contingent incentives to enforce grain contract fulfillment. The effectiveness of these incentives is analyzed in this paper.

Data collected in Jiangsu Province are used for the empirical analyses.[4] The study area consists of three villages in two counties, Gaoyu and Xinghua, located in Yangzhou prefecture. These two counties have been among the most productive grain areas in China since the late 1960s, due to the completion of water projects during the Maoist era. Until the late 1970s, the agricultural sector accounted for over 80 percent of the gross value of industrial and agricultural output (GVIAO). The economic reforms and the improvement of infrastructure during the 1980s have fostered rapid growth in the rural industrial sector. By 1988, industry's share of GVIAO in this area had risen to 50 percent.[5] Hence, this area can be characterized as a well developed agricultural area with a fast growing rural industrial sector. This characteristic makes the area an excellent case for the purposes of our study.

The remainder of this paper is organized as follows. Section 2 examines the reasons for, and implications of, development of a particular local institution—the "Unified Management System"—in response to decentralization. The contractual arrangements between village leaders and farmers within this system are analyzed. Section 3 examines the role of major factors (market conditions, incentives, and household characteristics) in sustaining these arrangements. Section 4 empirically analyzes the impact of these factors on agricultural contract participation and describes their consequences for production performance and fulfillment of grain quotas. Section 5 draws some policy implications for the grain sector.

2. Village Institutions and Contractual Arrangements

At the bottom of the government hierarchy, village leaders hold ultimate responsibility for the survival of village industries and for grain quota fulfillment. The following analysis is limited to local governments at the village level.

Village Institutions: The Unified Management System

From the point of view of village leaders, the FRS has conferred both the right to use revenue retained at the village level and the responsibility to fulfill grain obligations. On the one hand, village leaders' highest priority is to develop income-generating activities—and, compared to grain production, rural industries are obviously more lucrative. On the other hand, village leaders are responsible for delivering grain quotas. As the state's representatives, they have to meet quota targets in order to avoid economic and political sanctions.[6] Since they cannot now use direct political coercion as they did in the collective era, their task is to somehow encourage farmers to increase grain production so as to fulfill village quotas.

Village leaders solve this problem by using the authority gained from decentralization. They have tightened their control over production by establishing a "unified management system" (*tongyi jingying*), in which they exercise controls over land allocation, crop mix, irrigation, and pest control. They also control the labor and other inputs to be used in village factories.

Village leaders are involved in the agricultural sector primarily to balance land use. Village factories often require inputs that are costly to obtain in markets but can be produced in the village's fields. Hence, it is in the interest of village leaders to see that sufficient land is allocated to production of these crops. Since they are unable to expand village land, they must promote high productivity in grain production, so that less land is used to satisfy grain contract obligations and consumption needs and more land can be used to produce crops with high cash values. Village leaders attempt to coordinate both agricultural and industrial activities within the village, much as if it were a vertically integrated business corporation.

The political and economic foundations of the new village institutions are constrained input markets, state ownership of land, and restrictions on labor migration. Given constrained input markets, village leaders have been able to use distribution of subsidized fertilizers, pesticides, and other agricultural inputs to attract grain contract participation. Under the premise of the state ownership of land, they have been able to use land adjustments based on production performance as effective threats in enforcing contract

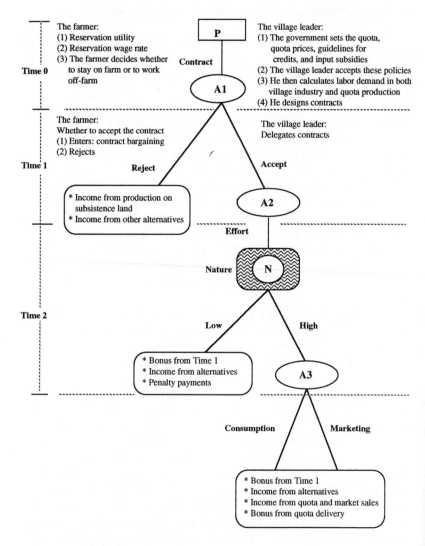

The farmer:
(1) Reservation utility
(2) Reservation wage rate
(3) The farmer decides whether to stay on farm or to work off-farm

Time 0

The village leader:
(1) The government sets the quota, quota prices, guidelines for credits, and input subsidies
(2) The village leader accepts these policies
(3) He then calculates labor demand in both village industry and quota production
(4) He designs contracts

The farmer:
Whether to accept the contract
(1) Enters: contract bargaining
(2) Rejects

Time 1

The village leader:
Delegates contracts

Reject

Accept

* Income from production on subsistence land
* Income from other alternatives

Effort

Nature

Time 2

Low

High

* Bonus from Time 1
* Income from alternatives
* Penalty payments

Consumption

Marketing

* Bonus from Time 1
* Income from alternatives
* Income from quota and market sales
* Bonus from quota delivery

Figure 1. The Decision-Making Process

Note: See text of Section 2 for explanation.

fulfillment. Lastly, due to the rapid growth of village industries and regulation of rural-to-urban labor migration, village leaders have been able to use off-farm employment opportunities as additional incentives.

At the bottom of the decision-making chain, farm households' decision-making power has been confined within a limited scope by the greater involvement of village leaders. Though an egalitarian land distribution rule applied at the beginning of the Household Responsibility System (HRS), the newly evolved village institutions have since undermined farm households' land-holding security. Now, a farm household's land can be expropriated by village leaders in the event of default on contract obligations. Although farm households remain the basic production units in agricultural activities, the intervention of village leaders in production planning and management has limited farmers' strategies to dividing household labor and current inputs among assigned cropping activities and between farm and off-farm work opportunities.

Under these conditions, to farm households grain production is not really an objective in itself, but rather a means of access to material benefits. The next section sets out to explore the village contractual arrangements that emerge from this complex decision-making environment.

Village Contractual Arrangements

In order to capture the nature of village contractual arrangements, it is necessary to understand the sequence of events in the decision-making process. Interactions between village leaders and farm households should be seen as dynamic, in that land adjustment and off-farm employment opportunities awarded to the farm household in the current period are consequences of its production performance in the last period.

At time 0 (Figure 1), the government determines the quota target and the guidelines for terms of the contract. After negotiating with the next higher level, the village leader has accepted a quota contract for his village. At the same time, he has also received the subsidized input supplies that come along with the contract. In order to delegate the quota tasks to individual households, he then designs (or formalizes) contracts with them.

A farmer's reservation utility and wage rate are determined by his previous production performance. At time 0, the farmer will take land allocation and off-farm employment opportunities as given. At the end of time 0, depending on his land holding, labor availability, off-farm work opportunities, and other calculations, he will decide whether or not to accept a grain contract.

At time 1, the village leader offers a contract and the farmer makes the decision whether or not to accept it. The contract offered by the village leader is a comprehensive package of incentives and penalties. If the farmer accepts the contract, he receives advance credit and subsidized inputs at the end of time 1.

Table 1. Fertilizer Supply and Contract Participation

| | Type of Contract Participation | | | | All |
	Grain	Cotton	Both	Neither	
Expenditure on fertilizer, per household (yuan)	187.2	159.4	196.5	109.3	176.1
Subsidized fertilizer (%)[a]	51	56	53	38	53
Average fertilizer price (yuan per kg.)	0.20	0.19	0.21	0.23	0.21
Expenditure on other farm chemicals, per household (yuan)	62.4	47.1	52.6	29.9	52.4
Number of observations	24	12	59	19	115

a. The share of subsidized fertilizer in total fertilizer used.

Source: Farm household survey; see text.

During time 2, production occurs (i.e., the farmer exerts certain efforts). The outcome of his productive efforts depends on his labor input and the state of nature. If he fulfills the contract, in the next round he will be rewarded—for instance, with a favorable land distribution (increases in total land or cash crop land) or with jobs in village factories for members of his household. If the farmer defaults on the contract willfully, he will be penalized. Penalties often include downward land adjustment and loss of off-farm employment opportunities in the next period. Consumption and marketing decisions are made after quota delivery.

The above discussion shows that an important response to decentralization and incomplete markets has been the formation of complex contractual arrangements between village leaders and farm households. The variables of interest in this paper are the incentives that the village leaders provide to induce participation in these arrangements and to enforce fulfillment. In addition, households' socioeconomic conditions may also influence their participation decisions. The next section examines how each of these factors influences the contract participation decision of a farm household.

3. Determinants of Contract Participation

The previous section showed that policy levers used by village leaders are of three types: distribution of subsidized fertilizers and other chemicals, land adjustments, and off-farm employment opportunities. These variables are the major incentive measures in village contract design. Of course, household characteristics such as age, education, dependency ratio, current land holding and, particularly, labor-pool size may also affect a household's decision-making.

To examine the incentive variables empirically, we will use survey data collected in Jiangsu province. In this survey, three villages with the same agro-climatic environment were selected in Gaoyu and Xinghua counties. The villages are still predominantly agricultural, with a large proportion of land sown to grain and with a mix of hybrid and conventional rice varieties. The sample households engage in a variety of economic activities. Revenues are generated from grain sales, cash crop sales, livestock marketing, and off-farm wage earnings. Rice and wheat are the two major crops subject to contract procurement. In addition, cotton is also subject to state procurement, and can only be sold at state purchasing stations. Land distribution and the production of other cash crops are contingent on the rice and wheat production contracts.

Due to the nature of data collection, our study focuses on rice contracts. Other cash crop contracts in the same production period will also be taken into consideration. Sample households are placed into four groups, by type of contract participation: grain, cotton, both grain and cotton, or none. The impact of incentive variables and household characteristics on contract participation is discussed in the following subsections.

Incentive Measures and Contract Participation
Distribution of subsidized inputs. If the distribution of subsidized inputs were used to entice contract participation, we should expect households with contracts, particularly with grain contracts, to have better access to these inputs.

Table 1 confirms that sample households in contracts received more subsidized fertilizer and paid, on average, lower prices, as compared to non-contracting households. Among households in contracts, the differences in prices paid are very small. Although households in grain or both grain and cotton contracts spent more on fertilizers, the ratio of the amount of subsidized fertilizer to total fertilizer is low compared to that of households in cotton contracts. This indicates that fertilizers were rationed and distributed more or less equally among contract households.

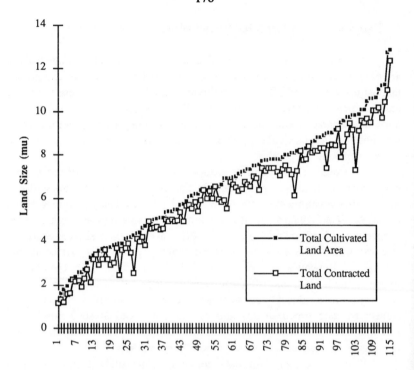

Figure 2. Total Cultivated Land and Contracted Land, by Household
Note: See Section 3 of text for explanation.

The fact that non-contracting households also received a certain amount of subsidized fertilizer may indicate the importance of personal connections in access to subsidized input supplies. Though village leaders could in theory use subsidized fertilizer as an enticement, individuals with "connections" may in fact have better access to these inputs in a dual marketing system. If this is so, using distribution of subsidized fertilizers as an incentive to attract contract participation may not be as effective in practice as theory would suggest.

Land adjustments. The land allocated to farmers is frequently divided into two types: subsistence land and responsibility land. Both types are "leased land" since they are received under lease from the government, and both types are subject to adjustment by village leaders. Since land adjustments have been used as one of the incentives for farmers' contract participation, a farm household's current land holding could be related to previous agricultural performance and contract participation. The differences between total land and leased land area are shown in Figure 2.[7]

Table 2. Deviation from Sample Land Holding per Capita

	Type of Contract Participation				
	Grain	Cotton	Both	Neither	All
Mean (mu)	-0.020	-0.203	0.142	-.0275	0.000
Standard deviation	0.391	0.598	0.497	0.753	0.558
Minimum (mu)	-0.472	-0.915	-0.688	-1.122	-1.122
Maximum (mu)	0.935	0.995	1.602	0.913	1.602
Number of observations	24	13	59	19	115

Source: Farm household survey; see text.

Table 3. Deviation from Sample Land Holding per Laborer

	Type of Contract Participation				
	Grain	Cotton	Both	Neither	All
Mean (mu)	-0.1034	-0.2917	0.2312	-0.4033	-0.0001
Standard deviation	0.8860	1.0073	1.0447	1.0588	1.0314
Minimum (mu)	-1.3700	-1.3500	-1.2357	-1.7500	-1.7500
Maximum (mu)	2.1600	1.8967	2.9500	1.7800	2.9500
Number of observations	24	13	59	19	115

Source: Farm household survey; see text.

These differences include two components: private plots, which have been very small and have existed since the collective era; and land changes since the beginning of economic reform in the early 1980s, which on average are probably larger and more varied.

Two proxies can be used to measure these changes. The proxies are based upon the two general criteria governing assignment of land use rights nationwide at the beginning of the reform era. One criterion is family size, according to which larger households would obtain larger amounts of land and per capita land holding would be roughly equal among farm households. The other criterion is the number of laborers in a household, by which land would be equally distributed on a per laborer basis. Changes in land

Table 4. Off-Farm Income, Labor Supply, and Wage Rates

Work	Number[a]	Income (yuan)		Number of Days Worked		Wage Rate (yuan per day)	
		mean	std[b]	mean	std[b]	mean	std[b]
Poultry	15	559.00	645.12	18.73	54.45	9.58	10.49
Fish farming	5	236.62	109.18	1.69	6.57	19.88	8.47
Food processing	2	600.00	212.13	4.29	23.49	10.00	7.07
Retail trade	8	1851.00	1509.74	25.11	60.17	14.01	10.27
Other commerce	7	447.00	167.41	22.00	54.71	3.98	3.21
Village factory	53	618.11	333.71	148.99	118.10	3.42	2.00
Construction	21	555.56	253.29	48.49	67.72	4.82	1.38
Forestry	3	1326.67	802.27	9.76	36.16	10.11	5.00
Government	13	460.29	405.58	33.33	68.16	3.23	1.86
Others	21	343.69	178.47	43.08	62.08	3.87	2.54
All	101	894.19	811.34	198.19	137.27	5.11	4.68

a. Number of households.
b. Standard Deviation.

Source: Farm household survey; see text.

holding, therefore, can be measured by the gap in per capita or per laborer land holding, obtained by subtracting the overall per capita (or per laborer) land holding from the corresponding land holdings of individual households. The gaps in per capita and per laborer land holding, grouped by contract type, are presented in Table 2 and Table 3.

Table 2 shows that, on average, households in both grain and cotton contracts made the greatest gains in landholding. Households in grain contracts but not in cotton contracts had almost no change in their land holdings. Non-contracting households had the largest decreases in per capita land holding. The gaps in per laborer land holding in Table 3 show a pattern similar to that in Table 2, with larger differences.

These data show the existence of land adjustments that may be closely related to contract, particularly grain contract, participation. Hence, we

Table 5. Labor Allocation, by Contract Type

	Type of Contract Participation				
	Grain	Cotton	Both	Neither	All
Total labor days	318	234	335	291	298
of which:					
on-farm (%)	40	56	49	29	47
off-farm (%)	60	44	51	71	53
Number of observations	24	13	59	19	115

Source: Farm household survey; see text.

would expect land adjustment to have a positive effect on households' contract participation decisions.

Off-farm employment. Given the state's restrictions on rural-urban labor migration, rural industries have become important for rural employment. In addition, farmers also engage in a variety of other off-farm activities. Average labor supply to, and income from, these activities are summarized in Table 4, for the sample households.

Table 4 shows that a majority of households engaged in village industries. Although work in a village factory provides relatively low wages and income, factory work is less risky than other off-farm activities. It also provides a highly stable number of working days, compared to other activities. Secure employment ensures stable and higher earnings in the long term, which are attractive to farmers. Hence we would expect positive correlations between off-farm labor allocation and contract participation.

The overall labor allocation is presented in Table 5. The table shows that, among contract participants, grain contract takers spent more days in off-farm work than others and cotton contract takers allocated the least amount of labor to off-farm work. This indicates that, among contract takers, grain contract takers do have better access to off-farm work.

Table 5 also shows that non-contracting households spent more time working off-farm. Since in each period of time, the contract participation decision is made *after* the off-farm labor participation decision, we would expect these households to have already secured their off-farm employment at time 1. Why didn't they participate in some form of contract just to ensure continuing employment in factories and to avoid downward land adjustments in the next round? First, since they supplied the least amount

Table 6. Household Characteristics, by Contract Type

| | Type of Contract Participation | | | | |
	Grain	Cotton	Both	Neither	All
Average household size (persons)	3.88	3.85	4.25	3.68	4.03
Average number of laborers	3.04	3.00	3.24	2.68	3.08
Average farm size (mu)	6.20	5.90	7.43	5.16	6.63
Dependency ratio[a]	1.24	1.40	1.44	1.47	1.42
Land area per laborer (mu)	2.25	2.06	2.58	1.95	2.35
Age of household head (years)	42.04	46.54	41.00	39.47	41.59
Education of household head[b]	1.96	1.62	2.00	2.11	1.96
Number of observations	24	13	59	19	115

a. Number of persons/number of laborers.
b. Number of years of schooling.

Source: Farm household survey; see text.

of labor in general, they may not have had sufficient labor to fulfill any contract and sustain efficient use of land after their off-farm labor allocation. And, second, they may have secure off-farm jobs due to their specific skills or experience and need not worry about job security.

The above discussion indicates that off-farm employment opportunities may have a positive effect on grain contract participation decisions. However, access to off-farm jobs may also be related to household labor-pool size and other household characteristics. This will be analyzed next.

Household Characteristics and Contract Participation

In addition to land, household labor is another important factor influencing contract participation decisions. Previous discussion shows that, after allocating labor to be used in off-farm work, if a household still has sufficient labor remaining it would engage in a contract in order to expand the resource base (land, and other inputs) on which that labor can be utilized. Hence, family labor-pool size is expected to be positively related to contract participation. Indeed, this can be seen in Table 6. Since overall land allocation is based on contract participation, households with larger farm size are also expected to have larger quota obligations.

The actual number of days worked is not only determined by family size and number of laborers, but is also affected by the dependency ratio. This ratio—i.e., the ratio of the number of consumers to the number of workers—determines both a household's consumption needs and its need to care for young children and the elderly. These two needs have opposite effects on the number of days a household laborer can work off-farm. On the one hand, a high dependency ratio may indicate a high demand for household income. In addition, if the land and other means of production available to the household are insufficient for full employment of the household labor, the household may seek off-farm work to augment its (insufficient) income from cropping. On the other hand, a higher dependency ratio may also require that members of the household's labor force serve as care-givers within the home. Because off-farm employment usually requires workers to stay away from home, a high dependency ratio may constrain such employment.

Table 6 shows that non-contracting households had the highest dependency ratio. Since they also had the least land, it is not surprising that most of their income came from off-farm earnings. The pattern of dependency ratios among all the contract types suggests that this ratio may have a positive effect on off-farm labor participation and therefore a negative impact on contract participation.

Household heads are responsible for making overall production decisions. The outcomes of contract negotiations and access to, and security of, off-farm jobs may be positively related to the household heads' status and experience (often indicated by age), and educational attainment. We would expect, therefore, these characteristics, in turn, to affect off-farm labor and contract participation.

The study so far has shown that incentive measures—land adjustments, subsidized inputs, and off-farm employment opportunities—may have positive effects on contract participation decisions. These effects may be enhanced or undermined by certain household characteristics. This raises questions about the joint effect of these various factors and their relative importance in off-farm labor and contract participation decisions. These questions are addressed through econometric analyses in the following section.

4. Model Estimation

A key purpose of this section is to answer two empirical questions. First, do the variables discussed above actually affect the decision to enter a contract? Second, do the variables have the same impact across contract alternatives?

Determinants of Contract Participation

In order to estimate the probabilities of contract participation, quantitative response models involving at least two possible discrete outcomes should be used. When individuals can choose only one outcome from among a set of mutually exclusive and collectively exhaustive alternatives, multinomial logit models are appropriate. The purpose of these models is to produce estimates of the probability that the dependent variable is equal to a particular value for any observation, and to identify those factors statistically significant in determining the value of that probability. The general framework of the probability models has the following form, where $j = 1,\ldots,J$:

$$\text{Prob[event j occurs]} = \text{Prob}[Y = j]$$
$$= F[\text{relevant effects: parameters}].$$

When the choice is modeled to be a function of demographic characteristics such as age and education and of other economic variables, a polytomous logit model is generated. This model can be thought of as being applied to the analysis of J separate populations; it is used to estimate the probability that an observation belongs to one of these populations, and produces a complete set of coefficient estimates for each possible value of the dependent variable except the one used as a reference point.[8]

The model to be used for our estimation can be expressed as follows.[9]

$$\log\left[\frac{P_{ij}}{P_{il}}\right] = x_i'\beta_j$$

The term on the left of the equation is the log-odds of falling into the jth alternative as compared with the reference category. For example, if P_j is the probability of choosing the grain contract and P_1 is the probability of non-contracting, then this model estimates the effects of x on the log-odds of choosing a grain contract as compared with not contracting at all.

Table 7. Definitions of Variables Used in Logit Estimations

Variable	Mean	Standard Deviation	Definition
AGE	41.59	10.78	age of the household head (years)
AGE2	1845.09	962.16	AGE squared
EDUCA	1.96	1.17	educational attainment of the household head (years of schooling)
EDUAGE	73.76	40.42	AGE × EDUCA
DEPRATE	1.41	0.42	number of persons/number of laborers
ZHONGDI	6.63	2.61	farm size (mu)
DLAND	0.00	1.03	difference between household's land holding per capita and sample land holding per capita (mu)
FEIRATE	0.53	0.31	share of subsidized fertilizer in total amount used
FNDAYS			dummy variable: participation in off-farm work
VD1, VD2			village dummy variables
ONE			intercept

Source: Farm household survey; see text.

The vector x in the logit model contains all the variables influencing household contract participation decisions. These variables are of three types: economic factors, such as farm size, the proxy for land change, and the ratio of subsidized fertilizer; household characteristics, such as the household head's age and education, and the dependency ratio; and dummy variables, such as participation in off-farm work and residency in different villages. The explanatory variables used in the following estimates are summarized in Table 7.

The estimations include two binomial logit models and a multinomial logit model. The two binomial logit models are used to compare the effect of explanatory variables on household participation in contracts of any sort and on household participation in grain contracts, as follows.

Table 8. Results, Binomial Logit: Contract Participation versus Non-Participation

Variable	Coefficient	Standard Error	T-Ratio	Prob: t > x
ONE	-9.03	7.21	-1.25	0.21
AGE	0.24	0.29	0.82	0.41
AGE2	-0.0012	0.0029	-0.42	0.68
EDUCA	2.13	1.26	1.69	0.09
EDUAGE	-0.048	0.030	-1.58	0.11
DEPRATE	-1.11	1.15	-0.96	0.34
ZHONGDI	0.21	0.19	1.06	0.29
DLAND	1.42	0.69	2.05	0.04
FEIRATE	0.93	0.98	0.96	0.34
FNDAYS	1.94	1.07	1.81	0.07
VD1	1.27	0.85	1.50	0.13
VD2	1.81	0.88	2.05	0.04

Note: Maximum likelihood estimates.
    Log-Likelihood: -39.04
    Restricted (slopes = 0) Log-L: -51.55
    Chi-squared (11):   25.02
    Significance level: 0.0091.

Source: Farm household survey; see text.

Binomial model (1): Contract versus non-contract. The dependent variable Y takes the value 1 when a household participates in grain contracts or cotton contracts or both; Y takes the value 0 when the household does not participate in any contract.

Binomial model (2): Grain contract versus non-grain-contract. The dependent variable Y takes the value 1 when a household participates in either grain contracts only or both grain and cotton contracts; Y takes the value 0 when the household either participates in only cotton contracts or does not partici-pate in any contract.

Table 9. Results, Binomial Logit: Participation versus Non-Participation in Grain Contracts[a]

Variable	Coefficient	Standard Error	T-Ratio	Prob: t > x
ONE	-9.27	6.37	-1.46	0.16
AGE	0.22	0.24	0.92	0.36
AGE2	-0.0018	0.0023	-0.79	0.44
EDUCA	1.61	1.11	1.44	0.15
EDUAGE	-0.034	0.026	-1.30	0.20
DEPRATE	-0.55	0.81	-0.68	0.50
ZHONGDI	0.29	0.14	2.12	0.03
DLAND	1.01	0.46	2.15	0.03
FEIRATE	0.42	0.81	0.53	0.60
FNDAYS	1.78	0.94	1.91	0.06
VD1	0.99	0.68	1.46	0.15
VD2	2.24	0.76	2.96	0.0031

Note: Maximum likelihood estimates.
Log-Likelihood: -52.48
Restricted (slopes = 0) Log-L: -68.00
Chi-squared (11): 31.04
Significance level 0.0011.

a. Participation in grain contract or in both grain and cotton contracts.

Source: Farm household survey; see text.

The multinomial logit model is used to estimate the effects of the explanatory variables on households participating in different contracts. The dependent variable Y takes the value 1 when households participate in both grain and cotton contracts; Y takes the value 2 when households participate in grain contracts; Y takes the value 3 when households participate in cotton contracts; Y takes the value 0 when households do not participate in any contract.

In the following estimations, $Y = 0$ is always used as the reference category to which other categories are compared.

Empirical results: binomial logit models. Land redistribution has a significant positive effect on contract participation (Table 8). Note that

Table 10. Results, Multinomial Logit: Participation versus Non-Participation in Contracts

Variable	Coefficient	Standard Error	T-Ratio	Prob: t > x
Y = 1 (participating in both contracts)				
ONE	-7.45	8.01	-0.93	0.35
AGE	0.073	0.31	0.23	0.82
AGE2	-0.00037	0.0031	-0.11	0.91
EDUCA	0.93	1.45	0.64	0.51
EDUAGE	-0.018	0.035	-0.52	0.59
DEPRATE	-0.73	1.24	-0.58	0.55
ZHONGDI	0.42	0.21	1.95	0.05
DLAND	1.41	0.74	1.89	0.05
FEIRATE	0.94	1.04	0.90	0.36
FNDAYS	2.78	1.23	2.24	0.02
VD1	1.94	0.94	2.05	0.03
VD2	2.69	0.99	2.71	0.0065
Y = 2 (participating in grain contracts)				
ONE	-21.88	10.95	-1.99	0.04
AGE	0.78	0.45	1.75	0.07
AGE2	-0.0065	0.0044	-1.46	0.14
EDUCA	4.31	1.76	2.43	0.01
EDUAGE	-0.099	0.042	-2.35	0.01
DEPRATE	-1.60	1.35	-1.18	0.23
ZHONGDI	0.094	0.22	0.41	0.67
DLAND	1.51	0.78	1.93	0.05
FEIRATE	0.71	1.14	0.62	0.53
FNDAYS	1.63	1.26	1.29	0.19
VD1	0.37	1.04	0.36	0.71
VD2	1.71	1.02	1.66	0.09

Table 10, continued

Variable	Coefficient	Standard Error	T-Ratio	Prob: t > x
Y = 3 (participating in cotton contracts)				
ONE	-7.27	9.97	-0.73	0.46
AGE	0.17	0.39	0.44	0.65
AGE2	-0.00058	0.0039	-0.14	0.88
EDUCA	1.41	1.61	0.87	0.38
EDUAGE	-0.033	0.036	-0.95	0.35
DEPRATE	-0.94	1.43	-0.65	0.51
ZHONGDI	0.027	0.24	0.11	0.91
DLAND	1.04	0.86	1.20	0.22
FEIRATE	0.94	1.33	0.71	0.47
FNDAYS	1.14	1.38	0.83	0.40
VD1	0.99	1.07	0.93	0.35
VD2	0.089	1.25	0.07	0.94

Note: Maximum likelihood estimates.
    Log-Likelihood: -110.04
    Restricted (slopes = 0) Log-L: -139.53
    Chi-squared (33):   58.98
    Significance level   0.0036.
Source: Farm household survey; see text.

households in Village 2 are more likely to participate in contracts. This is because households in Village 2 have smaller farms and smaller land holdings per laborer, as compared to the average. These households are probably more sensitive to the effect of land changes.

Off-farm employment opportunities also have a significant positive effect on contract participation. This confirms our earlier observation that off-farm jobs (especially those in village factories) are regulated by village leaders to manipulate farm households' contract participation. Although the effects of other variables are not statistically significant, the signs of all coefficients are as expected.

Previous discussions show that farm households in the pure cotton contracts are similar, in terms of household income, farm size, and per capita land holdings, to non-contracting households. The real difference between contract participation and non-contracting probably lies in the grain contracting (grain or both grain and cotton, versus cotton alone or neither grain nor cotton). The results for grain contracting versus not grain contracting are presented in Table 9. The variables that affect contract participation in general remain significant for grain contract participation. In addition, farm size is now an important factor; farm households participating in grain contracts are not only concerned about land redistribution but also about their total land holding.

Empirical results: multinomial logit model. The preceding discussion, along with earlier comments, shows that the same explanatory variables may have different effects on households' decisions to participate in alternative contracts. For this reason, a multinomial logit model is used to analyze farm households' decisions to participate in different contracts. The results of the estimation are presented in Table 10.

For households in grain contracts or in both grain and cotton contracts, farm size, land adjustment, off-farm employment opportunities, and village dummy variables have significant effects on contract participation. Although the other coefficients are not statistically significant, their signs are consistent with our hypotheses.

The results in Table 10 also reveal differences in the effects of exogenous variables on participation in these two types of contracts (grain versus grain and cotton). For farm households in the pure grain contracts, age, education, and land redistribution are the most important variables affecting their participation decisions. Whereas those households participating in both grain and cotton contracts are concerned about farm size, land changes, and employment opportunities, those participating only in grain contracts are most concerned about productivity and land changes. Households whose heads are senior and have higher education are more likely not to participate in grain contracts.

For households in cotton contracts, the results are disappointing. None of the explanatory variables can differentiate this group from the non-contracting group. Recall that, for the two groups, most of the household characteristics—and, especially, the size of the household's labor pool—are very similar. Non-contracting households secured most of their cash income from off-farm employment. Among cotton contract takers, the average age of household heads is higher and their educational attainment lower, indicating that they may not be able to find off-farm work easily. Since cotton is basically a cash crop, these households may take the contracts as an opportunity to earn cash income without being subject to grain quota obligations. The behavior of cotton contract takers, therefore,

Table 11. Household Income, by Contract Type

	Type of Contract Participation				
	Grain	Cotton	Both	Neither	All
Average household income (yuan)	4774	3582	4929	3496	4508
of which:					
farm (%)	53	39	46	25	43
rice (%)	30	5	19	4	17
wheat (%)	19	18	17	14	17
cotton (%)	1	13	4	1	5
other cash crops (%)	3	3	5	6	4
livestock (%)	25	24	22	31	25
off-farm (%)	22	37	32	44	32
Number of observations	24	13	59	19	115

Source: Farm household survey; see text.

differs from that of non-contractors only because the latter have better access to off-farm work.

The study so far has shown the impact of incentive variables and household characteristics on contract participation. The question that remains is how these contractual arrangements affect outcomes, such as income distribution and quota fulfillment, at the end of the production period. This will be examined in the following subsection.

Income, Output, and Quota Fulfillment

Household income. Household income refers to the payn ts a farm household receives at the end of a production season, both from agriculture and from other activities. Because information is lacking on unearned income, this component is not included; household income is limited to cash income and income in kind earned by members of the farm household in the course of the production year. Cash income is calculated by multiplying the amounts of quota, above-quota, and market sales by the respective prices. Income in kind is calculated on the portion of the total harvest that is not marketed, using the market price. To avoid double

Table 12. Grain and Cotton Yields, by Contract Type

	Type of Contract Participation				
	Grain	Cotton	Both	Neither	All
Grain (*jin* per *mu*)	1429	939	995	1069	1091
	(2032)	(170)	(205)	(225)	(948)
rice, conventional	696	528	673	545	640
varieties	(461)	(517)	(475)	(536)	(485)
rice, hybrid	1241	748	1014	1128	1050
	(1177)	(371)	(744)	(808)	(836)
Cotton (*jin* per *mu*)	33	155	134	69	104
	(59)	(47)	(40)	(84)	(70)
Number of observations	24	13	59	19	115

Note: Figures in parentheses are standard deviations.

Source: Farm household survey; see text.

counting, the value of home-grown feed grain is calculated at market prices and is subtracted from livestock income.

Farm household income and its sources by contract participation are presented in Table 11. Households that participated in both grain and cotton contracts have the highest household income. The next most well-off group is households with pure grain contracts. Agricultural income, particularly grain income, is the most important source of income for these two groups. Off-farm income is the second most important source of income for households with both contracts. For pure grain contract takers, it is not surprising that livestock income is the second most important income source, since most of the feed grain needed may be produced by the household. Both cotton and cash crop sales account for less than 10 percent of the total.

Household income for both cotton contract takers and non-contractors is below average (and is lowest for the non-contractors). For households in pure cotton contracts, cotton sales account for only 13 percent of total income. For households that do not contract, off-farm earning was the major source of income.

Agricultural output and marketing. Given the performance-contingent nature of the contracts, grain contract takers not only have to meet a quota target, but must also achieve some minimum yield requirement. We would therefore expect to see farm households in contracts reach higher yields than other types of households. Grain and cotton yields, by contract type, are presented in Table 12. Overall, households in pure grain contracts had the highest grain yields. Households in the other types of contracts had fairly similar performances. For those in contracts, it is obvious that the higher the amount of grain one contracts, the higher yield requirement one must achieve.

It is interesting that non-contracting households had higher yields than households with cotton contracts or with both contracts. There are two possible explanations for this. On the one hand, because these households have smaller farm sizes, household consumption and marketing demands may motivate them to achieve higher yields. On the other hand, the current smaller farm sizes may be due to poor performance in previous years, and these households may be trying to improve performance so as to get more land in the future. If gaining land is the major objective, we would expect these households, even though they were not in contracts, to sell a certain amount of grain to the state at quota prices. In later analysis, we will see that they did so.

Agricultural output and marketing rates are shown in Table 13. On average, 15 percent of total grain output was sold to state procurement stations at the quota price. Another 2 percent was also sold to the state, but at the above-quota price. Even though output was high, the marketing rates for rice in this area were fairly low; rice sold on free markets accounts for only 1 percent of total output. One possible explanation is that rice is the preferred household consumption staple. Another is that the market price was so low that it was more profitable to use rice as feed grain.

Production and marketing of individual crops differ sharply among farm households according to their choice of contract. The total production level was very high for households in the pure grain contracts, as a result of more land and high yields. About 21 percent of the grain they produced was used for quota and above-quota sales. Since these households produced mostly rice, they also sold more to free markets.

Total production levels and quota sales for households with both cotton and grain contracts are lower than for households with pure grain contracts. This is because they also have cotton obligations to fulfill. These households also had a relatively high level of cash crop production, the result of larger farm size and a higher percentage of cash crop land.

Households in cotton contracts produced the highest level of cotton. They sold most of their output to the state, due to the quota requirements in their contracts. These households also produced the smallest amounts of grain; interestingly, however, they sold 15 percent of their grain to the state procurement system. This may reflect their demand for subsidized inputs.

Table 13. Agricultural Output and Marketing, by Contract Type

	Type of Contract Participation				
	Grain	Cotton	Both	Neither	All
Average grain output (jin)	5564	2942	4949	3935	4683
	(2054)	(1373)	(2064)	(2130)	(2138)
of which:					
quota sales (%)	17	15	17	6	15
	(8)	(50)	(11)	(11)	(21)
above-quota sales (%)	4	0	2	2	2
	(7)		(6)	(8)	(6)
sold in free markets (%)	3	1	1	0	1
	(6)	(3)	(7)		(5)
Average cotton output (jin)	41	408	221	158	194
	(97)	(522)	(188)	(316)	(274)
of which:					
marketed (%)	13	98	54	28	46
	(37)	(105)	(67)	(71)	(72)
Average cash crop output (jin)	71	112	126	57	102
	(108)	(177)	(194)	(90)	(164)
of which:					
marketed (%)	16	52	50	53	44
	(3)	(73)	(189)	(113)	(145)
Number of observations	24	13	59	19	115

Note: Figures in parentheses are standard deviations.

Source: Farm household survey; see text.

Non-contracting households produced more grain than households with cotton contracts. This is due to the larger shares of land they allocated to hybrid rice. Note that these households also sold 8 percent of their grain to the state, probably also to meet their needs for subsidized inputs.

In summary, the patterns of total production and quota sales across different types of households are quite consistent with our previous discussion. The households in grain contracts have higher yields and higher levels of production; the grain quota requirements for this group are higher

Table 14. Farm Households' Quota Fulfillment

| | Rice Quota Fulfillment Rates (percent) | | | | | |
	<49.5	49.5-69.5	69.5-89.5	89.5-99.5	>99.5	All
Households selling grain on free market						
number of households	0	0	0	1	13	14
average fulfillment rate (%)	--	--	--	95	167	113
standard deviation	--	--	--	--	240	110
Households not selling grain on free market						
number of households	3	0	2	4	60	69
average fulfillment rate (%)	6	--	78	97	109	162
standard deviation	11	--	6	2	31	230

Note: Table includes only the 83 households entering grain contracts.

Source: Farm household survey; see text.

than for other groups. Households in contracts have higher levels of cash crop production; one of the rewards for contracting is cash crop land.

Quota fulfillment. Given the incentive structure and high levels of output in the study area, we should expect high fulfillment rates. Indeed, this is seen in Table 14. In this table, households are grouped according to whether or not they sold grain on free markets. The purpose is to determine if households sold grain on free markets before they fulfilled their quotas.

Of the 83 households engaged in grain contracts, only 14 households sold grain on the free market. Of the 83 households, ten did not fulfill their quotas. Note, however, that five households were very close to attaining their quota obligations; record-keeping errors probably account for part of the underfulfillment. Table 14 suggests that incentive measures were effective, in that the sample households reached a high rate of quota fulfillment.

It is interesting to note that on average, the fulfillment rates exceed 1, which means that households actually sold more grain to the state than they were required to. There are several possible explanations. First, overfulfillment could be due to the transaction costs of marketing. Although the quota price is lower than average market price, state procurement branches are usually located in nearby towns and are easily accessible for farm households. Unfortunately, we do not have sufficient information to compare the locations of markets and state grain stations in order to assess the costs of marketing grain through different channels. Second, as discussed before, farmers were encouraged, by village leaders or officials at the grain stations, to sell more grain to the state. One reward for doing so is usually a certificate for quota fertilizers.[10] Obtaining subsidized inputs may be one reason for higher quota sales, over market sales.

In summary, average household production levels and fulfillment rates were high in our sample. The village leaders in our study area were able to induce these high rates of quota fulfillment by linking delivery with land allocations, yield requirements, and current input supplies.

5. Concluding Comments

The second stage of economic reform in China has resulted in the continual growth of rural industries and decentralized decision-making. At the village level, in contrast to decentralization of decision-making at higher levels of government, decision-making power became *more* centralized in the hands of village leaders. In order to achieve overall balance in the rural economy, village leaders established the "unified management system," through which they were able to implement incentive mechanisms to elicit contract participation. Our study found that these incentives—off-farm employment opportunities, land allocations and adjustments, and input supplies—had a significant impact on grain contract participation and production.

The empirical analysis shows that, on average, the time farmers spent in off-farm activities and their income from these activities constituted major shares of total work time and total income, respectively. Hence, opportunities for off-farm work would seem to have motivated farm households to engage in contracts and to pursue high yields. On average, households in grain and/or cotton contracts gained land. Hence, inequalities in land holding per capita or per laborer may be the consequence of conscious land adjustments, based on contract performance, and maintaining land holding was probably another important motivation behind contract participation. Econometric results confirm the positive effects of the above two variables on contract participation decisions.

The presence of subsidized input supplies, however, showed no significant impact on contract participation. Variation of fertilizer prices across households indicates that they had different degrees of access to fertilizer markets—implying considerable scope for corruption in the distribution system, which diverts subsidized fertilizer supplies into sales at higher prices.

The study shows that the market failed to play its intended role in inducing marketing of surplus grain in the study area. Although the study area was a grain-base area, market grain sales accounted for less than 2 percent of total output. This outcome is probably attributable mainly to high input costs and low market prices; it became more profitable to use grain as feed, rather than marketing it directly.

The findings clearly indicate that the high quota fulfillment rate, and grain production, were motivated not by the potential profit from grain sales but rather by the desire to secure household land and by the potential gains from livestock raising and off-farm work, which compensate for the lower returns from grain production.

Given the current structure of the urban grain rationing and the procurement system, several specific reforms are suggested by this study. They include improving market infrastructure, to enhance incomes earned from grain sales; improving the supply system for fertilizer and other agricultural inputs, to strengthen input-supply incentives; and legitimizing labor hiring and land leasing, to increase labor productivity.

Market infrastructure. Recent policy debate has focused on whether grain market prices play an important role in inducing grain production. This study showed that, in our study area, quota sales still dominated—and strongly influenced overall grain marketing. After quota delivery, free market grain sales remained very small.[11] In our study area, rapidly-growing village factories may account for the fact that income shares from grain sales were less important. An increasing income share from livestock raising may indicate that using grain as feed is more profitable than direct marketing. In addition, because many barriers to interregional grain transfers still exist, local market demand for direct consumption in grain surplus areas had been saturated by the late 1980s.[12] As the consumption demand for livestock increases, returns from grain production can also increase through the use of grain as feed. Without increases in demand for direct grain sales (through interregional grain transfers), market price mechanisms will continue to play a less significant role in stimulating grain production in a surplus region, such as our study area. Production can only be stimulated by other incentives and through increases in livestock sales.[13]

Improving input supplies. Increasing farmers' participation in grain contracts requires a policy addressing two sets of issues: grain productivity and access to product and input markets. The study findings indicate that increases in rice output at the farm level would come primarily from increased yields; nearly all the available land has already been devoted to rice production. Yield increases call for increased use of current inputs and improvements in production technology and farm management. Fertilizer supply and distribution, then, have a very important bearing on yield increases. Subsidized fertilizer distribution tied to grain quota delivery may be important in theory, but it has not been effective in practice due to the high costs. Specific reforms should aim at increasing fertilizer supply, improving the fertilizer distribution system, and encouraging alternative input marketing channels.

Improving land and labor markets. Because the state has, in effect, retained land ownership and delegated land-use decisions to its representatives in the village, village leaders have been able to use land allocation as a control variable. Although this may be effective in terms of control, the current fragmented land distribution can be questioned on efficiency grounds.

The current land allocation structure, coupled with a restrained labor market, is a barrier to further improvement in farm organization and management. Under present land use rights—which grant no secure rights to buy, sell, lease in, or rent out—talented farmers find it difficult to operate their farms efficiently, to adopt the appropriate technologies, and to achieve economies of scale. Land transfer rarely occurs because of the risk that a temporary transfer may become permanent. Currently, agricultural laborers still engage in both agricultural and non-agricultural activities for several reasons. One is that the opportunity cost of keeping their land, while at the same time engaging in off-farm work, is still very low. Another reason is that village factories have not developed to the stage of absorbing surplus labor. Yet another is that the profitability and stability of village industries are still subject to external and internal constraints—external constraints including macroeconomic policies (which constantly change) and regulations on credit and taxes, and internal constraints including the lack of technology and management and insufficient levels of education and training of workers. Overcoming these constraints is contingent on broader economic reforms. In the meantime, for the majority of farm households land remains a safety net.

A related necessary condition for improving farm productivity is improvement in the labor market, both within and outside the agricultural sector. Our study showed that household labor-pool size is a constraint in grain contract participation. If regulations on labor hiring can be relaxed, more households—with smaller family size—may engage in grain contracts. On the other hand, policies directed at achieving more efficient farm organization will require a larger amount of labor migration out of farm activities.

Notes

1. Jean C. Oi, "Fiscal Reform and the Economic Foundations of Local State Corporatism in China," *World Politics*, 45, October 1992, pp. 99-126.

2. William A. Byrd, "Rural Industrialization and Ownership in China," *Comparative Economic Studies*, 32(1), Spring 1990, pp. 73-107.

3. Terry Sicular, "Plan and Markets in Chinese Agricultural Commerce," *Journal of Political Economy*, 96(2), April 1988, pp. 283-307.

4. The survey data used in this study were collected by Scott Rozelle, during the period from summer 1988 through spring 1989. His permission to use the data made this research possible.

5. Scott Rozelle, "The Economic Behavior of Village Leaders in China's Reform Economy" (Ph.D. dissertation, Cornell University, 1991).

6. Field interviews indicate that market purchase of grain to satisfy quotas was not allowed; credits and material supplies to village industries were often contingent on quota fulfillment.

7. The data are sorted by households' total cultivated land. In the figure, each dark dot indicates a household's current total cultivated land; the corresponding blank square indicates that household's total leased land.

8. Since the sum of the probabilities for all options must equal one, we need to estimate probabilities for only J-1 of the options. The remaining probability is then just 1 minus the sum of all the others. Mathematically, all the coefficients for one of the options can be normalized to zero, so these values are not explicitly produced.

9. Detailed discussion of the multinomial logit model can be found in William Greene, *Econometric Analysis* (New York: Macmillan, 1990); G. S. Maddala, *Limited Dependent and Qualitative Variables in Econometrics* (Cambridge: Cambridge University Press, 1983); and G. G. Judge et al., *The Theory and Practice of Econometrics*, 2d ed. (New York: Wiley, 1985).

10. In our study area, farmers delivering their grain quotas were to be provided with (1) credit advances of 20 percent of their total quotas (4.7 yuan for every 50 kg. of wheat quota and 3.5 yuan for every 50 kg. of rice quota), and (2) subsidized inputs (9 kg. of chemical fertilizer and 1 kg. of diesel fuel for every 50 kg. of rice quota).

11. A recent study of northern Henan Province showed much higher commercial rates for grain during the same period; see X. Yao, "Market and Farm Household Level Impacts of Grain Marketing Reforms in China: A Case Study in Xinxiang, Henan Province" (Ph.D. dissertation, Michigan State University, 1990). Differences in income sources and off-farm work opportunities between Henan and Jiangsu may account for the differences in grain marketing rates.

12. Nicholas R. Lardy, "China's Interprovincial Grain Marketing and Import Demand" (working paper, University of Washington, 1989).

13. In fact, free market prices for grain have come down in Jiangsu. According to a recent observation, the state quota price for grain was 0.4 yuan per kilogram, and the average free market price 0.38 yuan per kilogram.

Hybrid Organizational Forms in South China: "One Firm, Two Systems"

Su Si-jin

1. Introduction

The phrase "one firm, two systems" succinctly characterizes the hybrid organizational forms that have emerged in China over the last decade or so.[1] Within many firms today, the market and planning coexist: some subunits are operated according to the principles of a market economy, while others are still state- or collectively-owned and operated according to principles of a planned economy. Marketized subunits have formed various kinds of joint ventures and partnerships with both foreign and domestic firms. In these subunits, the external investors already own a significant share of total assets, and the profits earned are shared according to each side's investment contribution. Subunits that are still state- or collectively-owned are controlled by the central, provincial or municipal governments, with profits shared between the subunits themselves and their supervising agencies.

These two different ways of organizing business activities across subunits have become a salient feature of Chinese firms since reforms began in the late 1970s. A typical firm is now a hybrid; in one representative instance, for example, a single firm includes a state-owned subunit, a subunit engaged in a Sino-foreign joint venture, another subunit that is subcontracted out to individuals who have formed a partnership, and yet another that is a joint venture involving both state and collective owner-ship.[2] As the manager of a hybrid firm explains:

> If you look at our firm as a whole, it has become very mixed; some subunits are still state-owned as they were before, but others are no longer so. And if you look at a particular subunit, it has also become a hybrid: the state, as one partner, now jointly owns the subunit's business with one, or several, private partners.[3]

Table 1. Incidence of Hybrid Organizational Forms

Type[a]	Share (percent)[b]
Joint ventures (including Sino-Sino and Sino-foreign)	82
Partnerships (with foreign or domestic partners)	73
Contracting	79

Note: N = 53.

a. Pertains to types of hybrid organization observed in sampled firms' subunits.

b. Percentage of sampled firms having hybrid organizational forms in their subunits. Shares sum to more than 1 because many firms have more than one type of hybrid organizational form.

Source: Survey and interviews; see text.

Such hybrids have developed mainly through joint ventures, contracting arrangements, and partnerships. Table 1 shows that joint ventures are most common, with contracting and partnerships following close behind.

To date, studies of organizational forms in post-Mao China have tended to focus on the mixed economy at the national level or at the level of individual sectors or regions. And most such studies have proceeded on a fairly abstract plane. Victor Nee, for example, has studied how the transition to markets gives rise to a new diversity of organizational forms, spanning a continuum from formal and hierarchical state-owned enterprises to small private businesses.[4] He argues that the dynamics of market transition are driven by such factors as the spread of markets, the changing structure of property rights, and the shift from a redistributive to a regulatory state. During periods of rapid institutional change and, hence, economic uncertainty, hybrid organizational forms flourish because they exhibit superior adaptive capacity.[5] William Byrd argues that the mixed system has created an inherent dynamic that leads to a continual increase in the role of the market (as compared to that of planning) in coordinating economic activity.[6] The effects of organizational change and the emergence of a mixed economy at the local level have been traced by, for example, Christine Wong.[7]

The specifics of hybrid formation at the grass-roots level (i.e., in the firm) have, by contrast, received relatively little attention. The purpose of this paper is to examine interactions between the different kinds of subunits inside hybrid firms and the dynamic process that these interactions generate. I will first examine income differentiation across subunits inside the firms, because this differentiation seems to precipitate interaction among the subunits. I will then describe how the subunits inside firms, and entire firms, mimic one anothers' behavior, resulting in widespread diffusion of organizational structures, contract forms, and management methods.

The data used in this study, collected between September 1990 and January 1991, include: (1) interviews with 57 managers of Chinese firms both in Hong Kong and Xiamen, (2) a survey covering 60 Chinese firms, and (3) the firms' contracts.

2. Income Differentiation among Subunits

Income differs significantly across subunits within a firm. To understand this income differentiation, one needs to look first at the major components of individual income—namely, basic salary, subsidies, and bonuses.

Basic salary is related to educational background and work experience (usually years of work). In state-owned subunits, salary is based on scales set by the central and local governments. *Subsidies* are frequently related to particular workposts (e.g., "deputy manager"). There are also subsidies for transportation and meals and regional subsidies to compensate for differences in cost of living. Subsidies are provided by the central government, local governments, and firms themselves. *Bonuses* are related to output performance and are used as an incentive mechanism. Since 1978, they have become a major component of income. There are two types of bonuses: those issued by a firm's headquarters, and those issued by each of its subunits. Bonuses from headquarters depend upon aggregate output performance, whereas bonuses from a subunit depend upon the performance of that subunit alone. The firm-wide bonus may be zero (due to poor aggregate performance) even though the bonuses in a particular subunit are very high (due to excellent subunit performance); this outcome results from subcontracting systems internal to the firm.

Basic salary and subsidies are fixed, with no variations across subunits (or even across firms, if the firms belong to the same type of ownership). Bonuses, however, tend to differ, by organizational form. Income differentiation thus reflects differences in bonuses across subunits.

The structure of income, as described above, differs dramatically from that prevailing prior to 1978. Then, the income of an individual employee consisted primarily of basic salary. There were subsidies related to transportation and regional differences in cost of living, but they contributed a very small share of total income—approximately 5-8 percent

Table 2. Average Income in One Firm, by Subunit, 1990

Subunit	Basic Salary plus Subsidies[a]	Bonuses[a]
Sino-foreign joint venture	227.5	584.0
State-owned	120.9	87.0

a. Yuan per month, per employee.

Source: Interviews; see text.

then, as compared to 11-31 percent now. In many firms today, employees' income consists primarily of bonuses rather than basic salary. Bonuses range from 30-odd percent of basic salary plus subsidies to 200 or even 300 percent.

Table 2 illustrates income differentiation across subunits inside one of the interviewed firms. In 1986, Subunit A formed a joint venture with a firm in Hong Kong. This subunit is (partially) financially independent of the domestic firm's headquarters, and it enjoys autonomy in decisions related to production, marketing, procurement, and recruitment.[8] In addition, Subunit A is allowed to determine the amount of bonuses for its employees according to its own output performance.[9] Subunit B has also enjoyed autonomy in production, marketing and procurement, but not in recruitment or bonus-setting. Comparing the two subunits, we see that A has approximately 1.8 times the basic salary plus subsidies of B, and 6.7 times more in bonuses. Subunit A's bonuses amount to 2.57 times its basic salary plus subsidies, whereas Subunit B's bonuses are much lower than its basic salary plus subsidies. In other words, in the hybrid subunit income consists primarily of bonuses, whereas in the state-owned subunit income consists primarily of basic salary.

Many other firms and subunits show similar income structures. Sino-foreign joint-ventured firms, partnerships, and subcontracting firms or subunits all tend to have bonuses that exceed basic salary plus subsidies. Indeed, for many firms and subunits, there is no longer *any* basic salary plus subsidies; instead, income consists entirely of bonuses from profit-sharing, based upon their performance under responsibility contracts and subcontracts. And, for some firms, although there is almost no differentiation in basic salary plus subsidies across subunits, there are huge disparities in bonuses. These disparities stem from profit-sharing that has not yet led to reforms in salary and subsidy systems.

3. Employees' Complaints and Resource Reallocation among Subunits

Income disparities among subunits within a firm generate complaints from lower-income subunits. Employees in these subunits tend to complain either to their subunit heads or directly to the firm's managers. As one manager explained:

> When income differences among subunits are large, the employees from the lower-income subunits come to me to complain. They usually do not ask for more pay; rather, they ask why the employees in other subunits have such high incomes, and request treatment similar to that enjoyed by the higher-income subunits: 'If we (i.e., our subunits) were given similar treatment, we would have performed as well.'...They do not ask for higher income because they know that they will not get it. Our firm simply does not have the budget to pay them more if they do not perform as well as they can. Well, sometimes headquarters may use revenues from the higher-income subunits to subsidize the lower-income ones a little bit, but the ability to do this is quite limited due to independent financial accounting at the subunit level. Moreover, employees in the high-income subunits would complain.

Despite the limitations noted by this manager, when lower-income subunits ask for treatment similar to that of higher-income subunits, they are often successful.

Another manager explained some of the arguments deployed by lower-income employees:

> When the income gaps among subunits are large, employees in the lower-income subunits will not be happy—and they will raise questions about the sources of the gaps. For instance, they tend to ask if the firm's resources (both financial and material) are being used appropriately and to find fault with higher-income subunits. This forces the firm's managers to either reallocate resources or monitor them more closely; it also forces the higher-income subunits to use resources more carefully, since they know that others will question what they are doing.

Yet another manager described his attempts to mitigate income differences:

> When I see that some subunits have higher incomes than others, I tend to question why this is so; I am very concerned that employees in lower-income subunits will complain....To avoid such complaints, I used to reduce the bonuses in higher-income subunits. But in doing so, I would immediately receive complaints from the employees in these subunits. I would also be dampening incentives in the higher-income subunits. As a result, the firm's income from profit-sharing might decline, and our welfare programs [such as housing] and bonuses could be affected—and that would just generate more complaints. What I often have to do now is force the other subunits—the lower-income ones—to perform well.

Many managers recognized that income disparities are not always caused by differences in performance. Instead, they may be due to unfair distribution of resources and opportunities across subunits (a fact observed by employees themselves, as noted earlier).[10] Under profit-sharing systems, profits are related to responsibilities and rights, which are in turn linked to possession of resources. Suppose that subunit A owns more resources than B, and that the performance of each subunit is measured by output rate. Clearly, subunit A will be able to outperform B. When employees in disadvantaged subunits question the distribution of resources, existing resources may be reallocated across subunits or the subunits' performance norms may be revised. These measures result in a more equitable environment inside the firm.

Income differentiation between subunits also stimulates competition. Especially in firms where subunits are responsible for themselves financially (with bonuses depending upon performance), lower-income subunits tend to mimic the behavior of higher-income ones. When employees in a lower-income subunit complain, the subunit head may simply pressures those employees to improve their performance so as to earn larger bonuses. Alternatively, the employees may cooperate with managers, helping their own subunit compete with more profitable ones. For instance, employees with relatives overseas may try to generate business for their subunits by exploring overseas business ties. Or employees may help promote their subunit's products. According to one manager:

> Our competitive motivation originates in income differentiation. When you see someone with a larger bonus than your own, you will naturally think that you should have as much—or more. Bonuses are very motivating; to get bonuses,

you have to perform well, because under the current profit-sharing system bonuses are determined by performance.

Another manager put it this way:

> When there are no differences in income across subunits, ours will not care what others have done. But when such differences exist, each subunit tends to observe others; in particular, the subunits with lower incomes tend to look at those with higher incomes, and to mimic what the latter have done. Any difference can drive you, your employees, and others to question why that difference exists.

Further competition results when a higher-income subunit, finding its own behavior mimicked by others, tries to perform still better. For only when it does still better can it gain still larger bonuses for its employees.

4. Mimicking and the Diffusion of Organizational Forms

As the preceding discussion indicates, contract forms and management methods that are successfully used in some hybrid subunits will sooner or later be introduced into other subunits. One manager notes:

> In 1986, a Sino-foreign joint-ventured subunit was set up in our firm. Since then, I have been looking very closely at what that subunit does. I observe how its responsibility system is implemented—how it defines responsibilities and rights for its employees, how it sets up internal reward and penalty systems, what contract forms it uses—because I want other subunits to learn something from it. Indeed, from the joint-ventured subunit, we *are* learning, little by little. Last year, for example, the sales department formed a partnership with two domestic firms, and we introduced similar methods into this Sino-Sino joint venture. As our local government says, 'one major purpose of establishing Sino-foreign joint-ventured businesses is to use them as windows, through which we can learn advanced management experiences from the outside world.'

Another manager said:

As of 1983, my firm had only one subunit that had formed a joint venture—with a German firm, to develop a new product for international markets. By 1985, three other subunits had formed joint ventures, with a Hong Kong firm and two domestic firms, to upgrade some of our key products and to market them. Our firm is now totally joint-ventured, with each subunit having its own partners; four subunits are completely independent, financially. Sometimes, when one subunit sees that others have more profits from domestic markets than from overseas markets, it too will shift its focus to domestic markets in the hope that it can increase its profits. And, of course, the opposite shift can also occur. In other words, although all the subunits are joint-ventured, they still imitate one another.

Yet another said:

Now, hybrid subunits and non-hybrid ones no longer seem very different, in terms of management style—except that the former, of course, have mixed organizational forms.

It is typically pressure from employees in lower-income subunits that causes those subunits to mimic the behavior of hybrid subunits inside or outside the firm. But pressure to adopt more efficient methods—to mimic—may also come from the firm's managers and from employees in subunits with higher income, as well as from employees in the low-income subunits themselves. Subunits that lose money due to poor performance become a drag on the overall performance of their firms. It is usually the firm as a whole that enters contracts with government bureaus and other firms, subcontracting quotas to its own subunits. If some subunits fail to fulfill their quotas, it is the firm as a whole that sustains any penalties stipulated in the contracts it has signed. Losses of lagging units tend to be absorbed by more efficient ones—effectively resulting in cross-subsidies among subunits. Or the efficient subunits may have to help the laggards fulfill their quotas, so the profit-sharing of the firm as a whole will not be affected.

One subunit manager vividly describes the external pressures resulting from lagging performance:

The firm manager would often say to me 'you've got to do something to improve your subunit, otherwise you're going to become a financial strain on the whole firm.' Our section has been sustaining serious financial losses, due to mismanagement in marketing over a two-year period. The firm manager wanted us to start turning a profit within a year; otherwise, financial penalties would be imposed on our subunit's employees and on me. He has pushed us very hard, really very hard. Employees from more efficient subunits also came to me to complain, because they have had to use some of their profits to offset our losses....To be honest with you, the pressure on me is often intense. Facing such pressure, I tend to look at the more efficient subunits to see how they are run, in the hope that we can improve ourselves financially by copying them.

It is clear from our interviews that interactions occur frequently between employees on the one hand and their subunit heads and firm managers on the other. The interviews, however, reveal little about interactions between the employees in different subunits. One possible explanation is that, in general, only the complaints from employees to subunit heads and firm managers can actually force managers to take action.

5. Diffusion Paths

Among the most common objects of emulation are contract forms. Most frequently, the contract forms used in the sampled firms originated in their business partners, domestic or foreign.[11] One managers explained:

When we decided in 1984 to set up a joint venture in Hong Kong with a Hong Kong firm, we began to discuss the contract forms to be used within the ventured firm—among the firm's headquarters, subunits, and employees. Our partner gave us some contract forms used in many Hong Kong firms, suggesting that the joint-ventured firm could use them too. In fact, we used them as blueprints, discussing and revising each item to come up with the forms to be used in the joint venture. I found the contract forms quite useful, and suitable for our domestic firm, so I recommended them; our domestic firm began to use the same contract forms internally. The domestic firm has joint ventures with firms in Fuzhou and Quanzhou;

the contract forms have also been used in dealings with the domestic venture partners.

Many other managers told similar stories. Hybrid subunits with foreign partners seem to be the arena where new contract forms are first used.

It is natural that contract forms tend to appear first in business activities with foreign partners, because the forms are part of international practice. When you have business with foreign firms, you will certainly need to adopt such practice.

Sometimes contract forms and management methods also come to a particular firm from its local government. According to one manager:

When I was first asked by our municipal government to use the responsibility contract forms it preferred, I was very reluctant because I was not sure that doing so would help our firm. But I had no choice but to use them. After a while, I came to like them, and so did other managers, because any activities related to the municipal government were clearly specified. Our responsibilities and rights are clear to us, and so are rewards and penalties. This minimizes disputes later on.

Even in cases such as this one, though, the contract forms proposed by local government first originated in other firms' business activities with foreign counterparts.

Over time, the diffusion of organizational innovations appears to follow a characteristic sequence. Consider a single innovation. Early on, in phase 1, diffusion from foreign-invested firms (including wholly foreign-owned firms and Sino-foreign joint ventures) to domestic firms predominates. Gradually, more and more *domestic* firms become agents of diffusion—until the predominant path, in phase 2, is from some domestic firms (the early adopters) to other domestic firms. For example, beginning in 1987 the Xiamen government issued a series of documents suggesting various kinds of contract forms and regulations to govern the business activities of municipal bureaus and firms. These documents specified very clearly that the contract forms and regulations pertained to management methods in foreign-invested firms—the rights and responsibilities of parties to contracts, financial and labor management, import, export, and foreign currency management, accounting, and auditing. In fact, the government was extending to domestic firms the methods used in, or used to govern, foreign-invested firms, clearly an instance of "phase 1" diffusion.

Diffusion originates in foreign-invested firms for two major reasons. First, foreign partners tend to introduce international practices and management methods. Second, in their efforts to attract foreign firms, both the central and local governments tend to introduce regulations favoring foreign-invested firms and accommodating their methods. Domestic firms, impressed by the success of foreign-invested firms, then seek to adopt similar methods. This often leads to legalization, and even government promotion, of the methods in question, for domestic firms.

While the diffusion process within and among firms can be complicated, and varies from one case to another, our interviews show that it tends to occur most frequently and rapidly in forms of investment, forms of profit-sharing, reward and penalty systems, internal subcontracting systems, and labor management. In discussing forms of investment, for example, one manager said:

> Our firm had very limited knowledge of what our side might contribute to a joint venture, until one of our subunits entered into a joint venture with a foreign firm in 1981. In negotiating with the foreign partner, we realized that many resources in our firm could be used as contributions to an investment project. We contributed land to that project, because we then had a lot of land but were relatively weak in technology and capital. Suddenly, we came to see land as a very valuable resource, through which we could obtain technology and capital in ventured form. We also learned a lot about land values and rents. We applied this idea of using land as our contribution to a joint venture again in 1984—in that instance, to a venture with a domestic firm from Shanghai, which contributed an electronic production line as its share....In fact, in the Shanghai venture, we also adopted the contract forms used in our earlier Sino-foreign joint venture. We suggested these forms to our Shanghai partner; both sides then discussed them item by item to come up with suitably revised versions. Using the contract forms from the Sino-foreign venture greatly simplified our contract negotiations with the Shanghai partner, because we had an idea of what should be included in our contracts—even though the specifics of the contracts would be quite different from those of the Sino-foreign venture.

Both our Sino-foreign venture and our Sino-Sino venture were formed by subunits inside our firm. Recently, due to the expansion of the Sino-Sino project, it has begun to subcontract part of its production to other firms....In most cases of external subcontracting, similar contract forms and ideas are used, with revised profit-sharing ratios and the reward and penalty systems. Although external subcontracting arrangements differ from the joint ventures, the basic principles for profit-sharing and for the provision of responsibilities and rights are quite similar.

Firms borrow contract forms and management methods from others, and then revise or combine them so as to fit their own needs. A contract form used in one subunit or one firm may be a combination of several contract forms from several subunits and firms. Thus, the adoption process itself is hybrid. One manager explained:

When I look at a contract form used in subunit A, I may see some provisions that are quite useful to my subunit. Similarly, when I look at forms used by other subunits, I may find some additional provisions of use to us. I tend to incorporate the provisions I find into our own contract form. Other subunits or firms may do the same thing. In the end, everyone's contract form will be a combination of provisions from everyone else's.

Another manager described a similar process:

Currently, we have many foreign investors coming to our firm to discuss various projects. These investors are from Hong Kong, Taiwan, Macao, and other places. They usually present contract forms and management methods they think should be used in a proposed project. And sometimes we too propose contract forms and management methods. Having carried on discussions with several firms, we are now familiar with many contract forms. Often, we either choose the one that will be the most suitable for our firm's situation or work one out by combining suitable provisions from what we have seen and what we have at hand.

In short, adoption is a mutual process: that is to say, when A adopts from B, C, and D, they may also adopt something from A.

In revising contract forms to fit their own situations, firms tend to make changes mainly in provisions for profit-sharing and for rewards and penalties. For instance, a firm operating at a profit will be in a different position from a firm operating at a loss, as regards the provision on profit-sharing. For the former firm, rewards are based on profits realized; for the latter, rewards are based on the amount by which the loss is reduced. The fact that there are five distinct types of responsibility contracts reflects the diffusion of contract forms among subunits inside firms and across firms and regions, with adaptation to fit very different needs.[12]

Although I do not have enough evidence to specify exactly how long diffusion inside a firm, a local area, or a larger region will take, it is clear that diffusion is most rapid within a firm, and more rapid within a local area than across a larger region. First, there are more interactions arising from income differentiation among the manager, subunit heads, and employees inside a particular firm than there are interactions across an area or region. Second, local governments' policies tend to favor diffusion within their administrative areas, as compared to diffusion across administrative boundaries (and, hence, across a larger region).

6. Conclusions

Income differentiation among subunits in firms has resulted in interactions among employees, subunit heads, and firm managers; such interactions have in turn resulted in more equitable treatment across subunits and a more efficient environment inside firms. Perhaps more importantly, they have also resulted in a process by which successful organizational innovations are diffused among subunits (and firms).

By examining the adoption of new contract forms, this paper has shown that hybrid subunits play a crucial role in the diffusion process. The evidence surveyed also suggested the sort of dynamic—driven by profit-seeking, competition, and emulation, and facilitated by government action—underlying the observed pattern of diffusion.

The process of organizational innovation demonstrated here is probably not unique to contracts and to Xiamen. This case, therefore, may provide clues relevant to the larger process of market transition in China and to the forces that have sustained that process.

Notes

1. The author gratefully acknowledges support provided by the East Asia Program at Cornell, through an LT Lam Award for South China Research.

2. The firm in question is one of those sampled for this paper, as explained later in this section.

3. The "state" to which this manager refers is the municipal government. This quote, and those later in the paper, are drawn from a set of interviews conducted during 1990-91, as explained at the end of this section.

4. Victor Nee, "Peasant Entrepreneurship and the Politics of Regulation in China," in Victor Nee and David Stark (eds.), *Remarking the Economic Institutions of Socialism: China and Eastern Europe* (Stanford: Stanford University Press, 1989), pp. 169-207; Victor Nee, "Organizational Dynamics of Market Transition: Hybrid Forms, Property Rights, and Mixed Economy in China," *Administrative Science Quarterly*, 37, 1992, pp. 1-27; and Victor Nee and Si-jin Su, "Local Corporatism and Informal Privatization in China's Market Transition" (paper presented at the conference on "The Evolution of Market Institutions in Transition Economies," Graduate School of International Relations and Pacific Studies, University of California, San Diego, May 1993). See also Douglass C. North, *Institutions, Institutional Change, and Economic Performance* (Cambridge: Cambridge University Press, 1990), and Oliver E. Williamson, "Comparative Economic Organization: The Analysis of Discrete Structural Alternatives," *Administrative Science Quarterly*, 36, 1991, pp. 269-96.

5. Michael J. Piore and Charles F. Sabel, *The Second Industrial Divide: Possibilities for Prosperity* (New York: Basic Books, 1984); and Michael Storper, "The Transition to Flexible Specialization in the US Film Industry: External Economies, Division of Labor, and the Crossing of Industrial Divides," *Cambridge Journal of Economics*, 13, 1989, pp. 273-305.

6. William A. Byrd, "The Impact of the Two-Tier Plan/Market System in Chinese Industry," in Bruce L. Reynolds (ed.), *Chinese Economic Reform: How Far, How Fast?* (New York: Academic Press, 1988), pp. 5-8.

7. Christine P. W. Wong, "Between Plan and Market: The Role of the Local Sector in Post-Mao China," *Journal of Comparative Economics*, 11, 1987, pp. 385-98.

8. "Partially" financially independent, because the subunit assumes responsibility for part of its investment capital and all of its losses, with part of its investment capital coming from the firm's headquarters and with headquarters sharing in any profits.

9. The bonuses a firm can award are usually governed by regulations of the Ministry of Finance, the provincial government, and the municipal government. These regulations specify (1) which firms are allowed to link bonuses with their performance; and (2) the maximum annual bonuses they can award. The maximum limit regulation generally does not apply to Sino-foreign joint ventures.

10. For further discussion, see Si-jin Su, "Hybrid Forms in the South China Mixed Economy: Dynamics of Internal Subcontracting Arrangements and Negotiations" (paper presented at the conference on "Explaining Transitions from State Socialism," Cornell University, May 1992).

11. Su, "Hybrid Forms."

12. Si-jin Su, "Responsibility Contract Systems: The Nature of Chinese Firms" (paper presented at the conference "Asian Studies on the Pacific Coast," California Polytechnic State University, June 1992).

Taiwan's DFI in Mainland China:
Impact on the Domestic and Host Economies

CHUNG Chin

1. Introduction

There are two strands of empirical literature concerning the economic impact of direct foreign investment (DFI) upon the host (DFI-receiving) and home (DFI-originating) countries.[1] The first strand, usually adopting the view of the less developed countries, concerns itself mainly with the effects of DFI flows on the host economy's employment, output, technological progress, and balance of payments.[2] The second strand, on the other hand, centers around such issues as the possibility of industrial "hollowing-out" in investment-originating countries, the long-term competitiveness of their domestic industries, and the trespassing on national sovereignty by multinational corporations.[3] Despite conceptual reciprocity and almost identical analytical tools, these two strands of literature have been developed more or less independently, which in part reflects the asymmetry in social aspirations as well as in economic circumstances between the DFI-receiving and the DFI-emanating countries.[4] Another possible reason for this dichotomy may be a lack of proper samples that lend themselves readily to simultaneous reciprocal analyses. Take DFI by the U.S. in ASEAN for example: since it constitutes a small share in the world-wide network of U.S. multinational operations, it makes relatively little sense, or so it seems, for either the home or the host country to analyze the feedback effects on the U.S. economy of the said capital flow. Likewise, since U.S. DFI represents only a portion of total foreign resources injected into the host countries, local governments are typically more concerned with the aggregate volume and industrial orientation of foreign capital rather than with its country-specific origins.[5] A simultaneous study of the two sets of effects (i.e., those on the host and the home economy) becomes viable, and even necessary, when the originating and recipient countries mutually count "heavy" in their reciprocal roles with respect to DFI flows. Taiwan's

Table 1. Major Recipients of Taiwan's Outward DFI, 1984-91

	1984	1985	1986	1987	1988	1989	1990	1991
United States	30.5	35.7	46.0	70.0	123.3	508.7	428.7	298.0
Europe		0.9	0.2	10.2	17.0	73.3	265.9	350.2
Malaysia			4.1	91.0	313.0	815.0	2383.0	741.0
Thailand				70.0	300.0	842.0	871.0	761.0	124.4
Indonesia			18.0	8.0	913.0	158.0	618.0	902.7
Philippines			0.4	9.0	109.0	149.0	140.7	11.6
Mainland China				100.0	421.0	523.0	984.0	1385.2

Note: All figures in million US dollars.

Sources: Investment Commission, Ministry of Economic Affairs, Taiwan, April, 1992 (for U.S. and European figures); Industrial Development and Investment Center, Ministry of Economic Affairs, Taiwan, based on host-country BOI reports (for ASEAN); *China Economic News* (Beijing) various issues (for mainland China).

recent surge of DFI toward mainland China provides just this special analytical setting.

The initiation of Taiwan's outward DFI may be traced back to the 1960s. Overseas operations at that early stage, however, were sporadic in nature and did not show any obvious trend. The situation changed gradually over the '70s as the pool of surplus labor in the economy steadily drew near, and eventually passed, its point of exhaustion. Especially after the mid-80s, the escalation of domestic labor cost, coupled with pressure from currency appreciation, has forced export-oriented Taiwanese manufacturers to diversify their production bases into Southeast Asia, the U.S., the EC, and also mainland China, in an attempt to rehabilitate their threatened competitiveness in the world market.[6] Table 1 shows the growing momentum of DFI activities during the '80s. One observes an abrupt rise in DFI toward mainland China, which overtook almost all other destinations soon after 1987—when the Taiwan government lifted its ban on kinship visits to the mainland after a 40-year freeze.

While changes in domestic macroeconomic conditions constitute the "push" factor common to all recent DFI activities emanating from Taiwan, it is the traditional ties between the two sides of the Taiwan Strait that explain in good part the rapid movement of Taiwanese DFI toward mainland China, particularly for smaller-sized firms. Cultural and linguistic identity effectively lowers the implicit barriers to entry typically faced by

Table 2. Major Sources of DFI in Mainland China, 1979-91

	Hong Kong	U.S.	Japan	Taiwan
1979-84	64.9	10.2	11.5	
1985	41.3	11.5	4.7	
1986	14.4	5.3	2.1	
1987	19.5	3.4	3.0	1.0
1988	34.7	3.7	2.7	4.2
1989	31.6	6.4	4.4	5.2
1990	36.8	3.6	4.6	9.9
1991	75.1	5.5	8.1	13.9
1987-91, total	197.7	22.6	22.8	34.2
1979-91, total	318.3	49.6	41.1	34.2

Note: All figures are 100 million US dollars, contracted value.

Sources: Editorial Board of the Almanac of China's Foreign Economic Relations, *Almanac of China's Foreign Economic Relations and Trade* (Hong Kong: China Resources and Trade Consultancy), various issues.

a foreign investor. With negligible entry costs in this sense and an added convenience of geographical proximity, Taiwan's direct investment into mainland China soared from 0.1 billion US dollars in 1987 to 1.4 billion in 1991, with another 3 billion US dollars projected for 1992.

2. Characterization of Taiwan's DFI in Mainland China

According to official statistics from mainland China, Taiwan's cumulative DFI ranked fourth, behind Hong Kong, the U.S., and Japan at the end of 1991 (Table 2). In terms of manufacturing investment, however, Taiwan may be second only to Hong Kong, since U.S. and Japanese investments are more often tilted toward resource- and service-related activities. In particular, if we compare the figures after 1987, Taiwan clearly outperformed both the U.S. and Japan in its volume of investment on the mainland.

Unlike the western and Japanese multinationals that possess sophisticated technologies, well-known brand names, and oligopolistic market power in the international arena, Taiwan's DFI firms, like those of

Table 3. Registered Taiwan DFI in Mainland China, by Industry

	Industry	Invested Value (thousand USD)	Number of Cases	Average Size (thousand USD)
1.	Electric and electronic products	102,748	242	425
2.	Nonmotorized vehicles	78,923	202	391
3.	Footwear	58,751	306	192
4.	Services	56,472	62	186
5.	Plastic products	44,582	129	346
6.	Textiles	31,995	74	432
7.	Metal products	30,440	85	358
8.	Agricultural products and livestock	21,378	35	611
9.	Athletic products	20,348	59	345
10.	Apparel	17,876	106	169
11.	Lamp Decorations	17,566	67	262
12.	Handbags and suitcases	16,466	40	412
13.	Wood processing	15,688	46	341
14.	Food processing	13,807	39	354
15.	Electrical appliances	13,343	37	361
16.	Woolen textiles	13,012	62	210
17.	Handicrafts	11,062	48	231
18.	Clocks and timers	10,989	12	916
19.	Umbrellas	10,829	62	175
20.	Vegetable and fruit processing	10,609	36	295
21.	Pottery and china	10,214	54	189
22.	Bamboo products	10,210	48	213
23.	Machinery	9461	30	315
24.	Medical equipment	9251	10	925
25.	Mine and stone products	8964	28	320

Table 3, continued

	Industry	Invested Value (thousand USD)	Number of Cases	Average Size (thousand USD)
26.	Petrochemicals	7158	37	194
27.	Paper products	6920	15	461
28.	Leather	6680	58	115
29.	Paper-making	6680	11	607
30.	Sanitary products	6675	36	185
31.	Zippers	6490	10	649
32.	Rubber	6478	31	209
33.	Trade services	6393	37	173
34.	Spectacles	5593	14	400
35.	Toys	5126	56	92
36.	Knitting	4945	24	206
37.	Glasswork	4920	10	492
38.	Frozen fish	4557	19	240
39.	Kitchen and bathroom equipment	3761	22	171
40.	Pharmaceuticals	3007	11	273
41.	Furniture	2891	15	193
42.	Printing	2793	21	133
43.	Gloves	2247	15	150
44.	Motor Vehicles	2185	7	312
45.	Dyeing	2030	5	406
46.	Fertilizers	1800	1	1800
47.	Lacquer and paint	1655	15	110
48.	Educational materials	1518	6	253
49.	Fishery equipment	1328	2	664
50.	Hand tools	1318	6	220

Table 3, continued

	Industry	Invested Value (thousand USD)	Number of Cases	Average Size (thousand USD)
51.	Gift products	903	14	65
52.	Optics	751	4	188
53.	Pearls and jewelry	410	7	59
54.	Synthetic resins	400	3	133
55.	Aquatic breeding	185	2	93
56.	Others	980	98	15
	All industries	753,915	2503	301

Source: Investment Commission, Ministry of Economic Affairs, Taiwan, May 1991.

Hong Kong, are characterized by ample OEM (original equipment manufacturing) experience and by dexterity in labor-intensive production techniques. In fact, a successful drive to export labor-intensive products under the auspices of western and Japanese industrial conglomerates and trading giants explains, in good part, the miraculous growth of the Taiwan economy over the past 40 years. Now that comparative advantage has shifted against labor-intensive production at home, Taiwanese manufacturers have chosen to embody their production know-how and well-established OEM network in the form of self-initiated DFI operations based in another low-wage country. Table 3 presents a listing of DFI activities on the mainland that were registered with the Taipei authorities as of April 8, 1991. It is obvious that most of the investment projects fall within the labor-intensive categories. Moreover, the majority of these operations are export-oriented instead of being geared toward the local market. According to one survey of 153 Taiwanese DFI firms across 61 different industries, 85-90 percent of the output produced on the mainland in 1990 was shipped to a third market, about 6 percent was shipped back to Taiwan, and less than 10 percent was retained for sale on the mainland.[7] A more recent survey reveals that, on average, 88.63 percent of the output produced in 1991 was directly exported to a third market.[8] Thus the behavioral pattern of Taiwan DFI in mainland China, at least until recently, fits nicely with the "defensive" prototype (*a la* Kojima), which stresses cost-reduction in defending existing markets (in this case the world export market) as the underlying driving force of outward DFI.[9]

In addition to being "defensive" in nature, the investment projects listed in Table 3 are typically small-scale, reflecting in part the underlying enterprise structure of the Taiwan economy.[10] The scale factor, however, is more apparent on the mainland than elsewhere, probably due to political reasons (i.e., risk aversion under existing tensions across the Strait) and the lower barriers to entry mentioned previously. For example, the average size of a Taiwan investment in Malaysia (the largest ASEAN recipient of Taiwan's DFI) is 3.6 million US dollars, over 12 times the average size of an investment in mainland China (Table 4). On the other hand, the frequency of investment is clearly much higher on the mainland than in Malaysia—2,503 DFI projects, as compared to 339. This implies that mainland China stands out as an ideal destination for relocation of Taiwan's threatened labor-intensive lines of production, even though currently these investments are still being made on a trial basis due to political uncertainties. If political tensions across the Taiwan Strait continue to ease, one may expect a rapid expansion of the total volume of DFI on the mainland, as well as the average size and the range of manufacturing activities in which DFI occurs.

Another notable characteristic of Taiwan's DFI that has important implications for the host country is its tendency to rely heavily on home sources for intermediate inputs. Ouyang, Lin, and Chou reported in 1991 that, on average, 86.61 percent of the machinery and equipment and 69.94 percent of the raw materials, semi-products, components, and parts required in overseas production were shipped from Taiwan.[11] The remainder were procured from a variety of sources, including upstream DFI firms originating in Taiwan; however, only minimal amounts were furnished locally by mainland producers. This pattern of international sourcing is frequently observed for DFI operations worldwide, as it provides a ready channel for internal transactions between the parent firm and the overseas subsidiary when the two entities are vertically integrated production-wise. Even in the absence of substantial parent-subsidiary internal linkages, as is often the case with Taiwanese DFI whose parent firms are usually quite specialized, reliance on a long-standing network of customer-supplier relationships seems a better way to guarantee a stable supply of inputs and to ensure the quality of output in the face of fierce international competition. Several institutional factors peculiar to the mainland economy, however, also reinforce this tendency toward outward purchase by DFI firms. The first of these institutional factors is the virtual non-existence of a consumer-goods industrial base, especially in coastal areas of Fujian

Table 4. Taiwan's DFI toward Malaysia, 1987-89 (Cumulative)

	Industry	Invested Value (thousand USD)	Number of Cases	Average Size (thousand USD)
1.	Electric and electronic products	508,418	102	4984
2.	Chemicals and chemical products	112,480	10	11,248
3.	Textile products	103,062	26	3964
4.	Processed foods	101,901	8	12,738
5.	Lumber and wood products	68,223	32	2132
6.	Nonmetallic products	66,539	10	6654
7.	Rubber and rubber products	65,851	55	1197
8.	Furniture	48,192	24	2008
9.	Metal products	29,860	12	2488
10.	Basic metals	20,594	13	1584
11.	Plastic products	20,312	11	1847
12.	Machinery	13,520	6	2253
13.	Transportation equipment	12,143	7	1735
14.	Paper, printing, and publishing	4485	5	897
15.	Scientific and precision measuring instruments	2698	1	2698
16.	Leather and leather products	1585	1	1585
17.	Others	30,743	16	1921
	Total	1,210,606	339	3571

Note: All data pertain to contracted values.

Source: Malaysian Board of Investment, 1990.

and Guangdong where the four special economic zones are located, due to relative neglect of these industries by the mainland authorities prior to the policy reversal of 1979. As a result, very few indigenous producers are as yet capable of supplying semi-products, components, and parts in accordance with DFI firms' specifications. The second factor limiting the degree of local involvement is the predominance on the mainland of large-scale, low-efficiency, state-owned enterprises, whose potential to furnish local supplies is handicapped by red tape, poor management, obsolete techniques, and insufficient quality control. The third factor is the poor state of transportation, which causes frequent delays. These factors together cause the emergence of a DFI "export enclave," which has little spillover into the local economy, but which is viewed by DFI firms as a more efficient way to regain their competitive edge in the world marketplace.

3. Impact on the Taiwan and Mainland Economies: An Input-Output Analysis

If in fact the current Taiwanese DFI in mainland China is basically "defensive" in nature, one may expect to find a concomitant "export shift" from Taiwan to the mainland along with the transfer of production sites. That is, in the heavily-invested industries Taiwan's exports, as well as employment and output, will tend to shrink, while those of the mainland will expand. On the earnings side, however, since intermediate inputs have to be acquired from outside mainland China and little room is left for local spillovers, foreign exchange earnings for the host economy will consist mainly of wage bills and rental payments on land and factory units. The lion's share of the export earnings will be kept in the hands of Taiwanese investors and, more often than not, remain outside the mainland economy.

Over the past few years, Taiwan's output and employment did shrink in such labor-intensive industries as wearing apparel, leather products, wood products, and textiles. The manufacturing production index for these sectors, using 1986 as the base year, showed a steady decline after 1987 and plummeted to 63.48-92.05 in 1990 (Table 5). Even in the more strategic and dynamic sectors, such as electronics and precision instruments, there have been signs of stagnation during 1989-90. Recall also that Taiwan has experienced a severe labor shortage in recent years, particularly in the manufacturing sector. The extent of the problem is vividly shown in Table 6. For the manufacturing sector as a whole, employment dropped from 2,624,100 people in 1987 to 2,186,400 in 1991, a net loss of 437,700 jobs (or 17 percent of the 1987 employment level) in four years. Particularly traumatized were the labor-intensive industries, including textiles, apparel, leather, wood, plastics, non-metallic products, and electrical and electronic

Table 5. Manufacturing Production Index, Taiwan, 1987-91 (1986=100)

		1987	1988	1989	1990	1991
	All Manufacturing	111.19	115.39	119.28	117.28	125.27
1.	Processed foods	104.57	105.77	103.54	108.57	111.83
2.	Beverages and tobacco	105.85	111.69	123.16	138.43	151.10
3.	Textile products	104.73	94.03	97.55	92.05	98.77
4.	Wearing apparel	102.66	85.61	83.87	75.75	75.05
5.	Leather, fur, and articles thereof	100.88	95.85	93.46	85.98	90.14
6.	Wood, bamboo, and rattan products	103.48	93.20	86.75	63.48	66.06
7.	Pulp, paper products, and printed matter	106.29	110.02	120.79	126.37	133.35
8.	Chemicals	103.65	108.01	110.30	119.61	136.60
9.	Chemical products	117.66	127.89	136.45	129.55	152.46
10.	Rubber and plastic products	112.35	118.05	115.30	107.89	111.66
11.	Non-metallic mineral products	105.99	110.08	115.77	117.87	121.06
12.	Basic metals	107.46	120.34	126.99	129.67	143.45
13.	Metal products	111.50	120.01	126.64	122.41	131.92
14.	Machinery	117.81	134.03	135.35	139.46	149.40
15.	Electrical machinery and apparatus	123.68	136.27	142.60	141.15	153.97
16.	Transportation equipment	122.82	125.17	148.23	152.48	160.45
17.	Precision instruments and equipment	114.72	131.71	147.31	144.51	153.97
	Others	110.88	116.44	111.13	100.29	101.13

Source: *Industrial Production Statistics Monthly* (Department of Statistics, Ministry of Economic Affairs, Republic of China), April 1992.

Table 6. Manufacturing Employment in Taiwan, 1987-1991

		1987	1988	1989	1990	1991
	All Manufacturing	2624.1	2580.7	2452.6	2260.1	2186.4
1.	Processed foods	127.0	119.1	115.4	116.3	115.8
2.	Beverages and tobacco	16.0	16.8	18.2	20.2	20.5
3.	Textile products	291.9	279.6	254.7	215.5	201.5
4.	Wearing apparel	140.2	129.4	109.9	92.8	86.2
5.	Leather, fur, and articles thereof	69.7	66.5	59.5	49.9	45.9
6.	Wood, bamboo, and rattan products	120.8	114.9	103.7	84.2	74.8
7.	Pulp, paper, and printed matter	108.8	112.6	113.4	110.7	111.1
8.	Chemicals	61.5	62.3	60.1	60.0	59.9
9.	Chemical products	66.2	67.6	70.5	71.0	70.3
10.	Rubber and plastic products	334.6	331.0	301.5	253.8	238.3
11.	Non-metallic mineral products	102.7	100.1	96.8	91.1	88.1
12.	Basic metals	78.4	80.3	80.1	75.1	74.3
13.	Metal products	232.6	237.3	237.7	228.3	228.1
14.	Machinery	105.8	110.9	115.1	117.3	118.3
15.	Electrical machinery and apparatus	446.6	439.4	418.2	397.5	384.9
16.	Transportation equipment	127.0	128.2	127.9	125.8	125.2
17.	Precision instruments and equipment	39.7	39.8	38.6	37.4	37.8
	Others	154.6	144.9	131.3	113.2	105.4

Note: All data in thousands of persons.

Source: *Monthly Statistics of the Republic of China* (Directorate-General of the Budget, Republic of China), April 1992.

equipment, each of which suffered a loss of 10-80 thousand workers during that period. Similarly, the export performance of these sectors has been on the decline. Table 7 shows the changing structure of exports for all manufactured products between 1987 and 1991. Aside from generating much smaller shares in 1991 than in 1987, some of the above-mentioned industries (e.g., apparel and leather goods) actually saw an absolute contraction in their export volumes after 1989.

All of this, however, is not simply a consequence of surging Taiwanese DFI but rather part and parcel of its contributing factors: the causation here runs both ways and one tends to reinforce the other. Moreover, there may be cyclical movements around a trend of structural transformation, such that short-run and long-run adjustments are intricately intertwined. What proportion, then, of the observed aggregate changes may be attributed to the recent wave of Taiwanese DFI toward mainland China *per se*?

To answer this question, we conducted an industrial linkage analysis, based on the officially registered investment volume of 754 million US dollars (as of April 1991) and the 1986 input-output table for the Taiwan economy. Our purpose is to gauge the potential impact on both the domestic and host economies in terms of output and employment changes and the extent of subsequent "export shifts." Compared with the cumulative investment from Taiwan of 2 billion US dollars registered with the Chinese authorities (as of end of 1990), our figure of 754 million dollars seems to be a severe underestimate. It may nonetheless serve as a good approximation for the "realized" capital inflow, since the mainland authorities report an average realization rate of DFI (from all sources) of roughly 45 percent of the contractual amount.[12] More importantly for our purpose, the registration data from Taipei provide us with detailed information on the distribution of investment projects across industries, which is essential for our analysis.

To clarify ideas, the transplantation of production activities immediately leads to an increase in overseas production at the expense of domestic output. The two quantities need not be the same, however, for at least two reasons. First, the productivity of capital may be different at home and abroad. Entrepreneurs carry out foreign investment projects in order to seek greater profits, so it is reasonable to assume a higher return on capital abroad than at home. The fact that DFI firms usually adopt more labor-intensive techniques of production also tends to boost the average productivity of capital abroad.[13] Second, as mentioned above, Taiwan's current DFI operations on the mainland involve very few local linkages and rely primarily on home sources for raw materials and intermediate inputs.

Therefore, despite the displacement of "first-round" activities from a linkage-analysis point of view, the second and later rounds of spillover effects are retained domestically as long as the "home purchase" policy prevails. This tends to mitigate the net effect on domestic output while accelerating export trade from the home country to the host. Given production technologies, employment changes at home and abroad are a direct result of variations in the respective output levels. And given the size of overseas production, the extent of "export shifts" within the DFI sectors is determined by the average propensity to export of the DFI firms.

Equations (1) to (6) summarize these theoretical considerations:

(1) $\Delta Y^* = \Delta K_i(Y_i^*/K_i)$

(2) $\Delta T = \delta D \Delta Y^*$

(3) $\Delta Y = B \Delta T - B[\Delta K_i(Y_i/K_i)]$

(4) $\Delta L = \Delta Y(L_i/Y_i)$

(5) $\Delta L^* = \Delta Y^*(L_i^*/Y_i)$

(6) $\Delta X^* = \alpha \Delta Y^*$

where ΔY, ΔK, ΔT, ΔL and ΔX stand for changes in output, capital, investment-induced exports, employment, and exports of the invested industries bound for third markets, respectively. D is the 29-sector domestic input coefficient matrix, $B = [I-(I-\hat{M})A]^{-1}$ is the 29-sector competitive industrial linkage matrix (where $\hat{M}$ is the diagonal matrix of the import coefficient matrix M), Y_i/K_i and L_i/Y_i are the capital productivity and labor requirement ratios, and δ and α are the average propensities to purchase intermediate products from home and to export finished products to the third market, respectively. An asterisk is attached when the term refers to a foreign concern.

We obtained the relevant figures on Y_i/K_i and L_i/Y_i for each sector *i* from the 1986 Industrial and Commercial Census Report for the Taiwan Area. Lacking reliable empirical data, we tentatively assumed, on the basis of our previous considerations, that overseas capital productivity, Y_i^*/K_i, is 1.2 times its domestic counterpart, and that the overseas labor requirement per unit of output, L_i^*/Y_i, is 4-6 times that of Taiwan.[14] As to the values of δ and α, previous experience from DFI toward Southeast Asian countries indicates that overseas subsidiaries tend to maintain their former customer-

Table 7. Taiwan's Manufactured Exports, 1987-1991

		1987	1988	1989	1990	1991
		value (million US dollars)				
1.	Processed foods	2494	2331	2374	2302	2725
2.	Beverages and tobacco	19	22	22	20	37
3.	Textile products	3499	3859	4880	5504	6528
4.	Wearing apparel	5489	5155	5339	4481	5024
5.	Leather, fur, and articles thereof	1645	1857	1829	1389	1341
6.	Wood, bamboo, and rattan products	2230	2219	2208	1834	1937
7.	Pulp, paper, and printed matter	316	448	520	630	745
8.	Chemicals	974	1593	1804	1976	2333
9.	Chemical products	785	857	958	1025	1263
10.	Rubber and plastic products	5138	5631	5373	4778	5138
11.	Non-metallic mineral products	1156	1249	1197	1114	1166
12.	Basic metals	752	1314	1498	1366	1394
13.	Metal products	3228	3490	3966	4049	4764
14.	Machinery	2377	3190	3851	4232	4903
15.	Electrical machinery and apparatus	13,496	16,647	18,112	17,889	20,262
16.	Transportation equipment	2370	2521	3022	3434	3863
17.	Precision instruments and equipment	1054	1298	1552	1528	1822
	Others	5766	5869	5721	5118	5292
	Total manufactured exports	52,788	59,553	64,225	62,670	70,537

Table 7, continued

		1987	1988	1989	1990	1991
		share in total manufactured exports (%)				
1.	Processed foods	4.72	3.91	3.70	3.67	3.86
2.	Beverages and tobacco	0.04	0.04	0.03	0.03	0.05
3.	Textile products	6.63	6.48	7.60	8.78	9.25
4.	Wearing apparel	10.40	8.66	8.31	7.15	7.12
5.	Leather, fur, and articles thereof	3.12	3.12	2.85	2.22	1.90
6.	Wood, bamboo, and rattan products	4.22	3.73	3.44	2.93	2.75
7.	Pulp, paper, and printed matter	0.60	0.75	0.81	1.01	1.06
8.	Chemicals	1.85	2.67	2.81	3.15	3.31
9.	Chemical products	1.49	1.44	1.49	1.64	1.79
10.	Rubber and plastic products	9.73	9.46	8.37	7.62	7.28
11.	Non-metallic mineral products	2.19	2.10	1.86	1.78	1.65
12.	Basic metals	1.42	2.21	2.33	2.18	1.98
13.	Metal products	6.12	5.86	6.18	6.46	6.75
14.	Machinery	4.50	5.36	6.00	6.75	6.95
15.	Electrical machinery and apparatus	25.51	27.95	28.20	28.54	28.73
16.	Transportation equipment	4.49	4.23	4.71	5.48	5.48
17.	Precision instruments and equipment	2.00	2.18	2.42	2.44	2.58
	Others	10.92	9.86	8.91	8.17	7.50

Source: *Monthly Statistics of Exports and Imports* (Department of Statistics, Ministry of Finance, Republic of China), April 1992.

supplier relationships during their early years of operation and start to divert to local suppliers only after they have firmly established themselves in the host economy. Because Taiwan's DFI in mainland China is a relatively new phenomenon, and also because of the "DFI enclave" phenomenon discussed earlier, we assume $\delta=1$ for simplicity.[15] Finally, $\alpha = .70$ is a natural assumption for most of the export-oriented DFI in China today, since preferential tax treatment is associated with an export rate of 70 percent. In view of the previous survey results, however, one may take the estimates based on the assumed value of .70 as a lower bound on the actual extent of "export shifts."[16]

Table 8 presents our results. From column 5 of the table we see that, for Taiwan, the initial loss of output value due to production transplantation together with its multiplier effects on other sectors of the economy adds up to a total of 4.646 billion US dollars annually. This is nevertheless partly offset by increased overseas demand for raw materials and intermediate products (column 3), together with backward linkages totalling 2.400 billion dollars (column 4).[17] As a result, the net loss for the home economy in terms of static output decline is 2.246 billion dollars per annum, as shown in column 6 of Table 8. This figure is roughly 1.4 percent of Taiwan's actual GDP of 164.1 billion US dollars in 1990.

On the other hand, Taiwan's DFI operations directly generated an output value of 2.647 billion dollars on the mainland in 1990, roughly 0.8 percent of mainland China's GNP and over 25 percent of all foreign contributions to the mainland's industrial production.[18] More importantly, the influx of Taiwanese DFI has created thousands of new job openings every month in coastal areas of mainland China. It is estimated that, as of the end of 1990, between 282,000 and 423,000 mainlanders had been employed in the manufacturing sector due to Taiwanese investment (column 8), while the same flow of investment had resulted in a net reduction of 53,900 manufacturing jobs in Taiwan (column 7).[19]

The apparent asymmetry of the employment effect for the home and host economies arises from two sources. The first is the asymmetry embedded in the output effect, discussed previously, for the two economies. The other is the tendency for DFI firms to revert to more labor-intensive methods of production in an attempt to exploit the comparative advantage element of the host economy. For Taiwan's DFI firms, labor-intensive production technologies are familiar from the "good old days" when labor abundance rather than labor shortage was a fact of life. As they venture into mainland China, Taiwanese entrepreneurs are quick to adapt these technologies to the new environment—which they find similar to one they experienced in Taiwan 15-20 years ago. This strategy of capitalizing on the crude labor of mainland China based on Taiwanese production proficiency promised to bring handsome returns to both the investing and the invested parties. Therefore, aside from ample OEM experience and established market outlets, dexterity in labor-intensive methods of production seems to have been the most important "intangible asset" possessed by Taiwanese firms in their recent surge of DFI toward low-wage countries.[20]

Finally, regarding the extent of the export shift, column 9 of Table 8 indicates that, as a result of the registered investment flow to mainland China, the annual volume of exports designated "MIC" (Made in China) will increase, and the volume designated "MIT" will decrease, by 1.8 billion dollars.[21] This amounts to a 2.9 percent gain in export performance for mainland China, evaluated at the latter's 1990 actual export level of 62.1 billion US dollars, or a 2.7 percent loss for Taiwan, evaluated at its 1990 export level of 67.2 billion dollars. As pointed out earlier, however, this transfer of exports is more apparent than real, since the bulk of hard currency earnings fall into the hands of Taiwan investors. An estimated 294-420 million US dollars (approximately 11-16 percent of the annual overseas production value) go to the mainland authorities in the form of workers' compensation, which is stipulated by law to be paid in foreign exchange.[22] This and other miscellaneous expenses currently constitute the bulk of hard currency earnings for mainland China from Taiwanese DFI.

4. Longer-Term Adjustments and the Trade Friction Problem

The above static analysis ignores the long-term impact of DFI on the home and host economies. For the home country, the long-term issue is essentially one of industrial restructuring called forth by changing comparative advantage in the international division of labor. Restructuring poses a particularly serious challenge for a newly-industrialized economy such as Taiwan, which still lacks a firm grasp of advanced technologies for competing effectively in the "up market," and whose past economic performance was largely based on the very industries that are now exiting the country. To prevent the exodus of labor-intensive production from hampering the growth prospects of the economy, indigenous entrepreneurs must endeavor to upgrade their technology and to explore the higher ends of their product spectrums so that a healthy new pattern of parent-subsidiary division of labor may be established. Short of this effort, Taiwan's manufacturing sector may gradually lose its competitiveness in the world marketplace and a discomforting process of "industrial hollowing-out" may be inevitable.

Table 8. **Estimated Impact of DFI on the Taiwan and Mainland Economies**

	Industry	ΔK (1)	ΔY^* (2)	ΔT (3)	$B\Delta T$ (4)	$-B[\Delta K_i \times (Y_i/K_j)]$ (5)
1.	Agricultural products and livestock	(2137.8)	--	2934.3	6576.3	-6877.2
2.	Forestry	(0.0)	--	330.3	595.9	-679.4
3.	Fisheries	(18.5)	--	454.7	723.8	-767.6
4.	Minerals	(0.0)	--	530.2	2305.0	-2181.1
5.	Processed foods	2897.3	7996.6	1428.0	4084.8	-12,286.0
6.	Beverages and tobacco	0.0	0.0	13.4	31.2	-35.7
7.	Fabrics	3897.0	9726.9	21,780.8	34,542.3	-37,029.5
8.	Garments and accessories	10,505.8	56,226.0	6634.1	9880.3	-55,156.0
9.	Wood and wood products	2878.9	9016.7	2145.5	3062.1	-10,559.0
10.	Paper and paper products, printing, and publishing	1640.3	3758.6	4658.4	10,214.5	-12,074.6
11.	Chemical materials	180.0	423.4	3980.3	14,752.8	-13,044.1
12.	Artificial fibers, plastics, and products thereof	5146.0	21,798.4	19,534.5	40,172.4	-52,363.5
13.	Miscellaneous chemical products	484.7	1425.1	4497.3	8758.9	-8913.3
14.	Petroleum products	715.8	1365.7	2561.9	8179.7	-9249.6
15.	Non-metallic minerals	2409.8	3730.4	1357.4	2523.3	-5620.6
16.	Iron and steel	0.0	0.0	7741.7	22,001.1	-19,367.0

Table 8, continued

	Industry	ΔY (6)	ΔL (7)	ΔL* (8a)	ΔL* (8b)	ΔX* (9)
1.	Agricultural products and livestock	-300.9	--	--	--	--
2.	Forestry	-83.5	--	--	--	--
3.	Fisheries	-43.8	--	--	--	--
4.	Minerals	123.9	--	--	--	--
5.	Processed foods	-8201.2	-1454.9	5674.4	8511.5	5597.8
6.	Beverages and tobacco	-4.5	-0.3	0.0	0.0	0.0
7.	Fabrics	-2487.2	-576.1	9012.6	13,519.0	6808.8
8.	Garments and accessories	-45,275.7	-17,340.4	86,137.1	129,205.7	39,358.2
9.	Wood and wood products	-7496.9	-3438.9	16,544.4	24,816.6	6311.7
10.	Paper and paper products, printing, and publishing	-1860.1	-468.5	3771.9	5657.8	2631.7
11.	Chemical materials	1708.7	145.4	144.1	216.2	296.4
12.	Artificial fibers, plastics, and products thereof	-12,191.1	-2987.3	21,365.7	32,048.6	15,258.9
13.	Miscellaneous chemical products	-153.4	-28.8	995.7	1493.6	997.6
14.	Petroleum products	-1069.9	-57.8	295.1	422.7	956.0
15.	Non-metallic minerals	-3097.3	-826.8	3983.3	5975.0	2611.3
16.	Iron and steel	2634.1	287.0	0.0	0.0	0.0

Table 8, continued

	Industry	ΔK (1)	ΔY* (2)	ΔT (3)	BΔT (4)	-B[ΔKᵢ× (Yᵢ/Kᵢ)] (5)
17.	Miscellaneous metals and metallic products	3171.8	9134.8	10,567.9	17,281.2	-24,184.1
18.	Machinery	946.1	2656.7	1387.5	2472.3	-4349.5
19.	Household electrical appliances	370.0	1638.3	504.9	886.1	-1960.0
20.	Electronic products	964.3	4269.9	2722.9	391.6	-6710.4
21.	Electrical machinery and apparatus	10,274.8	45,496.8	9723.9	12,452.3	-47,480.8
22.	Transportation equipment	8110.8	22,580.5	3783.9	5023.4	-24,260.5
23.	Miscellaneous products	12,356.5	52,638.7	4772.2	5389.9	-47390.1
24.	Construction	0.0	0.0	--	799.6	-1813.9
25.	Electricity	0.0	0.0	--	6418.4	-9930.3
26.	Gas and city water	0.0	0.0	--	216.9	-436.4
27.	Transportation, communications, and warehousing	0.0	0.0	--	3288.1	-6971.3
28.	Wholesale and retail trade	639.3	537.1	--	6320.1	-14,454.8
29.	Miscellaneous services	5647.2	10,300.5	--	10,883.1	-28,456.0
	Total	75,391.5	264,722.1	114,048.0	240,037.4	-464,602.3

Table 8, continued

	Industry	ΔY (6)	ΔL (7)	ΔL* (8a)	ΔL* (8b)	ΔX* (9)
17.	Miscellaneous metals and metallic products	-6902.9	-1403.3	7428.2	11,142.3	6394.4
18.	Machinery	-1877.2	-594.2	3364.0	5046.0	1859.7
19.	Household electrical appliances	-1273.9	-257.1	1322.8	1984.2	1148.8
20.	Electronic products	-6318.8	-1275.2	3446.9	5170.4	2988.9
21.	Electrical machinery and apparatus	-35,028.5	-7052.2	36,639.3	54,958.9	31,847.8
22.	Transportation equipment	-19,237.1	-3106.3	14,584.5	21,876.8	15,806.4
23.	Miscellaneous products	-41,991.2	-13,471.7	67,550.5	101,325.7	36,847.1
24.	Construction	-1014.3	--	--	--	--
25.	Electricity	-3511.9	--	--	--	--
26.	Gas and city water	-219.5	--	--	--	--
27.	Transportation, communications, and warehousing	-3683.2	--	--	--	--
28.	Wholesale and retail trade	-8134.7	--	--	--	--
29.	Miscellaneous services	-17,572.9	--	--	--	--
	Total	-224,564.9	-53,903.4	282,260.5	423,370.7	177,719.3

Note: All data in 10,000 US dollars, except columns 7 and 8, in persons. Column 8(a) is based upon the assumption that Y^*/L is four times Y/L, and column 8(b) upon the assumption that Y^*/L is six times Y/L.

The recent performance of the Taiwan economy provides some basis for optimism. The real growth rate of domestic manufacturing investment has revived since the second quarter of 1991, after a four-year plunge from 36.73 percent in 1986 to -2.56 percent in 1990. Exports of capital-intensive and technology-intensive products have been on the rise, filling the void caused by DFI-related "export shifts" in a wide array of labor-intensive products. Even some of the traditional labor-intensive sectors (e.g., wearing apparel and footwear) have witnessed a rebound in export values despite a continuous drop in export quantity; this development suggests that efforts to upgrade quality in pursuit of a higher unit price might be paying off.

For the host economy, on the other hand, two crucial aspects that will have a lasting impact are the extent of technology transfer and the creation of sectoral linkage effects over time. In the context of the mainland economy, both of these processes will involve the gradual emergence of a pool of relatively small, privately-run firms that produce to satisfy local, as well as export, demand.

One can hardly dispute that the type of technology being transferred to the mainland via Taiwan is "appropriate," in terms of its high labor-absorption rate. Moreover, Taiwan's past experience has shown that the type of technology being transferred is also conducive to a more equal distribution of income. As the technology itself is quite standardized, it is easy for local firms to replicate it—through labor mobility or through "coercive learning" on the part of state enterprises. However, if we broaden the concept of "technology" to include managerial efficiency, versatility in restructuring production lines in accordance with customers' shifting orders, and ability to engage in flexible intra-firm and inter-firm sourcing of production activities, all of which may be viewed as long-time imprints from a highly competitive, market-oriented economy, it is obvious that the present "export enclave" model of DFI on the mainland cannot fully exploit the potential benefits of a technological transfer. In order for the transfer to have a widespread and lasting effect on the host economy, local firms adopting the same technology and following a similar set of market incentives must be encouraged to develop as a matter of policy. Similar arguments apply in the creation of intersectoral linkage effects.

What is really at issue here is the need for systematic transformation toward a more competitive environment—one that is conducive to the growth of indigenous entrepreneurship. At the macro level, an extensive price reform that creates appropriate market signals is essential, as is greater freedom for entrepreneurs to engage in intra-national transactions and international trade. At the micro level, private and semi-private village and township enterprises should be further encouraged to take part in the economic process and contribute their rightful share. As Taiwan's experience has vividly borne out, these smaller-sized, highly motivated firms can be expected to perform much better than giant state-owned enterprises in various labor-intensive lines of production, if only for their innate responsiveness and flexibility with respect to market signals. A thriving pool of independent small- and medium-sized enterprises will not only provide fiscal relief for the local and central governments on the mainland, but will also absorb surplus rural labor and, therefore, foster the economic development of local communities. With the technological know-how and production hardware introduced by DFI, mainland China's indigenous entrepreneurs will then be well-equipped to face the harsh environment of the marketplace and to compete effectively not only with other indigenous producers but also with foreign-related firms, in providing for local as well as export market demand.

Finally, it may be emphasized that mainland China's current trade imbalances with the U.S. and with Taiwan are both induced in part by Taiwan's DFI operations on the mainland. As our calculations in the last section indicated, Taiwan has already "shifted" an estimated 1.8 billion US dollars' worth of exports from its own trade account onto that of mainland China as a result of 754 million dollars' investment—a relatively minor sum. If the total of 3.49 billion dollars of investment contracts signed by the end of 1991 were all to be realized, and if the same industrial distribution persisted, the potential "export shift" would soon mount to a dramatic 8 billion dollars. Since the U.S. has long been the prime importer of Taiwanese labor-intensive products, whether produced at home or abroad, an escalation of trade frictions between mainland China and the U.S. seems inevitable with the continuing injection of MIC products into the U.S. market fueled by Taiwanese DFI. This points to the limits of an export-oriented strategy as it applies to a country of vast scale. Mainland China must now choose between a more liberalized trade regime at home and an increasingly impeded market outlet abroad. Taiwan's DFI operations in the mainland only hasten the time of a showdown for the mainland.

Just as Taiwan's DFI has increased mainland China's trade surplus with the U.S., so it has aggravated China's trade deficit with Taiwan. The derived demand for intermediate inputs constituted over one-third of mainland China's total imports from Taiwan in 1990. With the ongoing investment flow, this share will rise further, putting additional pressure on the bilateral deficit situation of mainland China (which in 1990 registered 2 billion US dollars and in 1991 rose to 3.5 billion). This phenomenon is reminiscent of Japan's DFI operations in Taiwan during the 1960s and '70s, which resulted in Taiwan's heavy surplus with the U.S. and sustained deficit with Japan. In a way, Taiwan is now duplicating the same strategy of indirectly exporting to the U.S. through its production bases on the mainland and, to a lesser extent, in other Asian countries. Also reminiscent of the situation between Japan and Taiwan, where restricted access to the Japanese market explained a good part of Taiwan's long-term deficit with Japan, mainland China currently faces a high degree of import protection from Taiwan. Only 236 items, mostly agricultural products and raw materials, were allowed as legal imports from the mainland as of mid-1992. If this protective wall were removed, the current bilateral imbalance would be improved substantially, if not entirely reversed, by an increasing volume of return-purchases of semi-finished and finished products produced by Taiwanese DFI on the mainland.

5. Conclusion

The recent surge of Taiwan's DFI toward mainland China provides an exciting opportunity for economists to examine various aspects of DFI's impact on the domestic and host economies at one time. This paper examines the characteristics of Taiwan's DFI operations on the mainland and finds that they are mostly small-scale, labor-intensive, and highly export-oriented. These characteristics of Taiwanese DFI suggest that they are consistent with the "defensive" prototype, a la Kojima, who stresses cost reduction to defend existing markets as an underlying driving force for outward DFI. At a time when domestic labor cost has skyrocketed, Taiwanese manufacturers have brought their labor-intensive technology into full play by turning to another low-wage country to produce familiar products at an internationally competitive price.

Based on a registered investment volume of 754 million US dollars and the 1986 input-output table for Taiwan, we conducted an industrial linkage analysis to determine the static impact of DFI on employment, output, and export performance in the home and host economies. Our results suggest that the most significant short-run changes, in terms of proportions, occur in the external sectors of these economies. This is so because the phenomenon of an "export shift" from one country (the home) to the other (the host) is at the heart of a defensive-DFI strategy. The transfer of exports, however, is more apparent than real since the lion's share of foreign exchange earnings will fall into the hands of the investors, especially when the host economy is as yet unable to furnish the semi-products, components, and parts required in these DFI operations. The formation of "export enclaves" has also limited the extent of employment and output generation within the host economy, due to insignificant local linkage effects.

For the home country, the long-term challenge is one of reorientation based on changing comparative advantage. This will not be an easy task for Taiwan; huge effort is required to upgrade its technology in order for Taiwan to be competitive in the "up market" of the international arena. For the host economy, on the other hand, the challenge is one of absorbing in full the technology being transferred by DFI firms—including the element of entrepreneurship therein. This will provide the ultimate test of success of DFI operations in mainland China.

Notes

1. An earlier version of this paper was presented at the Third Annual Conference of the Chinese Economic Association (U.K.), London School of Economics, December 1991.

2. See, for example, Benjamin I. Cohen, *Multinational Firms and Asian Exports* (New Haven: Yale University Press, 1975); David W. Carr, "Impact of Foreign Direct Investment on the Economic Development of Australia" (Ph.D. dissertation, New York University, 1979); Chi Schive and B.A. Majumdar, "Direct Foreign Investment and Linkage Effects: The Experience of Taiwan," *Canadian Journal of Development Studies*, 11(2), 1990, pp. 325-42; Chi Schive, "The Foreign Factor: The Multinational Corporation's Contribution to the Economic Modernization of the Republic of China," in *Studies in Economic, Social and Political Change: The Republic of China* (Stanford: Hoover Institution Press, 1990); and Magnus Blomstrom, *Foreign Investment and Spillovers* (London: Routledge, 1989).

3. E.g., Raymond Vernon, "International Investment and International Trade in the Product Cycle," *Quarterly Journal of Economics*, May 1966, pp. 190-207; Raymond Vernon, *Sovereignty at Bay: The Multinational Spread of U.S. Enterprises* (New York: Basic Books, 1971); P J. Buckley and M. Casson, *The Future of the Multinational Enterprise* (London: Macmillan, 1976); and F. T. Knickerbocker, *Oligopolistic Reaction and Multinational Enterprise* (Cambridge: MIT Press, 1973).

4. Kojima may be a prominent exception. See Kiyoshi Kojima, "A Macroeconomic Approach to Foreign Direct Investment," *Hitotsubashi Journal of Economics*, 14, 1973, pp. 1-21; and Kiyoshi Kojima, *Direct Foreign Investment: A Japanese Model of Multinational Business Operations* (New York:

Praeger, 1978). Kojima's work on Japanese DFI has dealt with effects on the originating and recipient countries at both the theoretical and empirical levels.

5. The host countries usually do show a concern over the behavior patterns of different DFI-originating countries in terms of export propensity, average rate of local procurement, and type of technology being introduced. These concerns, however, do not go beyond the potential impact on the host economy and are not with the home country *per se*. See, for example, T. C. Chou, "American and Japanese Direct Foreign Investment in Taiwan: A Comparative Study," *Hitotsubashi Journal of Economics*, 29, 1988, pp. 165-79; and Robert Grosse, *Multinationals in Latin America* (London: Routledge, International Business Series, 1989).

6. From 1986 to 1991, the nominal average monthly wage rate in Taiwan's manufacturing sector increased by 77%, from 14,000 to 25,000 NT dollars; the value of the NT dollar against the US dollar has appreciated by roughly 50%, from NT$39.1:US$1 to NT$26:US$1.

7. C.S. Ouyang, Y. J. Lin, and W. S. Chou, *Trade-Warning System for Monitoring Taiwan-Mainland Economic Interdependence and Its Applications* (in Chinese) (Taipei: Chung-hua Institution for Economic Research, 1991).

8. T. T. Yen, Y. J. Lin, and C. Chung, *A Study of Taiwanese Investment and Trade Relations with Mainland China* (in Chinese) (Taipei: Chung-hua Institution for Economic Research, 1992).

9. Kojima, "Macroeconomic Approach."

10. Taiwan is renowned for its large pool of small- and medium-sized enterprises (SMEs) in manufacturing. SMEs play a leading role both in domestic production and in international trade. In 1988, for example, SMEs accounted for 98% of the total number of manufacturing firms in Taiwan, produced 44% of manufacturing output, and were responsible for 63% of total exports.

11. Ouyang, Lin, and Chou, *Trade-Warning System*.

12. Editorial Board of the Almanac of China's Foreign Economic Relations, *Almanac of China's Foreign Economic Relations and Trade* (Hong Kong: China Resources and Trade Consultancy, 1990).

13. According to a survey of Taiwanese electrical and electronics DFI in mainland China, the average scale of operation on the mainland in terms of invested capital is 650,000 US dollars, or roughly one-fourth that of the parent company in Taiwan (2,460,000 US dollars); however, the average number of workers employed on the mainland (312 persons) is 1.5 times that of the parent firm (210 persons). This amounts to saying that the average labor-capital ratio on the mainland is 5.6 times that of the parent firm. See Lee-in C. Chiu, Feng-cheng Fu, Chin Chung, and Lyang-chaw Chen, *A Feasibility Study of Integrating Intra-Industry Investment Toward Mainland China: A Case Study of the Electronics Industry* (in Chinese) (Taipei: Chung-hua Institution for Economic Research, 1991).

14. See note 13.

15. Note, however, that $\delta = 1$ together with the use of the D-matrix in our calculations only means that all of the intermediate inputs previously furnished by indigenous producers in Taiwan continue to be supplied by these same producers.

16. All of the above assumptions on Y^*/K, δ, and α have been relaxed and modified in Yen, Lin and Chung, *Taiwanese Investment*, according to a survey of 431 Taiwanese DFI establishments in mainland China in early 1992. The results, however, show a range of deviation from the present results of no more than 5%.

17. The estimated investment-induced exports (altogether 1.14 billion US dollars) accounted for about 35% of the actual export volume (3.287 billion US dollars) from Taiwan to mainland China in 1990.

18. In 1990, foreign-related industrial production in mainland China amounted to 10.4 billion US dollars, or 3% of the country's gross national output; see *Jingji ribao*, 17 July 1991. Note that this figure does not include output value attributable to DFI in the agricultural or tertiary sectors.

19. The reduction of manufacturing jobs, however, did not pose a threat to the employment situation in Taiwan. As a matter of fact, the unemployment rate in Taiwan has remained at about 1.7% since the mid 1980s. What is really occurring is a gradual yet persistent reshuffling of employment from manufacturing to the service sector as the economy slowly undergoes a process of structural transformation.

20. For discussion of "intangible assets" in DFI behavior, see, e.g., Stephen H. Hymer, "The International Operations of National Firms: A Study of Direct Foreign Investment" (Ph.D. dissertation, M.I.T., 1960; published by MIT Press in 1976); R. E. Caves, "International Corporations: The Industrial Economics of Foreign Investment," *Economica*, February 1971, pp. 1-27; and John H. Dunning, *International Production and the Multinational Enterprise* (London: George Allen & Unwin, 1981).

21. Foreign-related exports from mainland China totalled 7.8 billion US dollars in 1990. Taiwan's contribution would be around one-fourth of this total; however, if we include the value of offshore processing, which was not counted as part of China's exports by the Customs, Taiwan's DFI share would fall to approximately one-seventh.

22. The estimate is based on a monthly wage rate of 350-500 RMB per worker and a total employment of 350,000 workers due to Taiwanese DFI.

Economic Interdependence Between Taiwan and Mainland China, 1979-92

KAO Charng

1. Introduction

During the 1980s, there was a rapid increase in economic interdependence between Taiwan and mainland China. This increase was due in part to the mainland's policy of economic reform and its plan, adopted in the late 1970s, for building its economy through opening up to the outside world. It was also due to the mainland's more moderate stance regarding Taiwan, gradually adopted beginning in 1980.

Essentially, the Beijing authorities have encouraged bilateral trade between the two entities and have made great efforts to induce Taiwanese enterprises to invest on the mainland. The position taken by the Taiwanese authorities in response to mainland China's policies was predictable: they refused to "compromise, negotiate, or have contact with" the Chinese Communist Party in the beginning, and relaxed restrictions step by step later on. Economic interchanges between the two sides developed quickly because Hong Kong served as a convenient transfer port and because various economic and noneconomic factors—removal of exchange controls, appreciation of the NT dollar, labor cost increases, and the labor movement—drove Taiwanese small- and medium-sized enterprises to invest overseas. Geographical advantages, cheap labor, and nationalistic sentiments also attracted Taiwanese enterprises to mainland China.

This paper investigates current conditions and problems of, as well as prospects for, economic exchanges across the Taiwan Straits. It is hoped that the findings of this study will contribute to a better understanding of the economic relationship between Taiwan and the mainland. Section 2 analyzes the nature of, and trends in, bilateral indirect trade between the two sides. Section 3 analyzes the commodity structure of this trade. Section 4 further investigates the degree of dependence of Taiwan and the mainland on each other. Section 5 considers prospects for a deeper economic relationship between Taiwan and mainland China.

Table 1. Commodity Trade between Taiwan and Mainland China, via Hong Kong, 1978-92

	Volume (million USD)	Increase (percent)	Share in Total Exports	Share in Total Imports
from Taiwan to mainland China				
1978	0.05	--		
1979	21		0.13	0.14
1980	242		1.22	1.24
1981	390	61.07	1.73	1.77
1982	208	-46.65	0.94	1.08
1983	168	-18.98	0.67	0.79
1984	425	152.38	1.40	1.55
1985	987	132.13	3.21	2.34
1986	811	-17.91	2.04	1.89
1987	1226	51.27	2.30	2.84
1988	2242	82.81	3.65	4.26
1989	2896	29.18	4.38	4.90
1990	3278	13.18	4.88	6.14
1991	4679	42.74	6.14	7.34
1992	6288	34.39	7.72	7.80
from mainland China to Taiwan				
1978	47	--	0.41	
1979	55	19.42	0.41	0.38
1980	78	40.65	0.43	0.40
1981	76	-2.82	0.35	0.36
1982	89	17.90	0.40	0.48
1983	96	6.77	0.43	0.47
1984	127	33.04	0.49	0.58
1985	116	-9.16	0.42	0.58

Table 1, continued

	Volume (million USD)	Increase (percent)	Share in Total Exports	Share in Total Imports
1986	144	24.25	0.47	0.60
1987	289	100.47	0.73	0.83
1988	478	65.68	0.98	0.95
1989	586	22.60	1.12	1.12
1990	765	30.41	1.23	1.40
1991	1129	47.58	1.57	1.80
1992	1119	-0.89	1.32	1.55

Sources: Census Statistics Department, Hong Kong Government, *Transfer Trade Statistics*, various issues; Ministry of Finance, Republic of China, *Monthly Statistics of Exports and Imports, Taiwan Area, ROC*, various issues; State Statistical Bureau, *Statistical Yearbook of China* (Beijing: Zhongguo tongji), various issues.

2. General Characteristics of Mainland-Taiwan Trade

Because no official commercial relations exist between mainland China and Taiwan, the bulk of the trade carried out between them takes the form of indirect trade through other countries or regions—known as "triangular trade." It should be noted that all of the trade spoken of hereafter is indirect trade through Hong Kong. In addition to trade via Hong Kong, there is also indirect trade between the mainland and Taiwan through Japan, Singapore, Guam, and other third parties, and there is so-called "minor trade" that takes place directly between the two sides. Indirect trade routed via Hong Kong is estimated to account for about three-fourths of the total trade between Taiwan and mainland China.[1]

Table 1 shows the development of indirect trade between Taiwan and mainland China over the period 1979-92. Before the mainland authorities shifted to the policy of economic reform and openly started calling for exchanges with Taiwan, this trade was only marginal, with some minor purchases of mainland products by Taiwanese official organizations in Hong Kong and some purchases of Taiwan products by mainland trade corporations in the colony. As late as 1978, Taiwan's indirect exports to mainland China were worth only US$50,000, and indirect imports were worth only $47 million.[2]

Table 2. Major Commodities Traded between Taiwan and Mainland China, by SITC 2-Digit Code

	1979		1984		1990		1992	
Rank	SITC	Share[a]	SITC	Share[a]	SITC	Share[a]	SITC	Share[a]
from Taiwan to mainland China								
1	65	81.4	65	54.8	65	39.7	65	34.4
2	76	3.2	77	11.0	58	9.8	72	8.1
3	72	3.0	89	6.6	77	6.8	77	6.7
4	63	2.2	76	5.2	72	6.2	57	6.1
5	51	2.2	75	4.5	89	5.2	58	5.2
6	73	1.6	72	3.7	61	5.1	89	4.7
7	67	1.2	26	2.9	76	4.7	76	3.6
8	58	1.1	58	1.8	64	2.3	78	2.9
9	77	1.0	78	1.1	78	1.8	74	2.5
10	61	0.7	68	1.0	74	1.8	64	1.8
Total		97.6		92.5		83.4		76.0
from mainland China to Taiwan								
1	29	82.5	29	42.5	29	16.0	29	13.7
2	05	4.9	03	12.0	84	9.9	77	9.7
3	27	3.2	26	10.9	65	9.1	65	8.9
4	54	2.0	65	10.6	03	7.2	12	6.6
5	26	1.5	27	4.7	77	6.0	89	6.5
6	51	1.4	05	3.7	89	5.5	85	4.5
7	28	1.0	54	2.5	68	3.9	84	4.3
8	82	1.0	68	2.1	05	3.4	05	3.7
9	65	0.6	52	2.0	61	3.4	88	3.4
10	61	0.4	51	1.9	52	3.1	76	3.4
Total		98.5		92.9		67.5		64.8

Note: For definition of 2-digit SITC groups, see the Appendix.

a. Share in Taiwan's total indirect exports to, or imports from, mainland China, in percent.

Source: Charng Kao, Tzung-Ta Yen, et al., *A Study of Economic Exchanges between Taiwan and Mainland China: Current Situation and Perspectives* (Taipei: Chung-hua Institution for Economic Research, 1992), Table 2-3 (in Chinese).

Starting at the end of the 1970s, Beijing began to propose greater exchanges with Taiwan. This change was due to a major policy shift on the mainland, as revealed in the third plenary session of the 11th Central Committee of the Communist Party, held in December 1978. Specifically, the Party shifted the emphasis of its activities to economic construction and initiated major reforms. A look at the figures for trade via Hong Kong, as shown in Table 1, reveals that 1979 marked the start of a new phase in economic relations between the two sides. The total value of trade via Hong Kong reached US$76 million in that year, and subsequently grew rapidly and steadily, reaching a total value of $7.4 billion in 1992.

Taiwan and the mainland have been rapidly increasing in importance to each other as trading partners. In 1978, Taiwan accounted for just 0.3 percent of the total imports and exports of mainland China, and China accounted for 0.3 percent of the total imports and exports of Taiwan. By 1992, with total imports and exports reaching US$7.4 billion, these shares had increased to 4.47 percent of the total trade of the mainland and 4.48 percent of that of Taiwan, with Taiwan in sixth place among Beijing's trade partners and the mainland in fifth place among Taiwan's.

The overall characteristics of indirect trade between Taiwan and mainland China can be summarized as follows. First, the rapid increase of total trade between the two sides was due mainly to a sharp increase in exports from Taiwan to the mainland, which began in the early 1980s. According to the trade statistics shown in Table 1, the mainland's exports to Taiwan increased from US$55 million in 1979 to $1.12 billion in 1992—a 20-fold increase, or a 29 percent annual growth rate. During the same period, the mainland's imports from Taiwan increased from US$21 million to $6.29 billion—a 300-fold increase, or a 60 percent annual growth rate.

Second, trade has evolved from one-way to two-way. Until 1979, export of goods from the mainland to Taiwan accounted for the bulk of the total between the two sides. Since 1980, the reverse trend has taken hold and large quantities of products made in Taiwan have been exported to mainland China. The reason for this shift lies in the different policies that have been adopted over time by the two sides. In particular, Taipei has imposed controls on imports from the mainland, holding the rate of increase in imports from the mainland below that of exports to the mainland. These restrictions have been gradually relaxed since 1985.

Third, the mainland enjoyed a surplus in trade with Taiwan through 1979, but this changed to a deficit in 1980. The mainland has continued to record large deficits since—and, indeed, the trade imbalance is getting larger. As shown in Table 1, the deficit was about US$160 million in

1980, $870 million in 1985, and over $5.2 billion in 1992. As a result of this persistent imbalance, the mainland accumulated a trade deficit of US$18.6 billion over 1979-92. While some of this is due to restrictions on imports by the Taiwanese side, it is attributable mainly to the lack of competitive products on the mainland.

Fourth, during 1979-92 there were "three ups and three downs" in trade between Taiwan and mainland China. As shown in Table 1, the first cycle occurred in 1979-83. The trade volume first increased from US$76 million to $466 million, then decreased to $264 million. The second cycle occurred during 1984-86, when the trade volume increased from US$552 million to $1.10 billion, then decreased to $955 million. The third cycle, still incomplete, began in 1987. Trade volume increased from US$1.52 billion to $7.41 billion in 1992; although trade experienced continuous growth during this period, the growth rates of 1989 and 1990 were clearly lower than those of the first two years.

Obviously, trade fluctuations were related to policies adopted by mainland China, and by Taiwan as well. For instance, during 1982-1983 and in 1986, indirect exports from Taiwan to the mainland decreased considerably. These reductions can be attributed to changes in mainland China's economic policies. Due to overheating of the domestic economy and the trade deficit, the mainland authorities implemented deflationary policies, accompanied by tighter control of overseas trade and a reduction in imports. On the other hand, a six-fold jump in the total value of trade occurred during 1979-81. The main reasons for this jump were: (a) products made in Taiwan were imported free of duty into the mainland during these years, and (b) Taipei substantially relaxed its restrictions.

3. Changes in the Commodity Structure of Trade

Indirect trade between Taiwan and mainland China has shown rapid development since 1979, not only in total value but also in terms of commodity structure. Table 2 shows the main products traded between the two sides in selected years. Commodities of SITC groups 58, 65, 72, 76, and 77 have usually ranked among Taiwan's ten most important exports to the mainland; over time SITC groups 61, 64, 72, 74, 78, and 89 have become more important.[3] Furthermore, we find that Taiwan's exports to the mainland have experienced some diversification. As shown in Table 2, the share of the top ten groups in total exports decreased from 97.6 percent in 1979 to 76 percent in 1992.

Table 3 shows the top twenty commodities exported by Taiwan to the mainland through Hong Kong during 1989-91. In 1991, the total of these top twenty commodities was US$2.44 billion, or 52.1 percent of total indirect exports from Taiwan to the mainland.

With regard to indirect imports by Taiwan from the mainland, Table 2 shows that the top ten groups of commodities did not change significantly during 1979-90. Commodities in SITC groups 03, 05, 29, and 65 have usually been most important. The groups' shares in the total value of indirect imports, however, did change significantly. The top ten commodities imported from the mainland accounted for 64.8 percent of the total indirect import value in 1992, compared to 98.5 percent in 1979; again, the data reveal gradual diversification.

Table 4 shows the top twenty commodities imported from mainland China during 1989-91. As shown in Table 4, commodities such as toys (SITC 89423), electrical apparatus (SITC 77210), ferro-silicon (SITC 67162), and footwear parts (SITC 61250)—all industrial materials or manufactured goods—are becoming more important in terms of share. The total of the top twenty items imported from the mainland reached US$461 million in 1991, 40.8 percent of total indirect imports.

It is worth noticing that sixteen of the top twenty items in Table 4 (the exceptions being SITC codes 29240, 29196, 03410, and 27821) were banned from import into Taiwan from the mainland (Section 2, above). During the years in question, these sixteen items replaced more traditional imports; in 1991, imports of the sixteen totalled US$280 million, or 24.7 percent of the total value of indirect imports.

To sum up the above analysis, we find that compared to 1979, when the mainland imported mainly artificial fiber from Taiwan and Taiwan imported mainly Chinese herb medicines and specialty goods (such as tea) from the mainland, both sides are now exporting and importing a wider variety of commodities—a total of more than 10,000 different items. The mainland previously exported mostly primary products, but in recent years has been increasing its exports of finished goods. Currently, its major exports to Taiwan are agricultural and industrial materials such as crude animal and vegetable materials, yarn, fabrics, and made-up articles. Taiwan mainly exports manufactured and semi-manufactured goods to the mainland—yarn, synthetic fiber materials and synthetic fibers, fabrics, industrial machinery, artificial resins and plastic materials, cellulose esters and ethers, electrical apparatus and appliances, and electrical parts thereof.

The composition of imports and exports suggests that trade between Taiwan and the mainland is quite consistent with the principle of comparative advantage. The trade pattern reflects differences in endowments,

Table 3. Top Twenty Indirect Exports from Taiwan to Mainland China, 1989-91

Rank	SITC	Commodities	1991 volume[a]	1991 share[b]	1990 volume[a]	1990 share[b]	1989 volume[a]	1989 share[b]
1	65315	Fabrics, woven of continuous synthetic textile materials	496,493	10.61	385,723	11.77	289,833	10.01
2	65732	Textile fabrics impregnated, coated, covered, or laminated with preparations of cellulose derivatives or of other artificial plastic materials	344,616	7.36	239,732	7.31	175,716	6.07
3	65510	Knitted or crocheted fabrics, not elastic or rubberized, of synthetic fibers	239,913	5.13	174,580	5.32	118,298	4.08
4	58331	Polystyrene and its copolymers in primary forms	194,350	4.15	89,127	2.72	82,167	2.84
5	58343	Polyvinyl chloride in the form of plates, sheets, strips, film, or foil	171,677	3.67	127,185	3.88	89,187	3.08
6	65144	Yarn, textured, of continuous polyester fibers	169,907	3.63	84,074	2.56	39,371	1.36
7	61140	Leather of other bovine cattle	102,319	2.19	67,335	2.05	65,907	2.26
8	61230	Parts of footwear	94,892	2.03	71,044	2.17	60,576	2.09
9	78539	Parts, n.e.s., of and accessories for articles falling within heading 785	78,374	1.67	48,653	1.48	29,871	1.03
10	89949	Parts, fittings, trimmings, and accessories of articles falling within headings 89941 and 89942	67,067	1.43	51,270	1.56	34,188	1.18
11	72842	Machines and mechanical appliances for the rubber and artificial plastic materials industries, n.e.s.	59,142	1.26	46,780	1.43	77,226	2.67

Table 3, continued

12	77311	Insulated electric wire, cable, bars, strip, and the like, whether or not fitted with connectors	56,785	1.21	48,229	1.47	51,358	1.77
13	76493	Parts, n.e.s., of the apparatus and equipment falling within headings 761, 762, 7643, and 7648	56,636	1.21	53,074	1.62	61,160	2.11
14	65341	Fabrics, woven, of discontinuous synthetic fibers mixed mainly or solely with cotton	49,650	1.06	40,223	1.23	34,038	1.18
15	72480	Machinery for preparing, tanning, or working hides, skins or leather, and parts thereof, n.e.s.	47,887	1.02	39,397	1.20	48,793	1.68
16	68221	Bars, rods, angles, shapes and sections, wrought, of copper; copper wire	47,194	1.01	18,017	0.55	17,807	0.61
17	75990	Parts, n.e.s., of, and accessories for, the machines of heading 7512 or group 752	43,136	0.92	22,981	0.70	23,813	0.82
18	65148	Yarn of discontinuous synthetic fibers, not put up for retail sale	40,789	0.87	45,653	1.39	43,696	1.51
19	26652	Synthetic fibers, not carded, combed or otherwise prepared for spinning polyester	39,801	0.85	24,211	0.74	25,877	0.89
20	58259	Polyurethanes in other forms	36,860	0.79	26,421	0.81	17,571	0.61

a. In 1000 US dollars.

b. Share of commodity in Taiwan's total commodity exports to the mainland, in percent.

Source: Census and Statistics Department, Hong Kong Government, *Transfer Trade Statistics*, various issues.

Table 4. Top Twenty Indirect Exports from Mainland China to Taiwan, 1989-91

Rank	SITC	Commodities	1991 volume[a]	1991 share[b]	1990 volume[a]	1990 share[b]	1989 volume[a]	1989 share[b]
1	29240-1	Plants and parts of trees, bushes, shrubs or other plants, of kinds used primarily in perfumery and pharmacy	93,785	8.31	92,198	12.05	84,874	14.46
2	12220	Cigarettes	61,981	5.49	23,750	3.10	319	0.00
3	29196	Skins and other parts of birds, with their feathers or down	55,808	4.94	20,997	2.74	47,078	8.02
4	65341	Fabrics, woven, of discontinuous synthetic fibers, mixed mainly or solely with cotton	32,850	2.91	10,001	1.30	17,933	3.06
5	84513	Jerseys, pull-overs, slip-overs, twinsets, cardigans, bed-jackets and jumpers, knitted or crocheted, of synthetic fibers	22,793	2.02	12,713	1.66	8970	1.53
6	03410	Fish, fresh (live or dead) or chilled	21,722	1.92	51,974	6.79	31,935	5.44
7	65131	Cotton yarn measuring, per single yarn, not more than 14,000 me. per kg.	18,674	1.65	11,874	1.55	4395	0.75
8	05779	Edible nuts, fresh or dried, n.e.s., shelled or not	18,312	1.62	6172	0.81	3669	0.62
9	84621	Shirts, men's and boys', knitted or crocheted of cotton	16,108	1.43	6709	0.88	3391	0.58
10	65130	Cotton yarn	12,957	1.15	10,040	1.31	2998	0.51
11	89423	Toys, n.e.s., and working models of a kind used for recreational purposes	11,474	1.02	6454	0.84	2712	0.46

Table 4, continued

12	77210	Electrical apparatus for making and breaking, for protecting, and for making connections to or in electrical circuits; switchboards, and control panels, n.e.s.; parts	11,130	0.99	6106	0.80	1661	0.28
13	71610	Motor and generators, direct current	11,012	0.98	8540	1.12	6163	1.05
14	65166	Yarn of discontinuous synthetic fibers, mixed mainly or solely with cotton, not put up for retail sale	10,984	0.97	2732	0.36	4457	0.76
15	75990	Parts, n.e.s., of and accessories for the machines of heading 7512 or group 752	10,883	0.96	13,585	1.77	9849	1.68
16	89941	Umbrellas and sunshades	10,565	0.94	7219	0.94	7356	1.25
17	67162	Ferro-silicon	10,412	0.92	4367	0.57	6698	1.14
18	77118	Other electric transformers	10,054	0.89	3281	0.43	1410	0.24
19	27821	Clay, andalusite, kyanite and sillimanite, whether or not calcined	9937	0.88	7971	1.04	8500	1.45
20	61230	Parts of footwear of any material except metal and asbestos	9123	0.81	4227	0.55	579	0.10

a. In 1000 US dollars.
b. Share of commodity in Taiwan's total commodity imports from the mainland, in percent.

Source: See Table 3.

in stage of economic development, and in industrial structure. Furthermore, a look at the commodity structure of trade shows that a mutually complementary, vertical division of labor is being established between Taiwan and the mainland.

4. Trade Interdependence across the Taiwan Straits

Theoretically, the degree of Taiwan's trade dependence on the mainland can be measured by two indicators. The first is the share of Taiwan's commodity exports to the mainland in Taiwan's total commodity exports. The second is the share of Taiwan's commodity imports from the mainland in Taiwan's total commodity imports. In Table 1, the export share increased from 0.13 percent in 1979 to 7.72 percent in 1992, and the import share increased from 0.38 percent to 1.55 percent over the same period. Table 1 clearly indicates, then, that Taiwan's exports and imports have become more dependent on the mainland.

Using the same method, we can measure the degree of mainland China's trade dependence on Taiwan. The degree of dependence of mainland China's exports on Taiwan increased from 0.41 percent in 1979 to 1.32 percent in 1992, while in imports the degree of dependence increased from 0.14 percent to 7.80 percent during the same period. Comparing degrees of dependence across the Straits, we find that Taiwan was more dependent on mainland China than was the mainland on Taiwan.

The ratio of total commodity trade to GNP is usually used to measure a country's dependence on the external market. As an island economy, Taiwan has a higher degree of dependence on trade than does the mainland—about 80 percent in 1991, according to official statistics.[4] Since trade is more crucial to Taiwan's economic growth than it is to the mainland's, fluctuations in foreign trade affect Taiwan's economy more seriously. Owing both to this fact and to Taiwan's smaller economic scale, we might conclude that Taiwan occupies an inferior position in economic interchanges across the Taiwan Straits.

Chang Pei-chen has employed regression analysis to estimate the impact of changes in mainland China's external economic policy on the value of exports from Taiwan to the mainland.[5] Her analysis showed that there exists a positive relationship between policy changes and indirect exports. Indirect exports from Taiwan to the mainland decreased by about 30-40 percent whenever mainland China adopted a deflationary trade policy. Conversely, preferential measures, such as tax-free status for Taiwan businessmen, induced increases in Taiwan's exports to the mainland.

The main implication of Chang's study is that, to some extent, changes in mainland China's economic policies cause fluctuations in the course of economic interchanges between the two sides. As noted earlier, Taiwan is in an inferior position in these interchanges. Any ups and downs in bilateral trade can have severe impact on Taiwan, perhaps exceeding the absorptive capacity of the Taiwan economy. Since Taiwan is unable to control mainland China's economic policy, the higher Taiwan's dependence on mainland China, the more difficult it is for Taiwan to pursue steady economic growth.

The above analysis is based mainly on aggregate dependence. Now let us take a look at changes in the degree of dependence in terms of the main items traded between the two sides, based on 2-digit and 3-digit SITC groups. Table 5 reports that, for 2-digit groups, most ratios did not exceed 1 percent before 1985; after 1986, however, many items became more dependent on the China trade. To be specific, commodities such as edible products and preparations (SITC 09), plastics in nonprimary forms (SITC 58), beverages (SITC 11), crude rubber (SITC 23), yarn, fabrics and related products (SITC 65), and feeds for animals (SITC 08) all had ratios exceeding 20 percent in 1991. Five items (SITC 08, 58, 61, 64, and 65) showed rapid growth in their shares in total exports from Taiwan to mainland China and numbered among the top ten commodities after 1987.

With SITC 3-digit groups, some exports have shown even greater dependence on the mainland. In 1987, for rotating electric items and parts thereof (SITC 716), the degree of export dependence on the mainland was 64 percent; for machinery for the manufacture of paper (SITC 725), it was over 30 percent. Ten other groups had ratios above 10 percent. Most of these belong to the industrial materials and semi-finished products of SITC 6 and SITC 7—materials and products such as fabrics, woven man-made fibers (SITC 653), leather (SITC 611), specialized machinery and equipment for particular industries (SITC 728), textile yarn (SITC 651), and paper and paperboard (SITC 641).

Table 6 shows the degree of dependence of Taiwan's imports on the mainland (2-digit SITC). Before 1985, most of the ratios were fairly low. The top two items were fish, crustaceans, mollusks, and preparations thereof (SITC 03), and crude animal and vegetable materials, n.e.s. (SITC 29); for each of these, however, dependence on the mainland was below 3.5 percent. Since 1985, the degree of dependence of most commodities has gradually increased. By 1987, the ratios exceeded 5 percent for five commodity groups, and exceeded 20 percent for two (SITC 03 and 29). There were eight groups with ratios over 5 percent in 1989, and twelve in 1991. The ratios for apparel and clothing accessories (SITC 84), tobacco

Table 5. Taiwan's Export Dependence on Mainland China, by Commodity Group (SITC 2-Digit Code)

SITC	Share[a]	SITC	Share[a]	SITC	Share[a]
	1983		1985		1987
65	0.55	68	3.61	43	23.46
61	0.10	65	1.69	08	15.79
72	0.09	72	1.43	65	13.79
68	0.09	64	1.30	09	12.99
26	0.08	73	0.78	72	11.71
77	0.08	77	0.60	61	11.24
87	0.07	00	0.52	58	8.54
89	0.06	58	0.42	21	7.44
67	0.05	26	0.41	64	5.78
59	0.05	74	0.41	42	5.56
78	0.05	61	0.33	59	5.50
09	0.05	71	0.32	26	4.79
64	0.05	23	0.32	73	4.64
66	0.05	52	0.30	51	4.43
54	0.05	67	0.28	29	3.46
63	0.05	88	0.28	68	3.37
58	0.04	59	0.26	53	3.04
73	0.04	87	0.24	71	2.98
29	0.04	55	0.22	52	2.63
04	0.03	76	0.19	74	2.60
				23	1.03
Total[b]	0.67	Total[b]	3.21	Total[b]	2.30
	1989		1990		1991
08	20.08	08	23.81	09	33.57
61	19.72	09	23.77	58	27.64
58	19.00	58	21.64	11	24.56

Table 5, continued

SITC	Share[a]	SITC	Share[a]	SITC	Share[a]
72	18.24	65	20.79	23	24.55
65	17.37	59	16.67	65	23.63
59	13.97	61	13.48	08	22.17
64	9.18	23	12.76	59	17.33
68	8.39	64	12.19	64	16.91
51	8.04	72	10.13	68	14.54
73	6.48	68	8.42	61	13.34
26	6.18	51	8.33	72	11.89
52	5.71	55	7.82	51	10.32
09	5.19	26	6.26	43	9.88
29	5.13	29	6.14	52	8.60
56	4.75	73	5.02	26	8.50
71	4.20	52	4.92	55	7.97
77	4.12	53	4.42	73	7.66
74	3.94	43	4.31	53	5.95
55	3.90	63	4.29	34	5.18
23	3.35	76	4.04	02	4.77
53	3.20	87	3.96	63	4.70
78	3.13	71	3.66	54	4.58
76	2.85	74	3.51	87	4.57
67	2.75	77	3.10	76	4.23
63	2.64	54	3.06	74	4.06
87	2.57	81	2.68	78	3.98
Total[b]	4.38	Total[b]	4.88	Total[b]	6.14

a. Exports to the mainland as a share of Taiwan's total exports in each commodity group, in percent.

b. Exports to the mainland as a share of Taiwan's total exports in all groups, in percent.

Source: Kao et al., *Economic Exchanges*, Table 3-5.

Table 6. Taiwan's Import Dependence on Mainland China, by Commodity Group (SITC 2-Digit Code)

SITC	Share[a]	SITC	Share[a]	SITC	Share[a]
1983		1985		1987	
29	3.26	03	3.38	29	37.08
03	1.14	29	2.75	03	21.92
05	0.56	05	0.55	65	7.40
27	0.39	27	0.33	05	7.03
54	0.27	65	0.30	27	5.16
82	0.15	54	0.20	84	3.87
84	0.13	07	0.17	82	3.78
65	0.12	26	0.13	61	2.67
07	0.09	82	0.11	42	2.18
26	0.08	52	0.10	54	2.15
22	0.06	85	0.09	07	2.10
59	0.05	59	0.05	52	2.07
52	0.04	42	0.04	83	1.25
28	0.04	68	0.03	59	0.75
09	0.04	61	0.03	26	0.73
53	0.03	53	0.02	53	0.71
51	0.02	51	0.02	68	0.71
61	0.02	28	0.02	81	0.69
68	0.01	08	0.01	51	0.56
Total[b]	0.47	Total[b]	0.58	Total[b]	0.83
1989		1990		1991	
29	28.71	03	3.00	84	39.21
03	18.99	84	5.96	12	30.71
84	16.76	29	3.70	29	25.52
83	11.35	12	2.53	83	24.03
05	7.35	83	2.25	05	15.12

Table 6, continued

SITC	Share[a]	SITC	Share[a]	SITC	Share[a]
65	6.77	61	9.28	03	14.97
82	5.97	05	8.05	42	9.48
27	5.42	57	7.43	65	9.37
61	4.11	65	6.62	85	9.36
85	4.06	85	6.29	81	7.11
42	3.48	27	4.83	61	6.32
52	3.03	82	4.77	82	6.17
54	2.94	42	4.02	27	4.78
89	2.37	81	3.99	88	3.88
81	2.23	54	3.71	54	3.40
07	1.65	63	3.06	89	3.34
26	1.63	52	3.04	52	3.11
63	1.56	89	2.45	63	2.96
66	1.56	66	2.44	66	2.46
55	1.52	55	1.96	55	2.26
53	1.36	07	1.87	76	2.20
69	1.11	68	1.55	69	2.10
Total[b]	1.12	Total[b]	1.40	Total[b]	1.80

a. Imports from the mainland as a share of Taiwan's total imports in each commodity group, in percent.
b. Imports from the mainland as a share of Taiwan's total imports in all groups, in percent.

Source: Kao et al., *Economic Exchanges*, Table 3-6.

and tobacco manufactures (SITC 12), and travel goods, handbags, and similar containers (SITC 83) all increased markedly, breaking into the 20 percent range.

For SITC 3-digit groups, many imports—such as crude vegetable material (SITC 292, in which Chinese herbal medicines dominate), fish (SITC 034), and vegetables, roots, and tubers (SITC 056)—have shown high dependence on the mainland since 1985. Crude animal materials (SITC 291), vegetables (SITC 054), and fabrics (SITC 652, 653, 654)

Table 7. **Mainland China's Export Dependence on Taiwan, by Commodity Group (SITC 2-Digit Code)**

SITC	Share[a]	SITC	Share[a]	SITC	Share[a]	SITC	Share[a]	SITC	Share[a]
	1983		1985		1987		1989		1991
29	13.16	29	10.52	29	15.11	29	16.34	29	25.29
27	2.29	03	8.33	25	4.22	61	9.34	12	22.17
03	1.92	27	1.69	61	4.19	75	5.75	25	10.97
54	1.50	59	1.59	03	2.73	25	4.75	61	10.92
59	1.22	52	1.18	27	2.15	24	4.02	88	5.86
28	0.91	54	1.08	51	2.03	59	3.91	77	5.47
23	0.90	68	0.97	59	1.93	27	3.37	28	4.55
53	0.80	51	0.80	52	1.59	03	3.29	71	4.49
68	0.75	24	0.78	24	1.56	71	3.28	53	4.47
51	0.75	53	0.74	53	1.35	68	2.87	27	4.34
22	0.75	26	0.66	68	1.22	52	2.84	59	3.99
52	0.73	05	0.62	21	1.15	51	2.62	68	3.58
26	0.63	61	0.52	54	1.04	77	2.49	51	3.39
05	0.58	28	0.48	65	0.86	53	2.40	42	3.28
61	0.27	65	0.36	05	0.71	82	2.10	75	3.20
75	0.17	75	0.19	75	0.67	67	2.05	52	3.06
65	0.15	22	0.13	71	0.64	63	2.02	03	2.92
24	0.15	08	0.13	28	0.64	54	1.52	05	2.80
09	0.12	21	0.11	12	0.64	28	1.51	83	2.77
77	0.10	55	0.10	58	0.59	23	1.37	24	2.72
						89	1.33	81	2.31
						05	1.28	23	2.31
						55	1.20	63	2.17
						42	1.19	55	2.16
						66	1.06	82	2.16
								89	2.16
Total[b]	0.43	Total[b]	0.42	Total[b]	0.73	Total[b]	1.12	Total[b]	1.32

Table 7, continued

a. Exports to Taiwan as a share of mainland China's total exports in each commodity group, in percent.
b. Exports to Taiwan as a share of mainland China's total exports in all groups, in percent.

Source: Kao et al., *Economic Exchanges*, Table 3-7.

showed marked increases in dependence, breaking into the 10 percent range in 1991.

To sum up, it is clear that, for both exports and imports, the degree of dependence of Taiwan's trade on the mainland was not high prior to 1985, except in a few particular commodities. With the rapid growth of economic interchange between the two sides, Taiwan is gradually becoming dependent on the mainland for both exports and imports. Investing on the mainland has become common over the past few years, not only increasing the mainland's demand for Taiwan-made industrial materials and equipment, but also the supply of mainland-made semi-finished products to Taiwan.

Comparatively speaking, the degree of mainland China's dependence on Taiwan has been lower. As shown in Table 7, all commodities except crude animal and vegetable materials (SITC 29) had export dependence ratios below 10 percent before 1989. By 1991, there were three additional groups—tobacco and tobacco manufactures (SITC 12), pulp and waste paper (SITC 25), and leather (SITC 61)—with ratios of more than 10 percent. These four commodity items were also the top four in terms of growth in dependency ratio for these years.

The degree of mainland China's import dependence on Taiwan also shows an increase. According to Table 8, travel goods, handbags and similar containers (SITC 83) has shown the greatest dependence since 1987, reaching a remarkable 97 percent by 1991. There were three other groups—yarn, fabrics and related products (SITC 65), leather (SITC 61), and footwear (SITC 85)—with ratios above 30 percent by 1989. Thereafter, plastics in primary forms (SITC 57) emerged as a new force, with a ratio of almost 34 percent by 1991.

5. Prospects for the Economic Relationship

In the future, the scale of bilateral economic exchanges between Taiwan and the mainland will keep growing. This prediction rests upon the following observations. First, with the easing of political hostility between the two sides, the authorities in Taipei and Beijing can adopt policies that

Table 8. Mainland China's Import Dependence on Taiwan, by Commodity Group (SITC 2-Digit Code)

SITC	Share[a]	SITC	Share[a]	SITC	Share[a]	SITC	Share[a]	SITC	Share[a]
1983		1985		1987		1989		1991	
65	17.88	85	88.95	83	30.95	83	82.54	83	96.99
84	15.20	65	26.39	65	27.22	61	53.70	65	54.41
89	13.00	83	14.72	85	23.89	85	38.08	61	41.69
77	5.56	77	10.60	61	19.73	65	34.31	85	34.34
61	3.98	89	9.12	09	10.90	89	19.69	57	33.84
83	3.65	84	8.41	89	10.21	84	15.46	09	28.14
63	3.48	73	6.52	84	8.60	58	11.63	89	27.70
82	1.61	81	5.52	81	5.16	77	11.18	84	20.61
66	1.47	61	4.27	29	5.00	62	9.78	11	19.95
69	1.35	55	4.25	77	4.52	03	9.27	62	17.40
62	1.21	82	4.21	88	4.12	81	9.09	69	16.47
09	1.09	63	3.45	08	3.59	69	7.93	64	15.59
85	1.08	64	3.37	58	3.35	76	7.37	88	13.58
73	0.97	88	3.33	43	3.23	64	6.81	77	12.22
76	0.88	69	3.19	76	3.20	09	6.57	29	12.10
78	0.87	62	2.50	82	3.10	08	6.48	68	11.38
29	0.74	68	2.38	69	2.85	63	5.74	43	10.36
88	0.69	03	2.26	62	2.65	72	5.72	53	10.20
74	0.39	75	2.18	72	2.29	73	5.22	82	9.49
54	0.37	71	2.04	59	2.08	53	5.05	76	8.78
		76	1.79	63	1.96	75	4.66	59	8.19
		66	1.59	55	1.91	59	4.39	03	8.14
		74	1.58	73	1.90	88	4.16	78	7.87
		72	1.54	64	1.64	68	3.50	73	7.11
		00	1.41	71	1.61	78	3.26	63	6.85
		29	1.17	75	1.47	82	3.08	75	6.80

Table 8, continued

SITC	Share[a]	SITC	Share[a]	SITC	Share[a]	SITC	Share[a]	SITC	Share[a]
1983		1985		1987		1989		1991	
		58	1.05	53	1.40	66	2.74	52	6.61
				26	1.22	74	2.61	23	5.62
				74	1.08	71	2.44	72	5.08
Total[b]	0.79	Total[b]	2.34	Total[b]	2.84	Total[b]	4.90	Total[b]	7.34

a. Imports from Taiwan as a share of mainland China's total imports in each commodity group, in percent.
b. Imports from Taiwan as a share of mainland China's estimated total imports in all groups, in percent.

Source: Kao et al., *Economic Exchanges*, Table 3-8.

are more practical. Second, mainland China has undergone broad and deep reforms that are favorable to its economic growth and, in turn, create a better investment environment.

On the mainland, considerable progress has been made since 1979 in implementing "reform and opening up" and in introducing measures such as acceptance of foreign investment capital and liberalization of the trade regime. Because Taiwan and Hong Kong investment has played an important role in the process of economic growth on the mainland, we expect that Beijing's economic reforms will continue to emphasize attracting such investment. According to official statistics, mainland China's trade (in US dollars) increased at an average annual rate of 13 percent during 1981-92, while its gross national product (GNP) grew at 9 percent during the same period.[6] As a percentage of GNP, mainland China's trade rose from about 10 percent in 1980 to 38 percent in 1992. This expansion of trade, along with foreign direct investment (and also international loans), will be important for mainland China's economic growth well into the future.

On Taiwan, the authorities have gradually induced indirect trade and investment in mainland China by reforming regulations. Taiwan's economic policy toward the mainland has become looser and more practical. In 1991 alone, Taipei approved 38 projects to promote exchanges across the Taiwan Straits.[7] Fifteen of these related to economic affairs, dealing with, for example, increasing imports of agricultural and industrial materials (as well as semi-finished manufactured products) from the mainland, allowing residents of Taiwan to remit money to the mainland through third regions, and permitting banks in Taiwan to set up branches in Hong Kong.

It goes without saying that Taiwanese businessmen look forward to sharing in mainland China's markets. Essentially, deepening the "reform and opening up" would bring mainland China's economy into a market system, which to some extent implies that the risk of trading with the mainland could be decreased. As noted earlier, the Beijing authorities are working to attract additional foreign direct investment and induce transfer of advanced technology. Since most Taiwanese enterprises are concerned with market potential, mainland China's attitude towards opening its domestic markets will be the key factor determining the growth pattern of economic exchanges.

With the trend toward world economic regionalization and given the complementarity between Taiwan and the mainland, enhancing economic cooperation between the two sides will become more and more attractive. Furthermore, the economic performance of the Western countries is not predicted to be strong in the near future, and world markets are not considered as dynamic as they once were. Therefore, developing the domestic markets of mainland China will become more important as a way for Taiwanese enterprises to sustain and improve their performance.

We cannot, however, treat economic relations between Taiwan and mainland China as a normal case of international business. First of all, the political and economic systems are different. Under a largely planned system, mainland China's economic policies are directed through consideration of noneconomic factors. Such decision-making can be quite irrational in terms of market economic theory; thus, there exists higher uncertainty and risk in economic interchanges with the mainland. Second, although political relations between Taiwan and mainland China have eased somewhat, they are still hostile. The Beijing authorities frequently state that their main purpose in strengthening economic exchanges is to make Taiwan's economy highly dependent on the mainland—a dependence serving Beijing's political ends. (The Taiwan authorities, therefore, have advocated a prudent attitude in pursuing economic interchanges.) Third, since 1979 the mainland has changed its economic policy toward Taiwan many times, causing great fluctuations in the total value of trade, which in turn caused many bankruptcies on Taiwan. It is difficult to determine whether the reasons for such policy changes are political or economic; in any case, the changes are unpredictable and aggravate the uncertainty in exchanges between Taiwan and the mainland.

Ouyang and his collaborators estimated the economic effect of indirect trade across the Straits on Taiwan's economy.[8] They found that adding $1 to Taiwan's exports to the mainland would increase Taiwan's output of industrial products by $2. Chung Chin utilized data on approved indirect mainland investment (provided in May 1991 by the Investment Commission, Ministry of Economic Affairs) to estimate the effects of Taiwan's FDI in mainland China upon Taiwan's economy. Her results showed that such investment might account for over US$1 billion in indirect exports from Taiwan to the mainland—32 percent of the total indirect export value in 1990. Further, these induced exports would generate additional output effects and, thus, increase GNP by about US$2.2 billion, or 1.4 percent.[9]

Taiwan is a small, mountainous island with a poor natural resource endowment. On the one hand, the expansion of foreign trade is crucial for its economic growth; on the other, because Taiwan is so dependent on trade, it is sensitive to fluctuations in overseas markets. The more dependence Taiwan has on the mainland, the more impact Taiwan will feel from mainland China's economic fluctuations and/or policy changes. This unfavorable dimension of cross-Straits interchange could be minimized by diversifying—that is, by penetrating more overseas markets.

6. Concluding Remarks

The analysis of trade data in this paper shows that the economic relationship across the Taiwan Straits consistently developed and improved during the 1980s.

In general, due to its higher degree of dependence on the international market and smaller economic scale, Taiwan is in an inferior position in this interdependent relationship. Specifically, if economic interchanges between the two sides stopped for some reason, there would be far more harm to Taiwan's economy than to mainland China's. Further, some of Taiwan's exports and imports have seen their dependence on the mainland increase steadily and to high levels; such dependence creates risk, which is unfavorable for Taiwan's pursuit of stable economic growth.

Accompanying the promotion of contacts and exchanges on the nongovernmental level (including investment on the mainland by Taiwanese enterprises), trade between Taiwan and the mainland can be expected to develop even further in the future. The mutually beneficial nature of the relationship is the largest factor behind the growth of trade; although many obstacles still exist on both sides of the Taiwan Straits, growth is likely to continue in the coming years. Through trade with Taiwan, it is possible for the mainland to acquire equipment and industrial materials indispensable for its economic development. As for Taiwan, because the export competitiveness of its goods has decreased compared to other Asian NIEs (stemming from sharp appreciation in the value of the NT dollar over the past few years), the opening up of markets on the mainland and the supply of cheap materials for expanding its exports are particularly important. Another factor which could be important in Taiwan's future global trade effort is the possibility of setting up on the mainland, albeit indirectly, production lines and secondary plants.

Notes

1. For more details, see Charng Kao, T. T. Yen, et al., *A Study of Economic Exchanges between Taiwan and Mainland China: Current Situation and Perspectives* (Taipei: Chung-hua Institution for Economic Research, 1992), pp. 14-16 (in Chinese).

2. For more details, see Kao et al., *Economic Exchanges*, pp. 11-12.

3. See the Appendix for definitions of SITC commodity groups.

4. Council for Economic Planning and Development, *Taiwan Statistical Data Book* (Taipei: Council for Economic Planning and Development, 1992), Tables 3.2a and 11.4.

5. See Chang Pei-chen, "An Analysis of Indirect Trade across the Taiwan Straits, 1979-1988" (Economic Papers, no. 126, Chung-hua Institution for Economic Research, 1989), pp. 62-65 (in Chinese).

6. See Charng Kao, "Economic Reform, the Open-Door Policy, and the Economic Development of Mainland China" (paper presented, in Chinese, at the 19th Sino-Japanese Conference on Mainland China, Taipei, March 1992).

7. Mainland Affairs Council of the Executive Yuan, "Plans Put Forward by Executive Organs for Implementing the First-Phase Objectives of the Guidelines for National Unification" (Mainland Affairs Council, January 1992).

8. See Cherng-shin Ouyang, Y. J. Lin, and W. S. Chou, *Trade-Warning System for Monitoring Taiwan-Mainland Economic Interdependence and Its Applications* (Taipei: Chung-hua Institution for Economic Research, 1991), pp. 95-98 (in Chinese).

9. See Chung Chin, "Macroeconomic Impacts on the Domestic Economy of Recent Taiwanese DFI toward Mainland China (paper presented at the Conference on Investment Strategies and Policy-Making in Relation to Mainland China, Taipei, September 1991), pp. 12-16 (in Chinese).

Appendix. Classification of Commodities by 2-Digit SITC Code

00	Live animals, chiefly for food
03	Fish, crustaceans, mollusks, and preparations thereof
04	Cereals and cereal preparations
05	Vegetables and fruit
07	Coffee, tea, cocoa, spices, and manufactures thereof
08	Feedstuff for animals
09	Miscellaneous edible products and preparations
12	Tobacco and tobacco manufactures
21	Hides, skins and furskins (raw)
22	Oil seeds and oleaginous fruit
23	Crude rubber
24	Cork and wood
25	Pulp and waste paper
26	Textile fibers and their wastes
27	Crude fertilizers and crude minerals
28	Metaliferous ores and metal scrap
29	Crude animal and vegetable materials n.e.s.
42	Fixed vegetable oils and fats
43	Animal and vegetable oils and fats, processed, and waxes of animal or vegetable origin
51	Organic chemicals
52	Inorganic chemicals
53	Dyeing, tanning and coloring materials
54	Medicinal and pharmaceutical products
55	Essential oils and perfume materials; toilet, polishing and cleansing preparations
56	Fertilizers, manufactured
58	Artificial resins and plastic materials, and cellulose esters and ethers
59	Chemical materials and products n.e.s.
61	Leather, leather manufactures n.e.s., and dressed furskins
62	Rubber manufactures n.e.s.
63	Cork and wood manufactures

64 Paper, paperboard, and articles of paper pulp, of paper, or of paperboard

65 Textile yarn, fabrics, made-up articles n.e.s., and related products

66 Nonmetallic mineral manufactures n.e.s.

67 Iron and steel

68 Nonferrous metals

69 Manufactures of metal n.e.s.

71 Power generating machinery and equipment

72 Machinery specialized for particular industries

73 Metalworking machinery

74 General industrial machinery and equipment n.e.s., and machine parts n.e.s.

75 Office machines and automatic data processing equipment

76 Telecommunications and sound recording and reproducing apparatus and equipment

77 Electrical machinery, apparatus and appliances n.e.s., and electrical parts thereof

78 Road vehicles

81 Sanitary plumbing, heating and lighting fixtures and fittings n.e.s.

82 Furniture and parts thereof

83 Travel goods, handbags and similar containers

84 Articles of apparel and clothing accessories

85 Footwear

87 Professional, scientific and controlling instruments and apparatus n.e.s.

88 Photographic apparatus, equipment and supplies, and optical goods n.e.s.; watches and clocks

89 Miscellaneous manufactured articles, n.e.s.

The Market Transition in Taiwan: Any Relevance to the PRC?

Henry Wan, Jr.

1. Introduction

The current Chinese economic reform is one of the most dramatic events of our time. A communist regime, ruling the world's most populous nation, has gambled its future on market forces and has scored considerable success in several directions.

The reform has a *usual* goal—to modernize the economy with foreign technology, for the preservation of the Communist Revolution. Elsewhere, similar efforts have met a *usual* fate: the reform fails and the regime falls. The failure of the Chinese economy would be catastrophic, considering what happened in the former Yugoslavia (a Lilliput, by Chinese standards). What is *unusual* for the Chinese reform is its success—in decentralizing price and output decisions and in realizing rapid gains in income, employment, and exports. Suppose mainland China replicates the success of any other Chinese economy—i.e., of Singapore, Hong Kong, or Taiwan. The total Chinese Gross Domestic Product will then exceed the sum of any two other economies in the world (say, the US and Japan). This prospect is not entirely innocuous, in view of what has happened between China and four of its neighbors—Korea, India, the former Soviet Union, and Vietnam—even while the Chinese economy (and, hence, army) was relatively weak.

In spite of the significant successes the Chinese have achieved, significant hurdles remain. They are the same ones that plagued the former communist regimes in the Soviet Union and Eastern Europe before they collapsed—the heavy losses of public firms, the budget deficit of the state, inflation, the steady erosion of discipline and effectiveness in the bureaucracy. So far, the Chinese countermeasures against these ills have been ineffective. Since the government can no longer afford the customary subsidies and since rampant corruption continues to defy control, its key constituencies (farmers, workers, and public employees) are all alienated.

The repression is much milder now, but the lessening of fear does not win popular gratitude. People have more opportunities to make money on their own, but that does not inspire respect for the state, dedicated as it is to public ownership. Even as Western journalists marvel that the Chinese people have never had it so good, the government is deeply concerned with the possibility of open mass uprisings. Officers of the *People's* Government bemoan that "the *people* are troublesome."

So how will it all end? Will the Chinese economy join the ranks of East Asian miracles? Will the government collapse, following in the footsteps of fellow communist regimes? Can a regime collapse while the economy booms? Can a communist government survive while state ownership withers away? To the Chinese and to the rest of the world, the stakes are immense.

Those who are optimistic about the reform often point to the success of East Asian economies under authoritarian regimes—in particular, to Taiwan, ruled by a Leninist party originally organized on the advice of Mikhail Borodin. Among reforms already proven successful, this is the case most similar to the PRC.

But is this analogy valid? This we must consider seriously. Since the matter is complex, involving the nature of development, technology and markets, as well as the influences of politics, sociology and history, we shall first fashion a conceptual framework before taking up three questions:

How did the Taiwanese economy transform itself?
To what extent does "PRC, now" resemble "Taiwan, then"?
What lies ahead for the Chinese economy?

2. A Conceptual Framework

The economies of both Taiwan and mainland China belong to the developing world, lagging behind the advanced economies in income and resources per capita as well as in industrial technology.

In this century at least, sustained rapid growth is not so much producing more of the same outputs but rather producing more valuable outputs with the same inputs. Industrialization holds the key for stimulating such growth. This is a matter of both supply and demand. The expansion of agricultural production is limited by the immutable supply of land. Also, according to the Prebisch-Singer view, as world income rises, an ever higher income share will be spent on manufactured products, with ever higher quality. Much modern technology satisfies familiar human wants with outputs having more desirable characteristics—for example, substituting today's fashionable automobile for yesterday's horse and buggy.

For an economy that is technologically backward, the shortcut to affluence lies in acquiring foreign knowhow quickly and cheaply rather than reinventing it. This may be done by reverse engineering, by licensing foreign inventions, by entry into joint ventures with foreigners, by accepting foreign advice in the process of purchasing foreign equipment or supplying foreign clients, by hiring workers who have gained experience inside foreign outfits—in short, "by all means necessary."

In technology, innovation is admittedly risky and costly; effective imitation, however, is also far from free. If cost is not a problem, a nation can replicate intricate foreign technologies by self-reliance. The acquisition of nuclear and aerospace capability by the PRC, for example, was a technological *tour de force*, by any standard. The opportunity cost of such acquisition in terms of possible delays in industrialization, however, is hard to assess.

Technology acquisition is difficult. What matters is often much more than operating manuals and blueprints. An analogy may be useful for illustration. In "sexing the chicken," the famous incident cited in cognitive science, Japanese farmers could not—however hard they tried—describe to their American counterparts how they can uncannily determine the sex of a newborn chicken. Yet American farmers acquired considerable skill, simply by watching how their Japanese counterparts performed that task. In the industrial context, product design is often the easy part. The difficult questions come later: what precise composition of materials, what specific processes, what adjustments to make when such and such occurs. Transfer of technology is trickier to do than to say.

Furthermore, the transfer process is a contact sport, not for those eager to keep foreign influence at arm's length. To keep up with the advanced world on a broad front—even lagging by some constant distance—is not simple, since trial and error is costly in time and effort. Meiji Japan found keeping up difficult, in the field of electrical machinery.[1] India had difficulties, too.[2] The failure of Soviet Russia to keep up in automobile technology is another example. By comparison, the leading Japanese automobile and electronic firms today include operational units that were branches or joint ventures of American and European firms in times past.[3]

While the above argument favors international cooperation, the matter does not end there. Benefits from working with multinational corporations (MNCs) depend on both the product market such cooperation serves and the labor market in which the MNCs operate. As shown by Morawetz, open competition in the markets of advanced economies provides more valuable lessons than do sheltered markets at home or within a Third-World customs union.[4] And, when multinationals operate in a competitive labor market, the personnel they train may eventually relocate elsewhere, taking their experience with them.[5] The benefits, therefore, are magnified. The high labor turnover in Asian NIEs, in contrast with the Japanese system of lifetime tenure, is often regarded as a weakness for developing firm-specific skills. Yet at this stage of development, it actually serves to spread new skills, ideas, and attitudes more rapidly, telescoping the Japanese development sequence into a much shorter period.

The argument can be carried further. Technology transfer is like heat transfer in physics. The efficiency of the process depends upon convection flows in both interacting systems. In this case, labor mobility in the host economy is one link in the transfer mechanism. If the local employees in foreign firms are fully aware that what they learn there can subsequently serve their personal interests, they will acquire knowledge with a vengeance. This happened in Taiwan, when the former employees of General Instruments left to set up eleven competing shops, giving rise to the term "hollowing out" in the business literature. The Chinese employees of Beijing Jeep, as described by Jim Mann, do not seem to have the same incentives; rather than focusing upon acquisition of skills from the foreign partner, they quibble instead about whether calendars should be printed in the PRC or in Hong Kong.[6] Information within the multinationals forms the other link in the transfer mechanism. If the product market being served is the competitive world market rather than the domestic market, the multinationals are motivated to transfer more advanced technologies—in our analogy, a more substantial flow.

Assessing the effectiveness of technology transfer is not simple. It may sound heroic to "capture the secrets singlehandedly, at last!" But "at last" may mean that what is captured is commercially obsolete. The object is the capability for timely and reliable delivery of commercial quantities, at competitive cost and with a tolerable defect rate. The object is not just to deliver presentable samples for touring VIPs. The test of technical prowess occurs in the competitive market; the market, further, provides automatic feedback for those who learn and a screening device against those who do not. No inspecting official can possibly be an adequate substitute. Thus, the market is far more effective for the transfer process than government planning.

In this light, the approach of the Asian NIEs contains much more logic than meets the eye. These economies serve as export platforms and offshore sources serving markets in advanced economies. By so doing, they have acquired valuable technology through international cooperation, which reduces both difficulties and costs. MNC-guided learning-by-doing pays its own way, step by step, and the effectiveness of the transfer process is guaranteed by Darwinian competition in the market. The NIEs' free labor markets provide a ready means of disseminating the fruits of learning. A favorable environment for spin-off firms provides incentives for local employees in MNCs to learn well and quickly. To offer low-wage local direct labor to MNCs is also to compel the MNCs to share trade secrets with local indirect labor supervising the working crew. Since MNCs compete against other MNCs, they cannot possibly rely only on high-cost expatriates for supervision—and, in any case, expatriates are probably less effective, due to cultural barriers. Thus, MNCs must allow their domestic rivals and domestic employees to observe their technologies and practices at close range. To be sure, proprietary parts of the technologies will be guarded as closely as possible; however, observation of the rest remains invaluable for a developing economy.[7]

So far, economic development has been regarded as an isolated process, independent of the forces of politics, sociology, psychology, and history. Of course, this is not really the case. We have concluded that markets form an effective matrix for transferring foreign technology. Yet markets do not arise and function in a vacuum. Appropriate laws must be provided by the state to nurture their operation. The state can do this only if its legitimacy is not undermined by chaos, social polarization, or general dissatisfaction. Thus, the degree to which markets can assist economic development depends upon politico-social institutions. Parliamentary democracy may or may not be the answer; the democratic regime of Chang Myon in Korea could not resist Park's march on Seoul, because Chang's ineffectiveness had forfeited the *vox populi*.

Equally valid is the Marxian claim that economics can be the foundation of politico-social evolution. The transfer of technology is not an innocuous process. It can undermine the institutions under which it initially takes place, just as the heat exchange process can melt away one or both of the systems involved. Specifically, institutions set up by a redistributive, revolutionary state may not survive intact the full (re-)introduction of the market. Moreover, the very fact that people enjoy prosperity may heighten their demands for less social restriction and more political freedom. This has happened in Korea as well as Taiwan (to the concern of the present rulers of Singapore). The recent political changes in Japan can also be seen in this light.

This being the case, the vested interests of a regime need not favor economic development, given the knowledge that foreign ideas accompany foreign technology. As in biology, the unchecked introduction of foreign bodies may well subvert the host. Yet, comparison with more successful neighboring societies raises popular pressure for change, thus threatening a recalcitrant regime.[8] As Chen Yun, a redoubtable senior leader of the PRC, has said, "the ship [of state] will capsize if the economy is not handled well or if propaganda work is not done well." Whether a regime can manage the transition decides its future. What latitude for manoeuvre a regime enjoys depends upon its history and the state of society. Our analysis must now turn to such matters.

3. The Transformation of Taiwan's Economy

Consider a Chinese *society*, ruled by an authoritarian *government*. The government has been dominated by a Leninist *party* under a senior paramount *leader*. Most of the industries and all of the banks were state-owned. Both the government and the public enterprises were over-staffed with political appointees. Operations were bureaucratic and inefficient. Prices of most goods, and many other economic aspects of the society, were regulated by the state. Ostentatious consumption and certain elements of the Western lifestyle (e.g., social dancing) were frowned upon. Foreign ownership of firms was allowed only by special permit. Monopolistic capitalism was the *bete noire* of state ideology, and land reform was launched to get rid of the landlords. The CIA was suspected of being behind civil disturbances, which were put down with much bloodshed. Political dissidents were arrested, by appeal to an external threat.

Later, the leadership realized that the economy lacked vitality and that stability of the regime depended upon the performance of the economy. With deregulation, foreign direct investments were encouraged and private firms blossomed. Income, exports, and the export surplus relative to the U.S. all increased, *pari pasu*. A call for political reform arose, precipitating renewed, though milder, crackdowns.

This scenario fits mainland China, now. It also fits Taiwan in the 1950s and '60s. Of course, the ruling parties on both sides of the Taiwan Strait would protest the comparison: each claims to be the wave of the future China and each sees itself as incomparably superior to its old rival.

By the 1990s, Taiwan has become a role model for the developing world and for the formerly communist states. The ruling party maintains control by the ballot, rather than the bullet. Political reform under Chiang Ching-kuo and Lee Teng-hui has been as breathtaking as economic reform under Chiang Kaishek. In fact, one may argue that Taiwan would not be able to maintain the fruits of the latter without the former. After all, at some level of prosperity people naturally demand more liberty. Moreover, maintaining the growth of wages requires continuously rising productivity. And that may require a reverse brain drain—a tapping of overseas Chinese technical manpower; that, in turn, surely requires liberty.

Will mainland China evolve the same way? Our comparison will first focus upon society, government, party, and the leadership, then study how these four elements affect the market and hence economic development.

Society

In the 1950s, Taiwanese society had a traditional Chinese substratum with some Japanese influences, subsisting under martial law. For present purposes, the key point is that, despite their primitiveness and the restrictions surrounding them, markets in Taiwan were qualitatively no different from those in other market economies (such as Hong Kong). For the bulk of the population, the work ethic and customary concepts of property rights and employment relationships were alive and well. A sizable proportion of the urban industrial labor force was never part of the state sector and was never sheltered by any state welfare program.

There was no political freedom under martial law, but personal freedoms always remained essentially intact. In the aftermath of the February 28 uprising, there was a purge of part of the Taiwanese elite, judged subversive or unreliable. But by and large, by no stretch of imagination did this have an impact on society comparable to that of the "class struggle" in a communist agenda.

The court system was sometimes ineffective, tainted by corruption, and subject to political influence. Yet a conventional legal framework was always present and amenable to strengthening under the proper circumstances.

Government

The government in Taiwan was then the personal government of President Chiang Kaishek. On the mainland, Chiang was only the first among equals; each Kuomintang (KMT) military leader, such as Vice President Li, had a private army and a territorial fief. Moreover, even within the government bureaucracy that Chiang headed, interest groups vied for power and Chiang's control was less than absolute. The evacuation to Taiwan changed all this. Those with dubious loyalty parted company with Chiang (some, like Mayor Wu of Shanghai, coming to Taiwan for a while), and political infighting was brought under control. Chiang then enjoyed more freedom to make policy changes than ever before: as in the Korea of

President Park or the Singapore of Premier Lee Kuan Yew, there was little hindrance for any necessary change.

Party

The KMT that dominates the government was founded by Sun Yat-Sen, whose eclectic ideology (the Three People's Principles) contained certain social democratic elements taken from Henry George. Under such a platform, monopolistic capitalism should be banned and key industries should be publicly owned; however, there is nothing in the platform targeting private business as such, in theory or practice. Similarly, the domestic economy should be free from foreign domination, but there is nothing to preclude foreign investment that can contribute to development of the national economy.

Sun's central criticism of Marx remained relevant for the Taiwan of the 1950s and '60s: people should enjoy equality of opportunity, not of attainment. Hence, "material incentives," private enterprise, and differences in income due to effort or luck are all legitimate. To be sure, in *Tatung* (an ancient, apocryphal Confucian classic), Sun found his motto in the precept "from each according to his ability, to each according to his need." (*Tatung*, of course, predates Marx by two millennia). But this state is to be achieved through moral suasion, not forced upon the people by dictatorship of the proletariat. In short, no about-face was needed for a KMT regime to embrace private enterprise or parliamentary democracy—despite past flirtations with national socialism.

Like the Chinese Communist Party (CCP), the KMT once attracted members who risked their lives for the party's ideology. But it was for broad nationalistic goals, rather than specific economic platforms, that those members joined the party. Hence, the KMT can adopt a protean economic policy without alienating any significant portion of its membership.

Leadership

The transformation of Taiwan's economy was presided over mainly by President Chiang Kaishek in the late 1950s and throughout the 1960s, while the political reform was carried out during the later part of his son's presidency.

Though Chiang Kaishek was a military man by training and vocation, his model was Tseng Guofan, the 19th-century conservative and intellectual who suppressed the Taiping rebels. Chiang knew full well that a strong economy was needed for political stability and for sustenance of the armed forces. After the U.S. Seventh Fleet separated the combatants in the

Taiwan Strait during the Korean War, Chiang's priority naturally devolved to economic, rather than military, matters.

In economics, Chiang was never an ideologue. He stood ready to reach out to academia for advice. Indeed, this had been so on the mainland, as well as during his exile on Taiwan. But, as compared to Western leaders like John F. Kennedy, Chiang encountered problems in finding the right advisors. Some eight years after he had retreated to Taiwan and four years after S. C. Tsiang (no relation to Chiang) had presented a proposal for "libertarian" reform, much of Tsiang's plan was accepted and implemented. The Taiwan miracle is history; for those who puzzle over Chiang's failures on the mainland and his subsequent achievements in Taiwan, we can report that there was no instant conversion on the Damascus Road.

Summary

In both institutions and popular attitudes, Taiwan was better positioned, for economic liberalization, than any communist or formerly communist economy. In the Chiang Kaishek of the 1950s and '60s, one finds an undisputed political leader willing to seek the best available economic advice. In S. C. Tsiang, one finds a brilliant advisor, and one who, in fact, disagreed with the conventional wisdom of his day: he rejected export pessimism, the "big push" doctrine for heavy industrial development, and the nurturing of industrialization through low interest rates. History has shown that Tsiang was right, as was Chiang to accept essential components of his advice.

Furthermore, when the Taiwan government's adventures in supporting shipbuilding and the automobile industry turned sour and its adventures in steel-making were only moderately successful, policy makers accepted humiliation rather than gamble on Pyrrhic victory. A vibrant private sector was allowed to overtake inefficient state industries—but not asked to take them over. A gradualist growth path spawned Taiwan firms like the Evergreen Marine Line, a world-class container carrier; Acer, a rising star in the computer industry; many spin-off firms in electronics, which have successfully transferred technology from foreign companies; and shoe producers that sell in markets around the world. In many ways, Taiwan's approach is a valid alternative to the Korean development strategy, which subsidizes heavy industrial exports—with higher resource costs, more foreign debt, more price instability, and more industrial strife.

4. Comparing "PRC, Now" and "Taiwan, Then"

"PRC, now" differs from "Taiwan, then" in the nature of *society*, *government*, (ruling) *party*, and *leadership*. We first discuss such differences, before asking what they mean for economic reform.

Society

Mainland Chinese society today cannot be understood without keeping the Maoist era in perspective. In the name of the dictatorship of the proletariat, Chinese society was continuously reconstructed, over a period of three decades.

Profit was evil, wage contracts were sinful, and material incentives were corruptive for the soul. Private ownership was banned for farms, firms, and real estate. All means of production should be under the ownership of all the people; cooperatives might be expedient, but not ideal. Valuable personal effects, bought with income from prior ownership of productive assets, reverted to use by the state (through confiscations, bond subscriptions, or voluntary contributions). Owners, children of owners, and grandchildren of owners were stigmatized, targeted for reeducation, and barred from higher education; they were frowned upon as marriage partners even for the virtuous poor, let alone for party members. The stigmatized were potential enemies of the state, to be monitored with vigilance at work and at home by their coworkers, neighbors, and family members.

For constructing a Marxist-Leninist paradise, production was for defense and investment, with current consumption but an afterthought. With revolutionary logic, the quality and design of consumption goods could not be serious concerns. On the job, every Chinese was part of the ruling class, with the appropriate officious attitude; in private, each became the ruled, a supplicant of the state and at the sufferance of its officials. Having taken so much privacy, freedom, and creature comfort from the people, the state promised them—or, at least, the urban, industrial, and governmental portions of the populace—"iron rice bowls" and cradle-to-grave care.

Religions were not politically correct, as they might detract from revolutionary zeal. Art, literature, philosophy, and foreign connections received the state's *imprimatur* if and only if they advanced the revolutionary cause. Revolutionary justice was applied to reconstruct society; lawyerly wrangling would be a waste of the people's time. For the revolution, spouses could be assigned to jobs hundred of miles apart, to be reunited in short visits once or twice a year. The Cultural Revolution finally turned upon the children of the revolution themselves.

Like Khrushchev's reform, Deng's reform of 1978 was a brilliant compromise. Victory was finally declared, to end the class struggle. The excesses of past zealotry were rescinded, but not the revolutionary rhetoric. A full-fledged denunciation of one's predecessor would be too risky, alarming too many accomplices in past wrongs. It would also delegitimize one's own claim to power and the use of power to hold onto one's claim.

Every compromise has its price, and Deng's is no exception. More dogmatic comrades still share power, constantly braking against faster reforms. Lip service is still paid to orthodox positions, supplying rationales for the vested interests to obstruct progress. Past commitments to a welfare state must still be honored, dulling incentives and saddling the government with crushing financial burdens. Institutions and legal codes cannot be revised wholesale, since a modicum of consistency must be maintained with yesterday's slogans.

Most serious of all, the most dynamic economic activities—since they are driven by profit motives—must be conducted within the grey area of semi-legitimacy. Leaving their approval to the discretion of state officials encumbers business operations, corrupts the bureaucracy, and forfeits the people's respect for the state. And, with the legal system atrophied, the law is but a broken reed. Once law and order command little respect, impersonal trading becomes impossible, reducing the economy to a pre-modern state. To be sure, "respecting the law" is high on Deng's priority list. But behavior modification for an entire society must be launched with moral authority. This is difficult in a reform grounded in compromise.

Government

The government of the PRC is in a class by itself, in size, scope, and characteristics. Any Chinese government would have to rule a subcontinental land mass with over a billion residents. A *communist* Chinese government, dedicated to state ownership and insisting on an all-embracing role in every sphere from art to sport, must be a colossus. Governing becomes harder still when there exists no market to provide information. In principle, central planning coordinates activities; in reality, personal relationships and pairwise bargaining are of crucial importance. The central government bargains annually with the governor of a province, over the formula for revenue sharing. The governor of one province can blockade the shipping of a certain commodity to a neighboring province. What would be treasonous and insubordinate in other countries is the behavioral norm in the PRC. Conceivably, regional autonomy is a survival characteristic evolved in times of war, when isolated soviets must survive in the hills of southern China. In economic terms, such a *modus operandi* imposes tremendous transaction costs, in time and effort. Furthermore, it makes global planning at the center a nightmare, since simultaneous pairwise bargaining must be conducted with many regional administrations. Allocative efficiency is inevitably sacrificed. In addition, uncertainty about the outcomes from bargaining among government branches makes trading with China less attractive to foreigners. (Hence, to be competitive on world markets, the Chinese must accept worse terms.) It is for good reason that modern economies coordinate activities through hierarchies or markets, but not through pairwise bargaining on a global scale.

Balkanization occurs not only on a regional basis, but also along functional lines. In one instance, a vice-mayor of Shanghai promised to finish some jackets for a Japanese merchant. Half a dozen state enterprises had to be involved, since each controlled a necessary material; no two of the enterprises ordinarily dealt with each other. In the end, a special task force was organized for this order, to save the honor of Shanghai!

The well-known "cellular" (or Balkanized) nature of the Chinese economy is all the more harmful, given China's backwardness. Using our earlier physical analogy, heat exchange is effective only with a convection flow—not with compartmentalization. The fact that China lacks a highly integrated labor market means that experience acquired in one place must be reacquired again someplace else—a duplication of effort that China can best do without.

At the same time, the communist government retains an organizational relic from its infancy in insurgent war: at every level down to the academic department of a university, the unit leader is always paired with a party secretary. This practice is understandable for the Red Army of Trotsky, when commanders were mostly Czarist officers of questionable loyalty. But having been in power for more than forty years, the Chinese communists should by now have leaders who are both "red" and "expert." There is no need for this unwieldy divided command, a set-up cautioned against by strategists down through the ages.

While the government of the PRC is poorly organized for making timely decisions in the market, ironically a sizable portion of the Chinese economy is controlled by the government.

Party

The Chinese Communist Party may be understood from its Marxist ideology, its Leninist tradition, and the character of its members.

Founded on the orthodox (rather than revisionist) interpretation of Marx, the party's ideology has a philosophical and logical consistency without match. Yet, having denounced revisionism as the worst heresy imaginable, the party becomes a prisoner of its own rhetoric. Doctrine, once outmoded, takes an incredible amount of time, effort, and sophistry to reinterpret, in order to legitimize reform. Even then, the end result elicits cynical resignation from old comrades and secret smiles from the young and opportunistic.

Leninist "democratic centralism" sets up a top-down structure. Every aspect of life is controlled by the government, and almost all government units are headed by party members. Grassroot party members are guided by the opinions of the party center—not the other way around, as in Western parliamentary parties. This is a party designed for survival, and one that excels in meeting external threats. It can launch mass movements to work fundamental changes in society, but it cannot make timely responses to changes in the economic environment. But such changes arise constantly in the modern world. Thus, having concentrated all power in its hands, the communist-dominated state finds itself outperformed by the authoritarian regimes of President Park in Korea and the KMT in Taiwan.

At the beginning, the Communist Party was made of dedicated women and men ready to sacrifice everything for their revolutionary ideology and to take drastic and ruthless measures against others in the name of a cause. To be sure, there were schisms and internal purges, time after time. Yet it is the dialectic formalism, the revolutionary rhetoric and the cosmopolitan messianic vision, that gives communism a special power over its members. To true believers, temporary compromises with enemy forces may be acceptable as necessary expedients, but compromise on principle is anathema. The reintroduction of material incentives and private enterprises—in whatever limited or hybrid form—is dangerously close to apostasy. The issue is especially serious, because in mainland China capitalism was disposed of at tremendous human cost. Furthermore, the present leaders have claimed legitimacy by their stand against revival of capitalism. Thus, they are trapped. They can pacify their core believers by claiming the reform is a tactical retreat—but that would alarm foreign investors and send shivers down the spines of any domestic beneficiaries of reform, thus undoing all their incentive packages at one stroke. Or, they can ignore reservations from the fundamentalist wing of the party, thus risking the disillusionment of their staunchest supporters against any external challenge.

Leadership

Deng's leadership can be appraised from two angles: his position in the power structure, and the character of his leadership.

Deng's position within the ruling group is comparable to Chiang Kaishek's on the mainland, but not to Chiang's on Taiwan, President Park's in Korea, or, for that matter, Mao's during the Cultural Revolution. Although acknowledged as the paramount leader, Deng nonetheless has to pay attention to the views of his senior colleagues. This constrains what he can do.

Perhaps even more important is the character of Deng's leadership. Deng has always been respected for his political judgment and pragmatism, not his charisma. Even in his prime, he was never regarded as another Mao or Zhou Enlai. That may set an ultimate limit of how far Deng can successfully go. Specifically, even if Deng intends to make a sharp break with the past, redefining his "socialism with Chinese characteristics" as a Western European style of social democracy, it would take the personality of a Zhou to pull it off. In short, it probably was never in the cards for Deng to play the role of King Juan Carlos of Spain or Chiang Ching-kuo of Taiwan, shepherding a state into democracy. At any rate, Deng believes that China now needs stability, that only dictatorship can bring stability, and that only he can effectively exercise dictatorship.

Summary

Mainland China now differs from Taiwan in several important respects.

(1) China currently lacks both the social institutions and the popular attitudes favorable to development. Yet, in view of the achievements of the resettled Chinese in Hong Kong, these are soluble problems.

(2) The key elements of the ruling apparatus in mainland China are not such as to help in resolving current problems:

The government is all-embracing, yet its nature and organization are neither designed for nor suitable to economic development;

The party dominates all aspects of the government, yet its central ideological stance is not favorable to the needed reform;

The current leadership may have neither the intention nor the capability to effect a reorientation of the ruling apparatus.

At present, various reform programs are being carried out. Why all these fall short of their goals will be discussed in detail in the next section.

5. Prognosis for the Mainland Chinese Economy

The Chinese economy can be conveniently subdivided into four sectors: the agricultural sector, the sector of large- and middle-sized state enterprises, the sector of regional and rural enterprises and private businesses, and the foreign investment sector.

The Agricultural Sector

The agricultural sector remains quite large in output share, and even larger in employment share. It has been very successful in supporting the huge Chinese population on the limited arable acreage in modern China. It continues to play an essential role in any development program for China; by and large, the Chinese people must be fed by Chinese farms. But considering the severe resource constraints, the Chinese agricultural sector can neither provide a large portion of the populace with well-paid jobs nor generate sustained rapid growth of national income, all by itself.

The State Sector

The state firms of large and middle size are crucial for many reasons. First, their monopolistic incomes have been the main source of government revenue. Second, their hierarchies have provided the government with its principal outlet for placement of job-seeking youth. Third, their in-house welfare programs (rather than an overall government plan) have seen to the needs of the Chinese urban working masses—a group that the government views as politically decisive. Finally, the primacy of "ownership of the entire people" is enshrined in the preamble of the current constitution, alongside the leadership role of the Communist Party. Abandoning one diminishes the prestige of the other, especially after 1989.

Most state firms are inefficient and over-staffed. Their losses are now bleeding the treasury white, causing inflation as a consequence. Various plans to reform these firms have been tried, and have invariably failed. Politically, redundant employees cannot be unloaded, at least not at the current stage of development. That being so, overstaffed firms can neither be made profitable nor be sold to any buyer.

Operating under obsolete regulations and institutions and obligated to current employees and retirees, as well as spouses and children of employees, for housing, medicine, pensions, education and jobs, state firms might not make a profit even under the best management. Thus, clearcut malfeasance can be prosecuted, but mismanagement often cannot be.

Often, politically appointed managers are not equal to their tasks—and, in any case, they must always please the politically influential.

Serving short fixed terms, they have no reason to take a long view with regard to equipment acquisition and maintenance, let alone product development or customer service. Employee-elected managers cater to the short-term interests of the employees, not the profitability of the firm, resting assured that failed firms are always bailed out. Managers on responsibility contracts have won the right to do as they see fit during their terms. They are, however, motivated by personal short-term gain. Evaluation of their stewardships is always subjective.

It is not that public enterprises are destined to be inefficient. Some Western European firms in the state sector are competitive. But for that to happen, such firms must be managed with professionalism and overseen by an elected parliament of the people. In such organizations, there can be no role for political commissars connected to a self-perpetuating party.

Current plans for ownership reform envisage the owning of shares by each firm's own employees, or the selling of minority interests to the public. Neither has the same effect on efficiency as a free enterprise system, driven by impersonal, and hence objective, forces.

As time goes on, the plant and equipment of state firms become more and more obsolete, making their competitive positions ever worse. As the central government is severely strained for funds, modernization programs become more and more unaffordable.

Private Firms and Rural-Regional Enterprises

Private enterprise and wage contracts exist at the sufferance of the state. Maoist class struggles are merely suspended, not opposed as a matter of principle. Profit and capitalism are still evil in the official ideology. All this has consequences. The operation of a private business is subject to discretionary approval at every conceivable level, with each approval potentially requiring personal connections—if not outright bribes.

Private entrepreneurs can buy political correctness by adopting the guise of rural or regional ownership or by assuming cooperative forms. Continued operation depends on the favor of whoever is politically in power at the local level. The exchange of favors and the use of personal connections mean that transaction costs are high in terms of tangible resources, and probably even higher in terms of effort, time, and morale. Naked bribes must also be paid in daily operations, and bribery can still be viewed as high crime. Since "crime" is ubiquitous and endemic, its actual suppression must be selective. The selective application of justice, of course, admits discretion, and thus occasion for personal favoritism—and for more bribes. The precarious nature of business undertakings under these circumstances is incompatible with rational long-term planning of business operations.

But the drawbacks of the present institutions go beyond long-term concerns. In the short run, they also dilute the benefit of any price reform. The benefit of price reform depends upon the extent to which markets are competitive. Market competition is preserved via ease of entry by new firms. If prices are set by a small number of entrepreneurs who operate under the patronage of those with political power, resource allocation remains distorted.

The Foreign-Related Sector

Fully, partly, or supposedly foreign-owned firms form a class of their own. As potential providers of needed technology and capital for the Chinese economy, their taxes can be exempted or reduced and various special dispensations can be granted to them. Since, by their nature, they must practice capitalism in the land of "Chinese Socialism," officials can turn a blind eye to them with impunity. The defining qualification of such firms is that their owners include foreigners, Chinese resident in Hong Kong or Taiwan, or companies registered in these locations (not excluding fully-owned branches of Chinese state firms in Hong Kong). As a guise for genuine Chinese entrepreneurship, the foreign-invested or foreign-related form offers more legitimacy than the rural/regional enterprise. It cannot be simply taken over by the next village or county administration at whim.

It is not that such firms can operate unassisted in China, in the same fashion as firms outside the country. The cost of doing business in China is "notional"—and is high, for the ill-connected and the profitable. A firm can be billed by various branches of government for items created by imaginative officials and at rates set at their discretion. Appeals through official channels are likely to prove time-consuming and ineffective, but negotiation through appropriate intermediaries is always possible at some price. Decisions can be based upon a plethora of laws, precedents, committee resolutions, and administrative orders conveyed only via internal documents not fit for the eyes of the unauthorized. In short, whether foreign firms make huge profits or suffer losses in China depends partly on their ability to navigate the byzantine back channels of Chinese officialdom.

Still, since it is least shackled by the existing laws and institutions and favored by policies encouraging foreign investment, the foreign-invested sector is by far the most vibrant among the four sectors. Firms in this sector easily outcompete state firms or rural/regional firms in output and input markets. This worsens further the financial situations of state firms. In addition, many of those in power use their power to help family members make a quick buck in joint ventures with foreign capitalists, after obediently denouncing the evil, the decadence, and the foredoomed nature of capitalism. The irony and cynicism of it all eats away the very idealism on which the party and the government were built. Pursuing economic development and technological modernization requires a government that upholds the rule of law, under which market forces can work to full potential.

A Comparison with Taiwan

The Chinese reform is a success, compared with Eastern Europe and the former Soviet Union. The progress made in mainland China bears considerable resemblance to the early stages of the Asian NIEs (especially Taiwan). Rising wages in Taiwan, Korea, and Hong Kong now lead industries to migrate to the Chinese mainland, just as Japanese industries were forced to migrate to Taiwan by rising wages there, decades ago. Even today, there is a sizable section of the Taiwanese economy remaining in state ownership, still less efficient than the private sector, still with employees opposing privatization. Corruption is still a problem in Taiwan (as well as in Korea), just as it has always been. Yet important differences remain.

It is true that both Taiwan and mainland China are undergoing processes of transition. In Taiwan, a free press and a fledgling parliamentary democracy now offer means of cleaning up corruption; in mainland China, however, economic reform has introduced a broad range of new opportunities for corrupting those with political power.

Second, in spite of corruption of tax officials, Taiwan's government finance is not under constant strain. As a consequence, the real incomes of government employees have risen, and improved social welfare programs have been extended to the poor and the retired. In mainland China, the financial difficulties of the government have caused curtailment of welfare programs, and public-sector wages have lagged behind inflation. To be sure, many more opportunities have opened up for civil servants to surreptitiously supplement their incomes by taking on second jobs. But that fact has not endeared the government to the people.

Third, the fact that the private sector grows more rapidly than the public sector in Taiwan is cited by the ruling party as demonstrating the success of its own program. In comparison, the reintroduction of markets and private (and foreign) enterprises into the communist Chinese economy causes confusion and disillusionment among the more idealistic supporters of the government.

Fourth, local workers in foreign-invested firms in Taiwan are keen to learn foreign technologies and managerial practices, so that they can utilize such knowhow later in setting up firms of their own. This effective channel of technology acquisition does not operate in mainland China today. The Chinese employees in joint ventures with foreign firms have no prospect of using their experience in the future, after being transferred back to Chinese outfits.

Fifth, successful Taiwanese entrepreneurs can take the long view in developing their firms. The Evergreen Marine Line, Taiwan Plastics, Acer, and Tatung, to name a few, have achieved worldwide recognition, through efforts stretching over decades. In mainland China, state firms are inefficient due to the institutions within which they must operate. Private entrepreneurs can make profits only under various guises, and have little faith that they can be left alone for long, in a land where capitalism remains suspect. If this situation persists, the Chinese side must always bargain from a position of weakness in dealings with foreign enterprises (including the Chinese from Hong Kong and Taiwan), and must be content with the role of "hewers of wood and drawers of water."

In summary, unless some drastic change is made in mainland China, catching up with Taiwan is well-nigh impossible.

6. Conclusion

The facts presented above are self-evident to careful observers—and people on the Chinese mainland certainly do observe such matters with care and interest. Having been told for decades that their brethren in Taiwan were suffering in "deep water and hot fire," their curiosity is aroused now by tens of thousands of visitors from across the strait. People may or may not believe that the present in China is better than the past, or that the past under Mao was better than the past under Chiang. What they want to know, though, is whether and when they can live like the Chinese on Taiwan. This lateral comparison puts great pressure on all mainland officials, especially those at the top.

Three of the four Asian NIEs are Chinese. They rank first, second, and third (by income per capita)—ahead of South Korea. If mainland China is less prosperous than Korea, the problem is not with the Chinese populace. Nor is it necessarily a matter of personalities among the leadership. Ideology and institutions are of greater significance.

Deng's rule has entered its final phase. History shows that after a long rule by a party leader there will be a collective leadership, and after that collective leadership there will be a power struggle. This was true after Lenin. It was also true after Stalin and after Mao. It will be true after Deng. To win room at the top, Paris may well be worth a Mass. True democracy may not be quite around the corner, but the Spanish style of political evolution is entirely within grasp.

We have emphasized that private enterprises are essential for rapid technology transfers and that, for public enterprises, efficient operation requires professional management—perhaps backed by the oversight of a multi-party parliament. It is not true that Marxism is incompatible with parliamentary rule. In the states of Kerala and West Bengal, the Indian Communist Party has repeatedly won provincial elections. For that matter, Mao in 1950 and Deng in 1980 probably could have won open elections in China. In both Lithuania and Poland, former communists have now regained power, by way of the ballot box. But in order to do so, they have had to provide policy environments favorable to entrepreneurial activities, commit themselves to parliamentary democracy, and respect the free press.

Notes

1. H. Uchida, "The Transfer of Electrical Technologies from the United States and Europe to Japan," in D. J. Jeremy (ed.), *International Technology Transfer* (Brookfield, VT: Edward Elgar, 1991).

2. S. Lall, *Learning to Industrialize: The Acquisition of Technological Capability by India* (Hampshire, UK: Macmillan, 1987).

3. R. Komiya, "Direct Foreign Investment in Postwar Japan," in P. Drysdale (ed.), *Direct Foreign Investment in Asia and the Pacific* (Toronto: University of Toronto Press, 1970).

4. D. Morawetz, *Why the Emperor's New Clothes are not Made in Columbia: A Case Study in Latin American and East Asian Manufacturing Export* (New York: Oxford University Press, 1981).

5. S. Watanabe, "Multi-National Enterprises and Employment-Oriented Appropriate Technologies in Developing Countries" (International Labour Organization, Multi-National Enterprise Program, Working Papers, no. 14, 1980).

6. Jim Mann, *Beijing Jeep: The Short, Unhappy Romance of an American Business in China* (New York: Simon Schuster, 1989).

7. Watanabe, "Multi-National Enterprises."

8. Victor Nee, "Organizational Dynamics of Market Transition: Hybrid Property Forms and Mixed Economy in China," *Administrative Science Quarterly*, 37, 1992, pp. 1-27.

About the Contributors

Chung Chin is an Associate Research Fellow at Chung-hua Institution for Economic Research in Taipei. Her research focuses on Taiwan-mainland economic interaction and its implications for both economies.

Graham Johnson is an Associate Professor in the Department of Anthropology and Sociology at the University of British Columbia. His research focuses on the Pearl River delta region of Guangdong province. He is currently studying the consequences of massive migration into the region.

Kao Charng is a Research Fellow at Chung-hua Institution for Economic Research in Taipei. His current research concerns the development of economic relations between Taiwan and mainland China.

Echo Heng Liang is a consultant at the World Bank. Her research concerns rural development in China and, in particular, organizational change at the village level.

Thomas P. Lyons is Associate Professor of Economics at Cornell University. His current research concerns the economic development of Fujian province.

Victor Nee is Goldwin Smith Professor of Sociology at Cornell University, and director of Cornell's South China research project. His research uses interviews and large-scale surveys to examine the transition to markets in South China.

William L. Parish is Professor of Sociology at the University of Chicago. He is co-author or editor of several books on Chinese urban and rural society, and is currently completing research on family life, women's work, and aging in Taiwan and mainland China.

G. William Skinner is Professor of Anthropology at the University of California, Davis. His current research includes a comparative analysis of regional systems in Second Empire France, early Meiji Japan, and contemporary China.

Su Sijin is a Postdoctoral Fellow in Sociology at Cornell University. His current research concerns organizational change in Chinese enterprises and, in particular, the evolution of incentive schemes, contracting arrangements, and governance structures.

Henry Wan, Jr., is Professor of Economics at Cornell University and a former president of the Chinese Economics Association in North America. His areas of interest include international trade and economic development in the East Asia region.

Weng Junyi is Associate Professor of Economics at the MBA Center, Xiamen University. His current research includes a study of local development patterns in Fujian province.

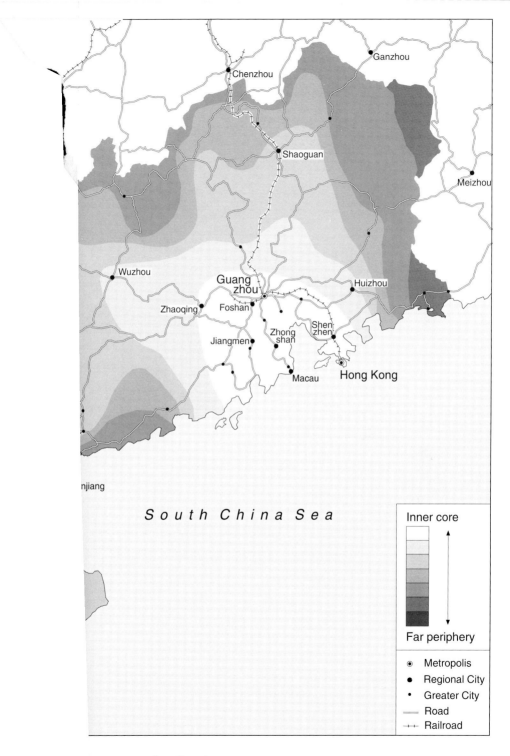

Cities, railroads, and major roads, 1985.

Chenzhou	
Ganzhou	
Shaoguan	
Meizhou	
Wuzhou	
Guangzhou	
Huizhou	
Zhaoqing	
Foshan	
Shenzhen	
Jiangmen	Zhongshan
Macau	Hong Kong

South China Sea

njiang

Inner core

Far periphery

⊙ Metropolis
● Regional City
· Greater City
— Road
+++ Railroad

ın macroregional system,
ıd major roads, 1985.

CORNELL EAST ASIA SERIES

For ordering information, please contact the Cornell East Asia Series, East Asia Program, Cornell University, 140 Uris Hall, Ithaca, NY 14853-7601, USA; phone (607) 255-6222, fax (607) 255-1388.

3-94/.2M cloth/.5M paper/BB

DATE DUE